J. C. RYLE

Prepared to Stand Alone

We want more boldness among the friends of truth. There is far too much tendency to sit still, and wait for committees, and number our adherents. We want more men who are not afraid to stand alone.

It is truth, not numbers, which shall always in the end prevail.

We have the truth, and we need not be ashamed to say so. The judgment day will prove who is right, and to that day we boldly appeal.

J. C. RYLE

J. C. RYLE

Prepared to Stand Alone

Iain H. Murray

THE BANNER OF TRUTH TRUST

THE BANNER OF TRUTH TRUST

The Grey House, 3 Murrayfield Road, Edinburgh, EH12 6EL, UK
P.O. Box 621, Carlisle, PA 17013, USA

✳

© Iain H. Murray 2016

✳

ISBN:
Print (clothbound): 978 1 84871 678 0
Print (paperback): 978 1 84871 679 7
EPUB: 978 1 84871 680 3
Kindle: 978 1 84871 681 0

✳

Typeset in Adobe Garamond Pro 11/15 pt at
The Banner of Truth Trust, Edinburgh

Printed in the USA by
Versa Press Inc.,
East Peoria, IL

J. I. Packer
Teacher, Guide, Friend
of so many around the world

Remember them …
who have spoken unto you the word of God.

HEB. 13:7

Contents

Illustrations   ix

Introduction   xi

1. Schooldays   1
2. 'The Greatest Change and Event in My Life'   13
3. Church and Homes Divided   25
4. All Doors Shut Except One   41
5. Peace Disturbed in Hampshire   53
6. Rural Suffolk: Stepping-Stone to the World   69
7. Puritans at Helmingham Rectory   91
8. Stradbroke: Twenty Fruitful Years   107
9. The Teacher   131
10. Liverpool   155
11. Standing Firm under Darkening Skies   177
12. The Last Years   197
13. What Does Ryle Say for Today?   215

Appendix 1. Extracts from Ryle   237
Appendix 2. Herbert E. Ryle   249
Index   261

Illustrations

Front endpaper: Cricket on the College Field (1830s) by William Evans. Reproduced by permission of the Provost and Fellows of Eton College.

Rear endpaper: from a secular cartoon, Manchester 1883.

Frontispiece: J. C. Ryle, about the age of fifty.

Park House, Macclesfield. Reproduced with permission from the Macclesfield Museums, *page 2*

Christ Church, Macclesfield, *page 2*

Portrait of Ryle in his youth. Reproduced by permission of the Provost and Fellows of Eton College, *page 14*

Old Henbury Hall. Used by kind permission of Mrs de Ferranti, *page 26*

District around Macclesfield, *page 42*

Area around Exbury, Hampshire, *page 52*

Exbury Church, *page 54*

St Thomas' Church, Winchester, *page 54*

The Protestantism of the Thirty-nine Articles: Extracts, *page 68*

St Mary's Church, Helmingham, *page 70*

Helmingham Church, from the park, *page 70*

Interior of Helmingham Church, *page 92*

Stradbroke School, *page 108*

Street scene in Stradbroke, *page 108*

Stradbroke Vicarage, as rebuilt in the time of Ryle, *page 130*

Ryle, when Vicar of Stradbroke, *page 130*

Ryle preaching to emigrants leaving Liverpool, *page 132*

The floating Landing Stage, Liverpool (1912), scene of his almost daily walk. Reproduced with permission from Colin Wilkinson, *Liverpool Then and Now* (Liverpool: The Bluecoat Press, 1993), *page 156*

Part of a press cartoon of 1883, *page 176*

At his desk in later years, *page 178*

Three generations of Ryles: Herbert, Edward, and JCR, *page 198*

Graves of John Charles and Henrietta Ryle, All Saints' Church, Childwall, Liverpool, *page 214*

J. C. Ryle, First Bishop of Liverpool, *page 216*

A page from *Home Truths*, *page 238*

Colour Inset between pp. 152-3

Cricket in the Playing Fields by William Evans. Reproduced by permission of the Provost and Fellows of Eton College.

Ryle's signature in an Eton entry book. Reproduced by permission of the Provost and Fellows of Eton College.

Helmingham Church and Manse.

Helmingham Hall, viewed from the church grounds.

Derwentwater, Cumbria, a place frequented by Ryle on holiday. Courtesy of Colin Roworth.

Introduction

'I F I HAD died before I was twenty-one, if there is such a thing
as being lost forever in hell, which I do not doubt, I certainly
should have been lost forever.'

So Ryle recalled his earlier years as he looked back in 1873 when
he was fifty-seven. The words were part of a record given to his family
as an explanation for them of his life down to the year 1860.[1] If his
children needed an explanation so do we. It is not self-evident how
one who could assert, 'I certainly never said my prayers, or read a
word of my Bible, from the time I was seven, to the time I was 21',
was the same man of whom it was to be said, 'Perhaps few men in
the nineteenth century did so much for God, for truth, for righteousness, among the English-speaking race and in the world.'[2]

Ryle's autobiographical account left the last forty years of his life
untouched, an evidence that it was only intended for his children and
not for publication. His later years they knew well enough. But it
remains the indispensable starting point for understanding the man.

[1] Although covering the years to 1860, the material dates from 1873 when it was
probably dictated and taken down by his wife. A third-hand copy, with minor editing by Dr Peter Toon, was published in 1975 under the title *J. C. Ryle, A Self Portrait:
A Partial Autobiography* (Swengel, PA: Reiner), though he had no access to the original text which he presumed to be lost. Ryle's original manuscript was rediscovered in
December 2015 and a new edition by Dr Andrew Atherstone is due from the present
publishers in 2016, entitled, *Bishop J. C. Ryle's Autobiography: The Early Years*. My
many unreferenced quotations of an autobiographical nature are from this source.

[2] 'Funeral Sermon by Canon Hobson', in *Richard Hobson of Liverpool: The Autobiography of a Faithful Pastor* (Edinburgh: Banner of Truth Trust, 2003), 342, originally published under the title, *What Hath God Wrought?* (1903).

He would have no biographers in his lifetime, and, surprisingly, there would be no attempt at serious biography for half a century after his death. One can only conjecture reasons for that long absence. No doubt the comment of James I. Packer that Ryle 'was widely written off as a dinosaur in his last years', enters into it.[1] He died at a date when the men who had been foremost in upholding biblical Christianity were to be, as Spurgeon anticipated, 'eaten of dogs for the next fifty years'.[2]

It was almost the middle of the twentieth century before a recovery of Ryle's life and work began with forty pages by M. Guthrie Clark, *John Charles Ryle, 1816–1900* (London: Church Book Room Press, 1947). This was followed by Marcus Loane, the future archbishop of Sydney, with sixty-two pages under the same title (London: James Clarke, 1953). These short biographies, sympathetic to their subject, whetted the appetite for more. Guthrie Clark mentioned how his own interest was awakened when he picked up Ryle's *Knots Untied* from a second-hand bookstall in Oxford. His first impression was enough to make him buy it: '"This man has got some convictions," I said to myself, "and his book will be worth reading."'

A new generation of Ryle readers had to wait until the 1970s for a fuller discovery of his life. It began with the first-time publication of Ryle's own, long-buried, partial autobiography, edited by Peter Toon. Toon and Michael Smout then provided another major advance in their *John Charles Ryle, Evangelical Bishop* (Swengel, PA: Reiner, 1976). Helped by the further detail, Marcus Loane published an enlargement of his original title (London: Hodder and Stoughton, 1983). What might have been the capstone in the way of a popular and detailed biography of Ryle was reached by Eric Russell in *That Man of Granite with the Heart of a Child* (Fearn: Christian Focus, 2001).

[1] J. I. Packer, *Faithfulness and Holiness: The Witness of J. C. Ryle* (Wheaton: Crossway, 2002), 10.
[2] C. H. Spurgeon, *An All-Round-Ministry* (1900; Edinburgh: Banner of Truth Trust, 2003), 360.

Yet the procession of books and of new information was not to end there. Russell's work was evidently written before he saw Ian D. Farley's in-depth account of aspects of Ryle's work in Liverpool in his title, *J. C. Ryle, First Bishop of Liverpool: A Study in Mission Amongst the Masses* (Carlisle: Paternoster, 2000), and the story has continued to be ongoing. Although Alan Munden's *Travel with Bishop Ryle, Prince of Tract Writers* (Leominster: Day One, 2012) was comparatively short, along with 150 colour photographs, it contained details not previously recorded. I am heavily indebted to all these authors for the much fuller portrait of Ryle which they have together provided.

In addition to the biographers of Ryle, just mentioned, I am thankful to the staff at the Evangelical Library, and the Dr Williams's Library, London, for their ready assistance. I thank Andrew Atherstone, Ian S. Barter, Susan Marshall, Alan Munden, and Derek Scales for giving me their time so generously in the reading and shaping of my account, together with aid in the clarification of occasional difficulties. I have especially valued on this title the assistance of my colleagues in the Banner of Truth Trust, John Rawlinson, Colin Roworth, and Jonathan Watson. As ever, my wife, has been indispensable; we have read Ryle together since teenage years.

Ryle appears to have discouraged the use of any of his personal archives, so that little of a personal nature to help a biographer has survived apart from the autobiography which he did not intend for publication. It was the message of his books, rather than a biography, that he wanted to see passed on to the future. For fifty years after his death his desire that his writings might serve that purpose seemed unlikely of fulfilment. Trends in twentieth-century evangelicalism were not conducive to keeping such authors as Ryle in print. Publishers assumed that the market for them had gone. But one London preacher, Martyn Lloyd-Jones of Westminster Chapel, disagreed and urged a hesitant London publisher, James Clarke, to believe that a republication of Ryle's *Holiness* would meet a real need.

Few anticipated at the time how significant the republication of that title in 1952 was going to be. In the Foreword which Dr Lloyd-Jones was asked to provide, he wrote:

> One of the most encouraging and hopeful signs I have observed for many a long day in evangelical circles has been a renewed and increasing interest in the writings of Bishop J. C. Ryle. In his day he was famous, outstanding and beloved as a champion and exponent of the evangelical and reformed faith. For some reason or other, however, his name and his works are not familiar to modern evangelicals. His books are, I believe, out of print in this country and very difficult to obtain second-hand. All who have ever read him will be grateful for this new edition of his great book on *Holiness*. I shall never forget the satisfaction—spiritual and mental—with which I read it some twenty years ago after having stumbled across it in a second-hand book shop.[1]

In the early summer of 1941 I saw a strange and awesome sight which has come back to me as I wrote these pages. From the coast of North Wales, looking some twenty-five miles east towards Liverpool, the whole skyline in that direction glowed fiery orange as that city burned under German bombing. Whether it was the night I watched I do not know, but it was May 1941 that brought the destruction of Church House, Liverpool, and with it Ryle's personal library which had been kept there. Now, in this bicentenary of his birth, we give thanks to God that the message lives which was housed in that library. What he once wrote of others who taught the word of God has proved true again in his own case:

> Some believers are 'rivers of living water' long after they die. They do good by their books and writings in every part of the world, long after the hands which held the pen are mouldering in the dust. Such men were Bunyan, and Baxter, and Owen, and George Herbert, and Robert M'Cheyne. These blessed servants of God do more

---

[1] *Holiness: Its Nature, Hindrances, Difficulties, and Roots* (1879; repr. London: James Clarke, 1952), iii. A new edition of *Holiness* was published by the Trust in 2014.

good probably by their books at this moment, than they did by their tongues when they were alive. 'Being dead they yet speak' (Heb. 11:4).[1]

IAIN H. MURRAY
Edinburgh
January 2016

.

---

[1] J. C. Ryle, *Holiness* (2014), 366.

I

Schooldays

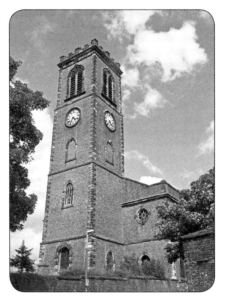

Top: Park House, Macclesfield

Bottom: Christ Church, Macclesfield

T WO hundred years ago John Charles Ryle was born on 10 May 1816, at Macclesfield, the eldest son of John Ryle who had married Susanna Hurt in 1811. Three sisters preceded the arrival of their first son, Mary Anne, Susan, and Emma, with another sister, Caroline, and a brother, Frederic, to follow. Their home, Park House, was on the south side of the town, not far from what is now Ryle Street, a short walk from Park Green where the London coach passed regularly on its journey north. On that Green his grandfather had lived, built a prosperous silk mill, and, on his death in 1808, left 'an immense fortune' to his eldest son. The times were propitious for Macclesfield in rural Cheshire which the manufacturing age had reached towards the end of the previous century. Mills, both for silk and cotton, had sprung up, raising the population from 8,743 in 1801 to 23,129 in 1831.

The Ryle family were leaders in the emerging new merchant class, their prosperity strengthened by intermarriages. Susanna Ryle, mother of the six children at Park House, was a distant relation of Arkwright, whose invention of the spinning-jenny had brought a fortune to that family. Another of their connections had come from the marriage of one of John Ryle's sisters to John S. Daintry. Daintry joined in partnership with his brother-in-law, to establish the successful Macclesfield and Cheshire Bank on Park Green in 1810.

As the family wealth grew so did their properties, and John Ryle became one of the best-known figures in the county; his positions were to include that of governor of the town's historic grammar school, treasurer of the Volunteer Fire Brigade, magistrate and, finally, High Sheriff of Cheshire. When Parliamentary boundaries were changed by the Reform Act of 1832, Macclesfield was allowed to elect two Members of Parliament, and it was no surprise that the owner of Park House was one of the successful candidates. His campaigning had included an address to an estimated 15,000 on Park Green, to whom he declared himself to be 'independent of and unconnected with any party'.[1] John Charles was to speak of his father as 'exceedingly popular in and around Macclesfield, and was almost king of the place'.

There are hints at the downside of this prosperity in Ryle's short autobiography:

> I remember generally that we were brought up in the greatest comfort and luxury, and had everything that money could get. My father took little notice of us, and was generally out all day. My mother was excessively anxious about us, and as angrily careful about our health, behaviour, and appearance, as a hen about her chickens.[2]

Such a respectable mother cannot have been pleased with her eldest son's first and unexpected announcement in the church they attended, Christ Church, Macclesfield. Admitting he was inclined to be 'excessively troublesome', Ryle referred to this incident on a Sunday in his childhood when his mother had given him a Pontefract sweet to keep him quiet during the service. But this he dropped, and was told to pick it up: 'I scrambled about under the seats of a large square pew and could not find it, and then shouted out to my mother's dismay, "I cannot find it anywhere."'

His first 'public speech', a few years later, was equally unexpected. It was the custom of a Colonel Parker, once a year, to put on an immense party for the fifty or sixty children from all the leading

---

[1] Peter Toon and Michael Smout, *John Charles Ryle, Evangelical Bishop* (Swengel, PA; Reiner, 1976), 28. The Reform Act by no means gave a general male franchise; the number voting at the 1837 General Election was only 777.

[2] In the following pages, all my statements from Ryle drawn from his partial autobiography are so numerous that I will not give the page references. They can be found in *Bishop J. C. Ryle's Autobiography: The Early Years*, ed. Andrew Atherstone (Edinburgh: Banner of Truth Trust, 2016).

families in the East of Cheshire. When the feast was over, about two o'clock, Ryle was to write: 'I suddenly astonished Colonel Parker, my mother, sisters, and all the company, by standing up on my chair and exclaiming at the top of my voice, "Well, Colonel Parker, I have had a good dinner."' The host was to speak of it as 'the greatest compliment ever … paid by his young friends', but it is more than doubtful whether Susanna Ryle thought the same about her seven-year-old's behaviour.

Ryle described his infancy as 'happy, and pretty harmless years'. The 'most painful thing' he recorded was Saturday nights when, in addition to their daily ablutions, 'we were all well washed and soaped in a huge wooden tub'. The pain lay in what followed, 'having our heads combed with a small tooth-comb. This was torture indeed.' A happier memory was connected with Christmas Eve, when, after yule cheese and 'an enormous apple pie', 'we danced country dances with the servants in the kitchen to the music of the dulcimer'. Then the 'men servants sang songs in the servants' Hall, with all the labourers, gardeners, and farm servants … and we did not go to bed until the clock struck twelve and the "waits" had come to the door and sung Christmas carols'.[1]

Much of his time seems to have been spent on his own or with his sister Emma, whom he names as the other 'troublesome' one. From the age of four, he 'could at any time be kept quiet with a book … Travels, Natural History, Battles and Shipwrecks, were the subjects I cared most to read about.' Apart from occasional visits to a farm they owned outside the town, it was on holidays that he saw more of his father. On the Yorkshire coast at Bridlington he was introduced to sea bathing, and to sailing in the North Sea in his father's yacht, *Seaflower*, on which he was tied to the mast to stop him falling overboard. His parents evidently endorsed sea air and swimming as the fashionable cure for poor health. Other destinations for that

---

[1] 'Waits': an old term for street singers and musicians at Christmas and New Year.

purpose were Bootle and Crosby ('then a very quiet watering place') near Liverpool, and Hastings, one winter, for his mother's health. Railways had not yet arrived and such journeys were made by coach or canal boats drawn by horses.

Macclesfield's grammar school was of high reputation but the class-conscious society to which Ryle's parents belonged looked for a more distinctive education. So Ryle had tutors at home. Of specific dates in his childhood, he remembered two especially. The very first was the coronation of George IV in 1821, and the second, 8 August 1824, when, at the age of eight, his mother took him—'My father took no part or interest in such matters'—to a private preparatory school run by a clergyman at Over, near Nantwich. As this was twenty miles away it meant that he would see much less of home in the next three and a half years. The merit of the school was the academic ability of its head, in whose home the sixteen boys—'from all the leading families in Cheshire'—who were to be his companions slept in two rooms. John Jackson's school was good for learning. Ryle was to comment: 'I was well grounded in Latin and Greek. … We were also taught writing very badly, arithmetic, history, geography, French, and dancing.' The demerit was the 'rough comfort' and the too-frequent absence of their tutor who also served the parish of Over. This left too much time 'to run wild over the country', to play cricket, to endure the 'petty bullying, and tyranny' which can accompany an absence of adult supervision. His physique was to help him, 'a very broad, stumpy boy', he described himself (later he would be over six feet tall). He recalled:

> I don't think I was an ill-natured bad-tempered boy, but I was sturdy, very independant, and combative. I had a very strong opinion of my own, and never cared a bit for being in a minority, and was ready to fight anybody however big if necessary. I don't think I was at all happy at school. I liked the holidays, and thoroughly hated going back to school.

Of his holidays at this period, he says he remembered little, except that they were too short, and 'I used to amuse myself as much as I could'. In the grounds of Park House,

> I was out of doors from morning till night and was always either fishing, making rigging or sailing little boats, working in the carpenter's shop, constructing water-wheels, shooting with bow and arrow, jumping with a leaping-pole, and constructing all sorts of carts and sleighs. … In the evening after dark, I would read all night long till I went to bed—travels, adventures, shipwrecks, naval and military memoirs were my chief literature.

He counted it a grievance to be interrupted in order to meet visitors, and 'particularly disliked being taken to call, or be shown off anywhere'. That he was 'not particular' about his clothes, and had his pockets 'stuffed with large knives, and quantities of string', contributed, he says, to his being 'a general nuisance to the house throughout the holidays'.

Ryle's later comments on his early schooling were clearly intended for the guidance of his own children when they became parents. Eight years of age, he told them, was at least two years too early for a child to be sent away from home. From experience, he urged, 'Love is one grand secret of successful training … Try hard to keep a hold of your child's affections.'[1] His conclusion about his prep school years was: 'I left Mr Jackson's school in December 1827, tolerably well grounded in Latin, and Greek, but having learnt a vast amount of moral evil, and got no moral good.'

* * *

Ryle's next school, save for the Latin and Greek, bore little resemblance to Jackson's vicarage at Over. For one thing it took him to a

---

[1] J. C. Ryle, 'The Duties of Parents', *The Upper Room* (1888; repr. Edinburgh: Banner of Truth Trust, 1977), 287.

distant part of England, as his two-day coach journey taught him at the end of January 1828. Eton College was twenty-one miles west of London, where it had stood beside the Thames at Windsor since 1441, and prided itself on being the nation's citadel of learning. It was with no exhilaration that the new boy from Macclesfield attended and had his name enrolled in the Entrance Book on 7 February by Dr John Keate, the headmaster. He was a few months short of his twelfth birthday.

> I did not like going at all. I did not know a single boy of the 600 in the school, and was awkward, shy, and young for my age. Moreover I had been brought up entirely in the north of England, and felt some-what out of my element in going to the south.

His father had arranged for his placement in the house presided over by Edward Hawtrey, one of the assistant masters. There could not have been a better choice but Ryle found it 'full of boys of noble family, or highly connected', and commented, 'It may well be imagined how awkwardly a raw Cheshire boy like myself would fit in, amongst such a set.' Yet it was not unusual for sons of the affluent merchant class in the North of England to be sent to Eton. Some of his cousins had already been pupils, and so had William Gladstone of Liverpool a few years before him. Ambitious parents who could afford it saw Eton as both a high citadel of learning and as an avenue to a lifetime of rewarding contacts for their offspring. The young Ryle saw it in no such light:

> I was thoroughly miserable for the first half year, and if my father had let me have my own way, I would gladly have been taken away. This however he wisely would not consent to, though I believe I caused him a good deal of anxiety.

Eton's pupils were divided into two groups of considerable difference. 'Collegers' were those who boarded on the school's central premises. They were seventy in number at this date, with twenty sleeping in one room, and fifty in another, 240 feet long. Ryle regarded it as a wretched and rough system and says that the Collegers, as a rule, were boys 'very inferior in rank and description'. The other and larger group were 'Oppidans', whose parents paid more for them to be in other residences about the town, one of which was Hawtrey's house. Here, with respect to 'temporal comfort' there was everything that could be desired, and Ryle had his own room. 'We were well fed, well cared for, and wanted for nothing.'

A system known as 'fagging' was operative throughout the school. In this arrangement, younger boys acted as servants to senior pupils at certain times of day. As a new boy the system was uncomfortable to Ryle, although as he went up through the school he was persuaded of the merit of compulsory fagging. Among other things, it could bring young noblemen 'to their proper level'.

> My opinion is distinct and decided, that a certain quantity of fagging in large public schools does no harm at all. On the contrary, I think that it often does good to young boys who have been petted and spoilt, and indulged at home, and taught to think that their own will is law. It obliges them to submit to the will of others, and teaches the great lesson which we all have to learn in life, that we cannot always have our own way.

This was evidently part of his own experience as a junior. 'I gradually', he says,

> fell into my place, and I have no doubt it was an excellent thing for my character, and taught me to bear, and forbear, and put up with much, and mortify my self-will, and accommodate myself to the various characters and temperaments of others.

'No one was formally sanctioned to administer corporal punishment except the head master.' If some thought that 'flogging Keate' did this too efficiently, Ryle does not seem to endorse that view, telling us, 'Dr Keat [*sic*] was a good disciplinarian, a good scholar, and kept good order.' Even so it is evident the boys themselves had to learn to keep order and it was an early lesson for Ryle in Hawtrey's house. He early had the misfortune to get too much attention from a young gentleman (later to become Lord Chamberlain to the Pope) of the bullying type and ever ready to tease the boy from the North. His fellow boarders advised Ryle that a fight was the best way to settle this, and so, one night 'we proceeded to settle matters at once in the usual manner, with our fists, before a small company of delighted spectators'. After two or three rounds the bully said he had had enough. 'This was', Ryle adds, 'my first, and only fight the whole time I was at Eton.' He must have had no part in settling other disputes in the College which was done by 'fighting in the playing fields before two or three hundred boys'.

His nearly seven years at Eton fell into two parts. In the earlier period, 'I did not come forward much in any way; I did not distinguish myself much in any game.' Much time was spent in silently watching, considering and reading. In terms of ability he took only a middle rank in the Fourth Form. The major change came in his last two years, when 'I suddenly came forward as a leading boy in the school.' In the select group of twenty-five who formed the Eton Society for Debating, in a room above Mrs Hatton's shop, he took a prominent part. His educational ability was now apparent. He was 'very high in the 6th Form', and 'surprised everyone' by taking fourth place in the examination for the prestigious Newcastle Scholarship (instituted at the College by the Duke of Newcastle in 1829). Perhaps his position would have been still higher had his place in the College XI not taken time, especially in his last year when he was captain of cricket. It was not his only sport; he enjoyed hockey, and was an oarsman on the river, but cricket was loved best. A friend who was his junior would later recall Ryle's prowess on the cricket field, telling us that he could strike balls with such force that, 'It was as much as a boy's life was worth to try to stop them; he was a hard hitter, a character which he kept up through life, and wherever I go into

Schooldays

battle, either in great or small things, I always hope to be at his side if he will take me with him.'[1] Although some would deride the words of the Duke of Wellington that the Battle of Waterloo was won on the playing fields of Eton, Ryle knew something of what he meant.

Before the end of his school career he could say, 'nothing was done in which I did not take a leading part'. It included breaking down the barriers between Collegers and Oppidans. 'I was', he would tell his family,

> ambitious, and fond of influence and power, attained power, and was conscious of it. Eton at that time so far as the boys were concerned, was a perfect republic. Rank and title, and name, and riches went for nothing at all, and a boy was valued according to his cleverness, or boating powers, or cricketing skill, or bodily strength, or good nature, or general agreableness, and pleasantness, and for nothing else at all.

At this date the reputation of the public school at Rugby was rising on account of the changes introduced by its young headmaster Thomas Arnold. Later, at Oxford, Ryle would note the difference which placed those from Eton 'at an enormous disadvantage'. The Rugby men came from a 'hotbed, trained and crammed to the uttermost', the product of Arnold's policy of taking boys 'by hand' and giving them much individual help and encouragement. Ryle, at Eton, had benefitted from the personal guidance of Edward Hawtrey, who had broadened his reading, outside the Greek and Roman authors, yet the attention given was not close: 'no boy ever dreamed of looking up to his tutor as a friend or adviser'. However, perhaps not without a touch of prejudice, Ryle was not ready to regard Arnold's policy superior in this area. In the end, he thought, the Eton system probably produced

---

[1] C. W. Furse, vicar of Staines, quoted in Ian. D. Farley, *J. C. Ryle, First Bishop of Liverpool: A Study in Mission Amongst the Masses* (Carlisle, Cumbria: Paternoster, 2000), 46. Furse was a fag to Ryle, a system adopted in all the public schools and not without value in the maturing of boys.

11

a greater number of men able to take their position, and fit it well in any place of life. We were all thrown upon ourselves, and obliged to think for ourselves with very little help of any kind and I think the system made us more independant and able to do our duty anywhere, than the Rugby system did.

One lifelong lesson Ryle gained at Eton was not to be impressed merely by anyone's name or title. He left the College with 'an instinctive dislike to the custom of honouring people because of their rank or position, if they had no intrinsic merit'.[1] This was no small acquisition in the class-conscious world of nineteenth-century England and he would need it in days ahead.

> I left Eton with unfeigned regret. The last year and three quarters that I was there were perhaps in a natural point of view one of the happiest periods of my life and did most for the formation of my natural character. But I believe it was high time I should leave and I should have got no good by staying there any longer. I was master of as much Latin and Greek as I ever knew in my life, and was fit to compete for anything in Classics at either Oxford or Cambridge. If I had stayed longer at Eton I think it would have been bad for me, and would have developed perhaps much that was evil in my character.

So in the summer of 1834, he took the Windsor coach into London for the last time, and then back to home in Cheshire.

---

[1] 'Nothing used to annoy me so much, as being invited to Windsor Castle, by my cousin John Ryle Wood, in order to be playfellow to Prince George of Cambridge, of whom I did not form a very high opinion.'

2

'The Greatest Change and Event in My Life'

Portrait of Ryle in his youth

'IN OCTOBER 1834, I entered Christ Church, Oxford, and remained there exactly 3 years.'

Ryle's introduction to this next stage of his life gives no hint of how momentous the time was to be before it was over. Many of the things of these years his family record would leave to one side. If he was proud of the college to which Eton men commonly went, he does not say so. Christ Church, founded in 1524, had long been among the most privileged of the Oxford colleges. At the time Ryle entered Christ Church there had been twenty-two British Prime Ministers and six of them had been its students. In 1831, of the ten men awarded first-class degrees in the university examinations, five were Christ Church men. Overshadowing the Tom Quad, in which Ryle had his first room, was the tower supporting Great Tom, a huge bell which struck every night 101 times, being the number of students when it was first heard in 1681. One writer of Oxford memories thought,

> The tolling of Great Tom is like a symbol of the predominance of Christ Church over the University. It is easily the most important, the most delightful of all Oxford's foundations. It has the largest revenues, it provides the best food and the most spacious rooms, and it sends forth the most successful alumni of any college.[1]

The number of scholars when Ryle came was considerably higher. There was a traditional division of the number between gentlemen commoners (also called nobleman-commoners), who paid extra fees, and others. He makes no mention of this, but there is oblique

---

[1] Toon and Smout, *Evangelical Bishop*, 19, quoting from C. Hobhouse, *Oxford as It Was and Is Today*.

reference in his words,

> I never saw such an amount of toadying, flattering, and fawning upon
> wealth, and title, as I saw amongst the undergraduates at Oxford. It
> thoroughly revolted me, and almost made me a republican. There
> was also a coldness, and a distance, a want of sociability and sym-
> pathy amongst undergraduates, which to a boy fresh from Eton was
> extremely offensive.

His other main criticism concerned the poverty of the help and
advice he gained from the tutor assigned to him; indeed he formed
the opinion, 'the College authorities really did not seem to care
whether we took a College degree, or took honours'. 'My first two
years at Oxford were practically thrown away. I read desultorily, and
spasmodically, kept up few friendships, kept myself to myself very
much.' Yet despite a first year with no sense of purpose, and a tutor
who was 'perfectly useless', he got one of the Fell Exhibitions at the
end of his first year. Yet the same tutor had led him to suppose that
he would get no more than a third-class degree. Henry Liddell, on
the other hand, proved 'a very good tutor', and urged him to sit for
the Craven University Scholarship, which he did successfully at the
end of his second year.

Even so, Ryle judged himself as comparatively unprofitable
in those first two years, and his examination success he attributed
chiefly to the knowledge he had gained at Eton. The one area in
which he was certainly not aimless concerned his first love. During
the summer time, he tells us, he played cricket 'incessantly, from 12
o'clock in the morning till dark, every day in the week'. He belonged
to the University XI all his time at Oxford, in his second and third
years as captain. He had much to do with making a match against
Cambridge, first played in 1827, a permanent fixture, and in the two
innings' match against that rival in 1836 he took ten wickets.

Sparing though he might be in making friends he was certainly
not a loner. 'At nights', he says, 'I idled a great deal of my time away

in the rooms of my friends.' In holiday periods from Eton it was the days when younger relatives and friends, male and female, came to stay at Park House, that were the high spots. With these frequent visitors, he tells us,

> we almost always played at cards or danced, and occasionally had dancing parties by gathering together all the young people in the neighbourhood. I was always passionately fond of dancing from the time I was 15—and especially fond of waltzing, reels, country dances, Sir Roger de Coverley,[1] and anything that had steam, and life, and go in it.

It was much the same during vacations while he was at Oxford. The summer of 1836, before the start of his final year, he spent largely at Malvern, the guest it seems of Colonel Parker, at whose former Cheshire home he had made his first speech. There he met with 'two handsome Miss Leycesters, who waltzed very well'. 'Between dancing with the Miss Leycesters in the evenings, dining … at the Hotel, playing at billiards, and reading Byron's works, my recollection is, that I wasted a great deal of time.' The connection with the young ladies he mentioned was evidently so noted during his three months' stay that 'it made so much talk, that at last I left Malvern and went home, and never saw them again'.

This way of life went on, he says, until he discovered that he 'had got a soul'. The remark seems surprising given he had been at church with his parents all his life, that he had been confirmed while at Eton, and both there and at Christ Church experienced daily services of worship. But the explanation lies in the conception of Christianity in which he had been brought up. He recalled:

> My father's house was respectable, and well-conducted, but there really was not a bit of religion in it. We had no family prayers at all, excepting on Sunday nights and that only occasionally. … Conversation on Sunday went on much as on a weekday. Letters were read

---

[1] Sir Roger de Coverley is the name of a country dance.

and written, and newspapers read just the same as on weekdays. ...
The plain truth is, that for the first 16 or 17 years of my life, there
was no ministry of the gospel at the Churches we attended. ... The
clergymen were wretched high and dry sticks of the old school, and
their preaching was not calculated to do good to anybody. ... We had
no real religious friends or relatives and no real Christian ever visited
our house. ... The plain truth is that neither in my own family, nor
among the Hurts or Arkwrights with whom I was most mixed up
when young can I remember that there was a whit of what may be
called real spiritual religion. ... We sometimes heard rumours when
we were children, of certain strange clergymen who were called Evangelical, but we never came across any of them; and were sedulously
brought up to regard them as well-meaning, extravagant, fanatical
enthusiasts, who carried things a great deal too far in religion. ... To
sum up all, I wish my children to remember that for about the first 18
years of my life, neither at home, nor school, nor college, nor among
my relatives or friends, had I anything to do good to my soul, or to
teach me anything about Jesus Christ.

The distinction he is making was between nominal, notional
religion and real Christianity. This needs to be kept in mind with
respect to his statement on not praying or reading a word of the Bible
till he was twenty-one. Clearly he had opened Bibles many times, but
not once so that it was alive and life-changing.

As Ryle spoke of this in later years, he was conscious that his
family had been a kind of microcosm of general spiritual conditions.
Apart from one thing, the Christianity of the previous hundred years
had been too generally asleep over the real meaning of Christianity.
The one thing that broke that slumber for numbers had been the
recovery of the New Testament message by George Whitefield, John
Wesley, and others in the so-called 'Methodist' revival. That movement had come to Macclesfield, shaking formal beliefs and changing
lives. Wesley first preached there in 1759, when 'a multitude of people
ran together but wild as colts untamed'. From beginnings in a cottage, a Methodist 'society' grew and one of the earliest to belong to it

was a Mrs Ryle. Her son, John (1744–1808) became an earnest sup-porter of Wesley. We read such entries in Wesley's *Journal* as: (April 1774) 'I went to Macclesfield, and came just in time to walk to the old church with the mayor [John Ryle]. The rain drove us into the house in the evening—that is, as many as could squeeze in—and we had a season of strong consolation'; (April 1776) 'I preached on the Green, near Mr Ryle's door. There are no mockers here, and scarce an inattentive hearer.' Three years later Wesley found the society 'increasing both in number and strength'; (1787) 'I preached at the new church [in Macclesfield] in the morning … Mon. 16 the house was well-filled at five in the morning. At noon I took a view of Mr Ryle's silk mill, which keeps two hundred and fifty children in per-petual employment.' Nor was it only John Ryle with whom Wesley visited. In another brief entry at Macclesfield he noted, (May 1783) 'at sister Ryle's, tea, conversed', and the next day, 'with E.R., etc. … conversed, christened, prayer'.[1]

Of this John Ryle, his grandson, J. C. Ryle, would later say, 'he was a very good man and an earnest Christian'. And of his grand-mother he would hear that 'she also was a very shrewd, sensible, Christian woman'. This being the case, how can it be that their son's house 'had not a bit of religion in it'? Had the son forgotten all he had seen and heard from his parents? On this point J. C. Ryle would later express a decided opinion:

> Poor dear man! He ought to have known better. My grandfather was a really good man, but my grandfather died unfortunately when he was young, and he came into his fortune unfortunately too soon, left the Wesleyans, and got thrown into the company of men who did him no good. But I always think that he secretly remembered what he used to hear when he was a boy, and knew more about religion than he cared to confess or practise.

[1] The references can be readily traced from the Index in vol. 8, *Journal of John Wesley*, ed. N. Curnock, Standard Edition (London: Kelly). It is possible that the 'E.R.' refers to Elizabeth Ryle, sister of John Sr, and that 'christened' refers to the baptism of John Ryle who was born in that year 1783.

The grandfather had died in 1808, when his son was twenty-four. The eight years between that event and the birth of J. C. Ryle was long enough for a major change in the house on Park Green. It may be that the fortune inherited, and a society marriage, contributed to the alteration in the second John Ryle, but fashionable public opinion, which stigmatized Methodist living as fanaticism, was still more influential. Evangelical experience is not hereditary, and what John Ryle Sr was strong enough to withstand, his son was not. The result was that J. C Ryle grew up without parental guidance in what was of first importance. This does not mean that without personal prayer and Bible reading he grew up dissolute, but, he confessed,

> It is only a special mercy that I had no taste for low company, or for the coarse vices and habits into which many young men run. For these things I had no natural inclination, my taste revolted against them, though I really do not think I had a bit of principle to keep me right.

He was like his father, a worldly gentleman, and it was only as he returned to Oxford for his last year that he discovered he was on the broad way which leads to destruction.

In the following century what would become the common account of Ryle's conversion was drawn from 'Canon Christopher's Reminiscences' published, after Ryle's death, by *The Record* (15 June 1900). Alfred Christopher, rector of St Aldate's, Oxford, wrote:

> God opened his eyes to the gospel in a very simple way. Not by a sermon, a book, a tract, a letter, or a conversation, but by a single verse of His Word impressively read by a clergyman unknown to him. It was in 1837, near the time of his final examination, that he was getting more serious than he had been in the earlier part of his undergraduate course. One Sunday his more serious state of mind led him into a parish church in the afternoon. A stranger read the prayers and lessons, whose name he never knew. He did not preach, and Mr Ryle told me that he remembered nothing about the sermon. But the stranger read the second chapter of St Paul's Epistle to the Ephesians

very impressively, and placed a short pause between each two clauses of the eighth verse: 'By grace are ye saved—through faith—and that not of yourselves—it is the gift of God.' How much can God do by one verse of His Word![1]

But Canon Christopher was unaware of the autobiography which Ryle had left for his children, in which nothing of this account of his conversion appears. Rather he said:

> The circumstances which led to a complete change in my character were very many and very various … It was not a sudden immediate change but very gradual. I cannot trace it to any one person, or any one event or thing, but to a singular variety of persons and things. In all of them I believe now the Holy Ghost was working though I did not know it at the time.

One of the circumstances to which Ryle refers was the start of a new Church of England congregation in Macclesfield unlike the two already existing 'where you might have slept as comfortably in those churches under the sermons of their ministers as you might in your own armchairs. with nothing to wake you up'.[2] In contrast, the ministry of John Burnet at St George's brought

> a new kind of religion into the Church of England, in that part of Cheshire … It certainly set many people thinking who never thought before about religion, even though they were not converted, and of these I was one. There was a kind of stir among dry bones, and a great outcry, and kind of persecution was raised, against the attendants of this new Church.

One of the attendants was his close friend and relative, Harry Arkwright. Another was his sister Susan. When both embraced what they heard, 'Evangelical religion in one way or another began to be talked of, and too often ridiculed and abused in our family'.

---

[1] *The Record*, 15 June 1900, 572. A very similar account appears in the volume by W. H. Griffith Thomas, *The Work of the Ministry* (1913), 185.
[2] *Abstract of Report and Speeches at the Forty-Fifth Annual Meeting of the Church Pastoral-Aid Society*, 1880, 8.

The disturbance which followed Susan's coming to faith prompted Ryle's attention, but he was not in any regular attendance at St George's, and 'still neither read my Bible, or said my prayers'. From services he attended at Oxford he gained a little—not the university sermons, 'so exceedingly dry, and lifeless', but those of the two clergy at St Peter's who 'were much more Evangelical men then, than they afterwards were when they became Bishops'.

One incident stood out as 'one of the first things that I can ever remember that made a kind of religious impression upon my soul'. During his days at Eton he had drawn close to the Coote family. He had spent the summer months with them in Ireland in 1834. About a year later, when he was nineteen, he received a rebuke from his friend Algernon Coote for swearing. 'He was the first person who ever told me to think, repent, and pray.' From that point he began to take seriously the sinfulness of sin.

When he returned to Oxford in the autumn of 1836, he says that for two years he had not been 'comfortable inwardly, and was rather perplexed by things that I saw and heard, but there was no change in my habits or outward behaviour'. At this stage his mind was set on gaining a first-class degree the following year. With this before him, there was no more socializing in the rooms of friends in the evenings; rather in the lodgings he now had at Jubbers, in High Street, opposite St Mary's Church, he could be found at his desk till one o'clock in the morning. Later he would doubt the wisdom of such practice for a student's health, but, mistake or not, the Holy Spirit was to use the ill health he came to experience for his good. The Christ Church archives record that in his last academic year Ryle was '*Aeger*' (sick).[1] Ryle dates this more specifically:

> about midsummer [1837] a severe illness … of inflammation of the chest confined me to bed for some days and brought me very low for some time. That was the time I remember distinctly when I first

[1] Toon and Smout, *Evangelical Bishop*, 26.

began to read my Bible, or began to pray. It was at a very curious crisis in my life—it was just about the time that I was taking my degree, and I have a strong recollection that my new views of religion helped me very greatly to go through all my examinations very coolly and quietly. In short, from about Midsummer 1837, till Christmas in the same year, was a turning point in my life.

The two references to 'Midsummer' in this quotation are significant. Midsummer Day was June 24. The second Scripture reading appointed by the Lectionary in the Book of Common Prayer for evening (or afternoon) the next day, June 25, was Ephesians chapter 2. This brings Ryle's account very close to the one Canon Christopher reported. The latter did not say that the hearing of Ephesians 2 was Ryle's conversion experience but that it 'opened his eyes to the gospel'. Ryle gives the same date as the time 'I first began to read my Bible, or began to pray'. It would appear that the 'some days' of illness followed that Sunday.

So Christopher's record is not in conflict with Ryle's, but the fuller information in the autobiography makes clear that the 'turning point' ran from 'Midsummer 1837, till Christmas in the same year'. Neither in his own experience, nor in that of anyone else, did Ryle think it important to date conversion to a particular day. As he would later preach, in the recognition of true conversion it is not the date which matters but its *nature* and *effects*. He summarizes:

Nothing I remember to this day, appeared to me so clear and distinct, as my own sinfulness, Christ's preciousness, the value of the Bible, the absolute necessity of coming out from the world, the need of being born again, and the enormous folly of the whole doctrine of Baptismal Regeneration. All these things ... seemed to flash upon me like a sunbeam in the winter of 1837, and have stuck in my mind from that time down to this.

People may account for such a change as they like, my own belief is, that no rational explanation can be given of it, but that of the Bible; it was what the Bible calls 'conversion', and 'regeneration'. Before that time I was dead in sins, and on the high road to hell, and from that time, I became alive, and had a hope of heaven. And nothing to my mind can account for it, but the free sovereign grace of God. It was the greatest event and change in my life, and has had an influence over the whole of my subsequent character and history.

'A first class honours in those days', Ryle commented, 'was a very serious affair.' He attained success with distinction when his final examinations came at the beginning of November. He was placed in the First Class *In Literis Humanioribus*.[1] This opened the way for him to take a teaching post at Christ Church, or a fellowship at Brasenose or Balliol. But, while seeing Oxford's buildings and colleges as 'things matchless in the world', life there had never appealed to him.

I left Oxford with a brilliant reputation for the honours which I had taken, but with very little love for the University, and very glad to get away from it. … In my foolishness I thought that I had a very different line of life before me, and left Oxford as soon as I could, never to return.

[1] His B.A. degree was conferred 22 February 1838. I am indebted to Derek Scales for this clarification of dates in 1837.

3

Church and Homes Divided

Old Henbury Hall

BEFORE we leave Oxford it is necessary to pause and notice something of what Ryle left behind him. It was during his time at the university that a movement was developing which would profoundly affect the Church of England. Although it was in the process of formation during his three years as an undergraduate, he makes no reference to it until his last term when, as a candidate for a first-class degree, he faced the examination of five days' paper work, and a one-day oral. At the oral, five students were taken in turn to be questioned on the Thirty-nine Articles, Bible, Prayer Book and Church History. With an audience of some fifty or sixty present, and three examiners asking whatever they thought fit, Ryle viewed this *viva voce* day as a stiff ordeal. 'For my own part, I remember being horrified by the questions which were asked of men who were examined before me, and kept wondering what I should have said.'

When it came to his turn, his examiner was Frederick Oakeley, 'since a pervert, and now a Roman Catholic Priest', he said in 1873.

> Curiously enough I remember to this day how many questions he asked me, about Tradition, the Fathers, the Creeds, Augustine, Pelagius, and other kindred subjects, all showing the direction in which his mind was going at the time.

That Ryle found himself able to answer every question 'with perfect ease', he attributed to his study of the Articles, with Hawtrey's help, at Eton for the Newcastle Scholarship, and subsequent study he had done at Oxford. The occasion was probably the first time he had spoken in public on evangelical principles.

Presumably Oakeley was required to judge a candidate's knowledge and ability, not his personal convictions. For in 1837, in his examiner's view, Ryle was representing opinions from which a number of Oxford's brightest men were dissociating themselves.

The change first became prominent in 1833, the year before Ryle came to the university, and in the form of three anonymous tracts, published under the name *Tracts for the Times*. The prime author was John Henry Newman, an Oxford don who became vicar of St Mary's the following year, by which time twenty-five such tracts had appeared. Where they might lead was at first not obvious. The motivation for their publication seemed to be opposition to the way the Church of England had become secularized, as an adjunct of the State, with her legislation, and the appointment of her bishops, controlled by the government and the Crown. What was needed, it was argued, was a recovery of the true nature of the church, and a higher view of its ministry and authority. Part of the remedy, as Tract One taught, was a recovery of the meaning of apostolic succession. The Church of England had not come into being in the sixteenth century, under the leadership of Elizabethan bishops who were 'henchmen' of the queen; rather it was catholic (i.e. part of the universal church) and apostolic.

Newman was by no means acting alone. He gained insight from fellow Oriel College tutor, John Keble, and from other Oriel men, E. B. Pusey, Richard Hurrell Froude, and Robert Wilberforce. They shared a common fear of rationalism in the Church of England, wanted to see orthodoxy strengthened and, at first, looked hopefully to evangelicals for support. Although this was not forthcoming, neither was opposition, at least not at the outset. Only gradually did it emerge that something more fundamental was involved in the programme of the Tractarians. To claim apostolic warrant for doctrine was one thing; it was quite another to say that the true church is to be identified in terms of an unbroken episcopal succession from the first century, and that only this succession guaranteed the authenticity of bishops and sacraments. The support of this case necessitated the elevation of 'tradition', derived from the Church Fathers, in order to supply what was not found in Scripture. The supposed justification for this was that no certainty about the church could be drawn from Scripture alone; there was therefore need to give tradition a coordinate position of authority, with the right to direct where Scripture is silent. Further, it was claimed, the church needed certainty to legitimise her divine calling because on her priesthood depended the efficacy of the sacraments which God has appointed for our salvation.

How far any of these points emerged in Ryle's oral examination in 1837 we cannot tell, but the real object of the Tractarian party was out in the open in 1838–9 when the *Remains of the Late Reverend Richard Hurrell Froude*, edited by Newman and Keble, were published. His letters to friends included such phrases as, 'that odious Protestantism', and 'I hate the Reformation and the Reformers more and more.'[1] Froude's feelings were not surprising because the Reformers' doctrine of the Church was in direct contradiction to what they were seeking to re-introduce, as witnessed by Article XIX of the Thirty-nine Articles, and more fully in the words of the Scots Confession of Faith (1560) which affirmed that 'The notes, signs, and assured tokens …[of the Church] are neither antiquity, title usurped, lineal descent, place appointed, nor multitude of men approving an error.'[2]

Shortly after Froude's publication, the evangelical leader Josiah Pratt, commenting on where the so-called Oxford movement was leading, observed:

Were the questions now awakened limited to the discipline of the

[1] Walter Walsh, *The History of the Romeward Movement in the Church of England, 1833–1864* (London: Nisbet, 1900), 96-7. Froude wrote to a ministerial friend in 1834: 'If you are determined to have a pulpit in your Church, which I would rather be without, do put it at the west end of the Church. … But whatever you do, pray don't let it stand in the light of the altar, which if there is any truth in my notions of ordination, is more sacred than the Holy of Holies was in the Jewish Temple' (*Remains of Froude*, 372).

[2] *The Confession of Faith*, in *Works of John Knox*, vol. 2 (Edinburgh: Banner of Truth Trust, 2014), 110 (spelling modernized).

Church, they might be left to their own level; but they affect the
vitals. The tendency, and I think the design of this agitation is to
form another way of salvation, beguiling unstable souls by the use of
old terms, but meaning by those terms quite different things; while
they rob the Lord Jesus of the glory of the sinner's justification … The
tendency of Tractarianism to Popery is everywhere seen. In its essence
it *is* Popery. Its rule of faith and duty is the same, for both interpret
and control Scripture by the traditions and opinions of uninspired
men: and acceptance with God is held, both by Popery and Tractarianism, to be on the ground of man's righteousness made perfect
by the righteousness of Christ; and so with an utter confusion of
Justification and Sanctification, and with the rejection of that which
is the great glory of the Gospel.[1]

Pratt spoke for all evangelicals in asserting the difference between
spiritual and formal religion. As the Tractarian movement developed
the emphasis was not on gospel preaching and truth received by faith.
Instead there was the steady promotion of sacramentalism, and the
place of the visual. In the words of one of their representatives: 'The
Tractarians turned to Ritualism. Eucharistic vestments, holy water,
candles, bells, incense and so forth were simply a way of showing
truth through symbols which anyone could grasp.'[2]

From the Roman Catholic standpoint, Ronald Knox stated the
contrast between the two opposing positions in the words:

An Evangelical Christian must ultimately choose in favour of direct
illumination of individual consciences rather than accept the idea
that Christ founded a Church that would be a faithful repository
of his message through the ages. A religion of experience displaces a
religion of sacraments; a religion of the Spirit supplants a religion of
authority.[3]

[1] *Memoir of the Rev. Josiah Pratt, by His Sons* (London: Seeleys, 1849), 340, 352.
[2] Penelope Fitzgerald, *The Knox Brothers* (London: Macmillan, 1977), 98.
[3] David Rooney, *The Wine of Certitude: A Literary Biography of Ronald Knox* (San
Francisco: Ignatius Press, 2009), 45. In the quotation I give it is hard not to wonder
if 'Spirit' is a misprint for 'spirit'. Knox's major work, *Enthusiasm*, works out the
theme that the evangelical experience, resting on feeling, is necessarily uncertain. He
ignored the certainty of faith which the Spirit of God works in the elect (John 10:4).

A crisis point came in 1841 with the publication of Newman's Tract Ninety. In it he claimed that the Thirty-nine Articles do not condemn official Roman Catholic teaching, only 'certain absurd practices and opinions which intelligent Romanists repudiate as much as we do'. This was a staggering argument in view of such Articles as VI, XIV, XXII, XXV, XXVIII, and it was condemned by the leading represent-atives of the university. Yet the teaching continued to gain ground. In 1843, a friend of Oakeley's, visiting Oxford, found among supporters of the movement 'a universal acquiescence in the Council of Trent, as being the only basis upon which an ultimate reunion will be effected, and a universal admission that the notion of independent national Churches is absurd'. When another Tractarian, W. G. Ward, went on to argue, with Newman, that, while he subscribed to the Thirty-nine Articles, he 'renounced no one Roman dogma', he was deprived of his degrees by the Convocation of the University. Oakeley, Ryle's examiner, at this time in charge of Margaret Chapel, London, agreed with Ward, and was prosecuted by the bishop of London. The result was the removal of Oakeley's licence to undertake any ministerial offices in the Province of Canterbury 'until he retracted his error'. In 1845, both Newman and Oakeley seceded to the Church of Rome. The latter could have been speaking for them both when he wrote that it had been his object to 'bring my own Church into the utmost possible sympathy and harmony with the Roman'.[1]

While some were to follow Newman and Oakeley, a majority of sympathizers remained in parishes across the country, and became known as Anglo-Catholics or ritualists. Dr Pusey remained at Oxford, and although suspended from preaching before the univer-sity for two years after a sermon upholding the Roman teaching of the Real Presence in the consecrated bread and wine, he continued to steer the Romeward movement in the Church of England. Pope Pius IX was to say of Pusey to Dean Stanley, 'I compare him to a

---

[1] For references, see Walsh, *History of the Romeward Movement*, 139-46.

bell, which always sounds to invite the faithful to Church, and itself always remains outside.'[1]

It is germane to the life of Ryle to note something of the reasons why the Oxford movement commanded the influence which it did. Prominent among those reasons was the comparative youthfulness of its leaders: Hurrell Froude was only thirty-three when he died; Newman was the dominant figure when in his early thirties. Ability, charm, and self-confidence, gave them influence, and the excitement of what they were proposing, coupled with a degree of hero worship, won the support of disciples who were their juniors. Perhaps most significant was the fact that numbers of the leaders acted with the zeal of converts, and what they were converted *from* was what they were working to see changed in the Church.

The Evangelical Revival of the previous century had started a recovery of belief in evangelical Christianity in the Church of England. None of the leaders of that revival survived to 1800, but their successors did, including such ministers as Charles Simeon, Richard Cecil, and Thomas Scott, and public figures, most notably, William Wilberforce. At the beginning of that century no group approached the evangelicals in what they were accomplishing both at home and abroad. It was evangelicals in the Church of England who led in the formation of the Church Missionary Society (1799), the British and Foreign Bible Society (1804), and the Church Pastoral Aid Society (1836). In Parliament it was evangelicals who did most to bring down the Slave Trade. At the Eclectic Society, London's gathering of evangelical clergy, one minister, in 1810, spoke of 'the most astonishing change in the public mind ever known'. Another observed, 'It is even disgraceful in some places not to profess religion.'[2]

---

[1] *The Protestant Dictionary*, eds. C. H. H. Wright and C. Neil (London: Hodder & Stoughton, 1904), 494.
[2] *The Thought of the Evangelical Leaders: Notes on the Discussions of The Eclectic Society London During the Years 1798-1814*, ed. John H. Pratt (Edinburgh: Banner of Truth Trust, 1978), 477.

Yet within two decades it was the sons of evangelical homes who repeatedly became leaders in the Tractarian movement. Newman in his *Apology for His Life* (*Apologia pro Vita Sua*) would speak of his youthful evangelical background and of his conversion whilst among that school. E. B. Pusey, in his early writings, two volumes on *Theology of Germany* (1828, 1830), spoke of how Luther turned from the 'meritorious performances of a Romish Convent' to 'the right understanding of Scripture, in whose doctrines alone he found rest'. And he upheld the Reformers and 'Their, or rather the Biblical, rule that "Scripture is its own interpreter"'.[1] I have mentioned Robert Wilberforce, one of the group at Oriel College. He was one of the three sons of the evangelical leader to become clergy in the Church of England and both he and his brother Henry would later be received into the Church of Rome. The third son who was ordained, Samuel, we will note below as rising to a distinguished career in the Church of England and from whom Anglo-Catholics would face little opposition. A friend of the Wilberforce sons was William Gladstone, mentioned above as the north-country boy who preceded Ryle to Eton. For a time the lives of Gladstone and Ryle ran parallel. Gladstone was also a leader in the Debating Society at Eton, and, like Ryle, went on to Christ Church, Oxford. But unlike Ryle, Gladstone came from an evangelical upbringing. He had originally thought of becoming a clergyman. Instead, among the Tractarians at Oxford, his views were to change and, in the words of one of his biographers, 'by the late 1830s he had moved far from the Evangelicalism of his youth'.[2] Instead of the Church, Gladstone was to spend sixty-two years as a Member of Parliament. He had a post in Peel's government in 1841, and would exercise influence on religious affairs through his long life. The evangelical leader Josiah Pratt would say of him in 1842, 'I wish Mr Gladstone were not a member of the Government. As a

[1] Walsh, *History of the Romeward Movement*, 77.
[2] Roy Jenkins, *Gladstone* (London: Macmilllan, 1995), 42.

man of talent and industry, he has weight; and though he is a man of religious feeling, yet his fallacious views of "*the Church*" lead him deplorably astray.'[1]

Two more examples of the same pattern will suffice. George Henry Ryder and Henry Edward Manning were both Oxford undergraduates from evangelical homes, the former at Oriel and the latter at Balliol. Both were drawn into the Newman circle. In 1833, we are told, 'Ryder's Evangelicalism was fast waning.' Keble teased him for the *volte-face* he was showing. Yet in that same year, in marrying Sophia Sargent, Ryder was linked to one of the best-known of evangelical households. John Sargent (1780–1833) was rector of Lavington, Sussex, a friend of Charles Simeon, and biographer of Henry Martyn. Henry Manning's views were slower in developing. Sargent had appointed him as a curate in 1831. At that date, Manning would later say, 'I had no view of the sacrament of the Body and Blood of Christ; and no idea of the Church.'[2] In 1833 he would marry another of the Sargent daughters, Caroline. Yet despite this marital unity with what Newsome called 'the purest Evangelical stock',[3] both Ryder and Manning would be received into the Church of Rome, Manning eventually becoming cardinal archbishop of Westminster, the first since the Reformation. It was Mary Sargent, mother of these two daughters, who outlived her husband by many years, who had the heaviest pain to bear in the spiritual dispersion of her family. The reader will find the story in detail in David Newsome's moving book, *The Parting of Friends*.

How is such a drain from the evangelical side to be explained? An explanation is to be heard from three sides. From the Roman Catholic, it was a case of individuals discovering that spiritual safety lay only within their fold, because a 'gospel without the Church' cannot

---

[1] *Memoir of Rev. Josiah Pratt*, 347.

[2] Quoted in David Newsome, *The Parting of Friends: The Wilberforces and Henry Manning* (Grand Rapids: Eerdmans, 1993), 200-1.

[3] *Ibid.*, 3.

save. Her sacraments promise the sure way to heaven: 'The priest renews the crucifixion of Christ every time he blesses the bread and the wine. In the sacrament of penance he conveys the power of God to forgive sin and heal the soul.'[1] Like many before and since, George Ryder, suddenly taken ill and facing death, trusted himself to this supposed certainty.

The Anglo-Catholic teaching was basically the same, and with the same appeal. But Anglo-Catholics differed from Roman Catholics in asserting that their Church also stood in unbroken succession from the apostles, with valid sacraments, yet, while reunion with Rome was desirable, it was not immediately essential.

The evangelical explanation of those who fall way was very different. It was that individuals or families may take the name 'evangelical' without knowing the reality of evangelical experience. Newman himself comes close to stating this thinking. Writing of himself in the third person, he was to say in 1874,

> And, in truth, much as he [Newman] owed to the Evangelical teaching, so it was he never had been a genuine Evangelical … the Evangelical teaching, considered as a system and in what was peculiar to itself, had from the first failed to find a response in his own religious experience. He had indeed been converted by it to a spiritual life, and so far his experience bore witness to its truth; but he had not been converted in that special way which it laid down as imperative, but so plainly against rule as to make it very doubtful in the eyes of normal Evangelicals whether he had really been converted at all … He was sensible that he had ever been wanting in those special Evangelical experiences which, like the grip of the hand or other prescribed signs of a secret society, are the sure token of a member.[2]

These words, however, cover a justification of Newman's position. He did not question the fundamental truths held by evangelicals

[1] Fitzgerald, *Knox Brothers*, 97. Any reader in doubt of the Roman Catholic teaching should go direct to the *Catechism of the Catholic Church* (London: Geoffrey Chapman, 1994).
[2] *Letters and Correspondence of J. H. Newman*, 1st edition, 122-3. Quoted by Walsh, 13.

but was challenging the 'narrowness' of their understanding. In the understanding which he rejected, he claimed that conversion had to be according to a 'special way', known only to an exclusive circle of devotees. This observation was common among those who moved away from evangelicalism. It was presented, for example, in the writings of James Stephen, son of the evangelical leader James Stephen. The son protested at how the successors of Wesley and Whitefield, who became the Church's

> most popular teachers had not merely been satisfied to tread the narrow circle of the 'Evangelical' theology, but had exulted in that bondage as indicating their possession of a purer light than had visited other ministers of the Gospel.[1]

It is certainly true that evangelical teaching was 'narrow' compared with the breadth of the one that Anglo-Catholics admired, namely, that all Church people are regenerate at baptism. But the question is, which is true to Scripture? To caricature evangelical teaching on conversion, as though there is a precise pattern to which every conversion must conform, was to avoid the real question. Certainly, conversion is a process in which experiences are not identical. But where there is real conversion, through the work of the Spirit in regeneration, there will be the same spiritual evidence which the unconverted do not and cannot share. At that point the New Testament is exclusive. The apostle John writes of defectors, 'They went out from us, but they were not of us; for if they had been of us, they would no doubt have continued with us' (1 John 2:19). For various reasons, people may for a time appear to belong to Christ and hold orthodox belief. Upbringing, self-advantage, and culture may hide for a while what is missing. But let the disadvantages of being an evangelical Christian come to be experienced and those unrenewed by the Holy Spirit will turn to whatever other system has greater appeal to their nature.

[1] James Stephen, *Essays on Ecclesiastical History* (1849; repr. London: Longmans, 1872), 447.

'Love not the world' is a comprehensive warning. It was no easy thing for students at Oxford, coming from evangelical homes, to identify with evangelicals when it meant being nicknamed 'Peculiars' or 'Methodists'. William Wilberforce had reason to warn his son, Samuel, when at Oriel, against the 'dread of ridicule' and the 'fear of singularity', reminding him, 'More perhaps depends on the selection of acquaintances than on any other circumstance in life.'[1] Lizzy, sister of the Wilberforce brothers at Oxford, wrote to Robert of her concern that Oxford was leading him to hide his religion, and not 'to see the distinction between the Christian and the amiable and good man of the world … I sometimes wish that you and dear Sam were where there is real piety.' 'The trouble', comments Newsome, 'was that both Robert and Samuel found the Evangelical set utterly unprepossessing.' With reference to the difficulty, Robert explained to his father,

> At Oriel there are not perhaps above two or three men whom you can call really religious … the men generally who are most religious belong (I believe) to Wadham or St Edmund Hall and are very low by birth and equally vulgar in manners, feelings and conduct. Would you have me form acquaintances with these?[2]

In a letter to Daniel Wilson, bishop of Calcutta, Josiah Pratt, summarised what he saw happening in the Church of England:

> Ignorance of the Gospel, with the accompanying worldliness of a great body of the Clergy, and the enmity of numbers of them to the distinguishing doctrines and the converting and spiritual power of the truth as it is in Jesus, have long prepared many for any system which should plausibly free men from the obligation of their just views of religion, and enable them to unite and settle down in a system more comfortable to the views and feelings of fallen man … though Popery makes large demands on the outward man, its compensations are so invaluable to the unrenewed man, as to make it the religion which he desires, if he must have any religion at all.[3]

[1] Newsome, *Parting of Friends*, 54-5.
[2] *Ibid.*, 77.
[3] *Memoir of Rev. Josiah Pratt*, 352.

The above may seem a lengthy digression from biography but, without this context, a life of Ryle would be like a life of the Duke of Wellington without the Napoleonic Wars.

* * *

While Ryle had frequent home-comings during school and university days, a number of changes had taken place. For one thing, before he left Oxford in 1837 the family residence had changed: home was no longer in Macclesfield. During his years at university his parents and family had moved three miles out into the country to the west. The manufacturing town had grown around Park House, where he was born, and his father had judged it time to move out and live among the landed gentry. The Henbury mansion and its estate was thus acquired, and John Charles on his home-coming found it 'a very pleasant place' and 'thoroughly in the country'. Standing outside the door, 'on any fine evening', the only distant sound to be heard was that of the dinner bell at other great homes in the area. Fields, woods, and water, he tells us, made up about a thousand acres of their land: 'there was much that was extremely beautiful about it both in the grounds, and in the distant views from them, and I soon became exceedingly attached to it.'

Part of his attachment was that, as the eldest son, he was heir of all he could see, and he saw Henbury Hall as his future permanent residence in the area which was his first love among the counties of England. He would later comment to a Lancashire audience, 'I lived in Cheshire, a fine county, no county breeds better and taller men than Cheshire does.'

Yet, while for most of the three and a half years after 1837 Henbury was to be his home, it comes as a surprise to us that Ryle would later comment to his children that these years 'were a season of very great trial to me, and I trust that no one of my children will ever have to go through the same'.

The problem was that, while the life of the household remained the same as at Park House, John Charles was not the same. His parents had no opposition to religion, and John Ryle Sr had contributed generously to St George's, but to see a repetition of their daughter Susan's singularity in their eldest son where they had never expected to see it, was very unwelcome. There was no doubting John Charles had come back from Oxford a different man. He would recall:

> The consequences of this change were very great indeed … it caused great uncomfortableness in my own family, and made my position very unpleasant indeed. In fact no one can tell what I had to go through, in hundreds of petty ways. … It made an awkwardness, and uncomfortableness, and an insensible kind of estrangement which no one can comprehend but those who have gone through it. … I had the constant uncomfortable feeling that on account of my religious opinions I was only a tolerated person in my own family and somewhat alienated and estranged from all my old friendships among my relatives.

It meant that what he could do in the way of Christian witness while living under his father's roof was greatly restricted. Any attempts at evangelization

> would have been strongly objected to, and would have given great offence. The utmost that I could ever do, was to read family prayers in the housekeeper's room before breakfast every morning to my sisters, the housekeeper and all the maids, but not to the men-servants. My father and mother tolerated this but never attended it.

The loneliness he now felt was not simply within the immediate family circle. Rather, the change he had experienced

> made a complete breach between all the friends and all the relatives I ever had before. I mean by this, that it made a kind of gulf between us, and there was a kind of tacit understanding that my tastes, and likings, and habits, had undergone a complete change. … It made … an insensible kind of estrangement which no one can comprehend but those who have gone through it … my friends thought me

wrong, and I thought them wrong. That they were annoyed at me, yet could not alter me; that I was sorry for them, and could not alter them.

A particular opponent was his cousin Canon John Ryle Wood, 'who was horrified at my change', and took a lead in arguing against evangelical religion.

No doubt, as a young Christian, Ryle's behaviour was not faultless and it may be thought he could have avoided some of the estranged relationships had his change of lifestyle not been so pronounced. Billiards no longer had any of his time; invitations to dances were all declined; and on a visit to London he mentions 'old Lady Keats being exceedingly cross, because I would not go with her and the girls to Drury Lane Theatre'. Would less rigour have made him more engaging to the friends he lost? This he did not consider as a possibility. From the beginning of his Christian life he was convinced of the 'indispensable necessity of holiness of life, being the only evidence of a true Christian', to which he linked 'the absolute need of coming out from the world and being separate from its vain customs, recreations, and standard of what is right'. Painful although these years were, he told his children,

> I have no doubt it was all for good. I believe it gave a decision and a thoroughness to my Christianity with all its defects, for which I shall always have reason to thank God.
>
> I think it well to remark by the way that Christians whom I recollect in those days strike me as having been much more decided and thorough-going than the Christians I have met of late years. The line of demarcation between religion and irreligion was much more distinct than it appears to be now. If a Christian was a Christian, there was no mistake about it. In fact, it made it more difficult to be a Christian; if, once you were one, in some respects it was more easy.

4

All Doors Shut Except One

District around Macclesfield, from a map of 1843

I N THE FOUR years between 1837 and 1841, from Ryle's age at twenty-one to twenty-five, there was a series of opportunities open to him which, for one reason or another he did not take. The probability when he came down from Oxford was that he would follow his father into Parliament. John Ryle Sr had relinquished his position as an MP that same year 1837, and it appears there were some who wanted the son to come forward to represent the borough of Macclesfield. The proposal had appeal to him, and he was currently doing a lot of reading 'of such subjects, as would prepare me for going into Parliament'. Many years later he would say of this date, 'I was on the point of entering Parliament.'[1] However, he decided that it would be premature to become a candidate for election and postponed taking the step: 'I declined to come forward, from a deep sense of my own inexperience, and from a natural backwardness which has clung to me all the days of my life.'

Politicians at this date were not the salaried professionals of modern times. John Ryle's parliamentary career had not entailed his living in London, and, like all MPs, he drew his income from other sources. In John Charles's case his thoughts of a good salary attracted him to the legal profession. This took him in 1838 to try his hand at law with Jonathan Christie in Lincoln's Inn, London, where he took lodgings in Pall Mall and lived 'chiefly', he said, 'at the Oxford and Cambridge Club'. While he had 'got off the rails' with his 'old worldly companions', the legal work was congenial, as was his attendance on

[1] W. F. Machray, *The First Bishop of Liverpool* (London: Thynne, 1900), 7. This is not strictly a biography but a series of helpful articles first printed in the *Liverpool Courier*.

the ministry of Baptist Wriothesley Noel at St John's, Bedford Row, where he became a regular communicant. Of this time, he recalled:

> I have reason to believe that I did pretty well in law, and it is curious to think what I might have come to, if I had been able to continue in it. But God ordered it differently, and would not allow me to be a lawyer.

His way forward was stopped after only six months, not by his own choice (though he did not like London) but by poor health. The chest complaint of his last year in Oxford came back amid the smoke and fog of the capital and a return to Henbury was his only option.

From what I have quoted above of the distance which had come between Ryle and his father it might be assumed that there was a breakdown of natural affection on the parent's part. This would be an unwarranted judgment. It must be remembered that Ryle's memories were recorded for his immediate family and were never intended as public statements about his parents. There is nothing to suggest his father was not proud of him and ready to advance his career. On the contrary, John Charles, back in Cheshire, was soon involved with the 'Daintry and Ryle Bank', as the local people called it. For a summer holiday he went with 'the whole of our family' to Beaumaris 'and saw a good deal of North Wales'. To get his eldest son settled in Cheshire, John Ryle Sr offered to purchase a house for him and give him £800 a year, if he married. No doubt it was with such thoughts in view that the parents also encouraged him to accept invitations 'for two or three nights at a time to many different houses in Cheshire' where there were eligible young ladies. For this course, Ryle says, 'somehow I felt no disposition'. For one thing, his education in exclusively male circumstances had left him 'very ignorant about women's characters'.

> I saw extremely few women that I fancied at all, although there were some that I liked better than others, but I could not fancy for a moment that anyone would marry me if I had asked them. … If I had known them then as well as I do now, I have not the least doubt I should have been married between 21 and 25.

But the spiritual factor also entered here. House parties which he would once have enjoyed, he now found 'a very great bore'. But, lonely though he became as compared with former days, his change brought him many new friends, 'kind-hearted excellent Christians', and he named seven families in particular:

John Thornycroft, and his two sisters, afterwards Mrs Henry Arkwright, and Mrs Massey—The two Miss Leycesters of Toft—Mrs Tollemache, then at Tilston; Admiral Harcourt, and his wife; Captain Hope, afterwards Admiral Sir Henry Hope.

Of some of these names we know nothing. Thornycroft and his sisters we assume belonged to the neighbouring estate where his dog Caesar would later go. Charlotte and Emma Leycester were daughters of the Leycesters of Toft Hall, an old mansion in the south of Cheshire with fine views of the Welsh mountains. One could confuse them with the Miss Leycesters with whom Ryle had danced so happily at Malvern before his conversion, but that cannot be, for he recorded that he never saw them again. The two from Toft Hall were serious Christians and it was probably they who introduced him to their cousin, Catherine Marsh, who became a lifelong friend of Ryle's as we shall see below. Mrs Tollemache was Georgina Louisa Best before she married John Tollemache in 1826 and lived with him in Cheshire. Ryle probably first saw them in the church he attended on Sundays during his preparatory school days at Over. She would play an important part later in Ryle's story, and in her future home he would also meet Admirals Harcourt and Hope again.

Of all these friends at this stage in his life Ryle says that they were

great helps to me in one way or another; strengthened me in my principles, encouraged me in my practice, solved many of my difficulties, assisted me by their advice, counselled me in many of my perplexities, and cheered me generally by showing me that I was not quite alone in the world. … they did me a great deal of good, and mightily helped my soul.

Ryle thought another companionship worthy enough to mention to his children. Lyme Hall remains today the greatest mansion in Cheshire and one of the few open to the public. What endeared him to the place was the gift of 'two huge Lyme mastiffs' he had received in his youth from the owner of a famous breed which traced its ancestry back to the Battle of Agincourt when one of them refused to leave his wounded owner. By these dogs, Ryle tells us, he was 'incessantly accompanied'. When one died its collar was carefully preserved, but at this stage of Ryle's life Caesar remained as his daily companion.

Precisely what role Ryle had in his father's bank is not clear. He was not a partner, and did not know the inner workings. 'My only business was to sign notes, use my eyes, and learn as much as I could generally of banking business.' The monetary notes were the equivalent of cheques which the Macclesfield and Cheshire Bank promised to honour to the amount the note stated. A record exists which says that on one day, 25 February 1841, Ryle signed at least 119 such bank notes.[1]

Besides this there was much to occupy his time. As a county magistrate he attended weekly sessions in the town; and, appointed captain of the 600-strong Macclesfield troop of the Cheshire yeomanry, he found it no easy thing to keep his men 'in a state of efficiency' needed in 'a world of trouble and vexation'. Once a year the troop went the thirty-five miles to Liverpool for ten days of exercise and inspection on the sands at Crosby where he had gone to swim as a child. At other times he was also at Crosby for cricket matches. Cricket was the one amusement which he kept up through this period, and he recorded taking part in 'gentlemen's matches in Derbyshire, Staffs, Notts, and Leicestershire'.

At the end of three and a half years, in June 1841, the routines and the tensions all came to a dramatic end: 'We got up one summer's morning, with all the world before us as usual, and went to bed that same evening completely and entirely ruined.' A London bank had

[1] Russell, *Man of Granite*, 27.

refused to accept a monetary note of the Macclesfield and Cheshire Bank on account of trouble in the bad debts of the latter's Manchester bank. At that point the Macclesfield branch was still solvent, but as the news was heard there was such demand on deposits at both branches that they both fell overnight. Anxious crowds, who had trusted Daintry and Ryle for forty-one years, waited in vain outside closed doors. 'Several people were injured in the crush and one man had his thigh broken.'[1]

John Ryle Sr was ruined. At the demand of creditors, all was lost—his properties, bank, and silk mill. 'My grandfather', Ryle was to tell his children, 'was the only Ryle who ever attained great wealth, and my father was the first Ryle who left Cheshire after losing every penny of it.' The son had not seen the letter which, months before, his father had sent to Ravenscroft, their Manchester manager, and knew nothing of an impending disaster. His father had written to that manager, 'If you knew a tenth of the bad effects of your management as I see it here, you would say you never heard of a more melancholy and heart-breaking case. … I am at my wits' end.'[2]

Unlike this letter, Ryle privately laid blame upon his father:

> I suspected my father was uncomfortable for two or three years before the crash came, but he never told me anything about it. I certainly cannot say I was surprised as much as some, and simply because I was a Christian I had long been vexed with the Sabbath-breaking which took place in connexion with the bank, visits to partners, and consultations about worldly business, and the like, and I had a strong presentiment that such a complete departure from my Grandfather's godly ways, would sooner or later be severely chastised.

Ryle traced the source of the eventual collapse to a loan of nearly £200,000 which his father had advanced to his brother-in-law, of the Wood family, some years earlier.[3] When the venture for which this

[1] *Ibid.*, 30.
[2] *Ibid.*, 29.
[3] Presumably the father of Ryle's cousin, Canon Wood.

money had been advanced did not succeed, the Woods persuaded him to open a bank branch in Manchester, where the Macclesfield and Cheshire's reputation was high, and where circumstances pointed to it becoming a source of 'immense wealth' which would retrieve the loss. It might have been so, had a better manager been appointed. Ryle Sr and Daintry hardly ever went near it and its funds 'were squandered away by hundreds of thousands, by loans and advances to people who ought never to have had a penny'. His father's mistake, Ryle advised his children, was to have too many affairs to be competently supervised, and more than that,

> my father was never fit to be a banker. He was too easy, too good natured, and too careless about details. The three great principles which a banker should never forget are these: first, He must be able to say 'No'; secondly, He must never change his mind; thirdly, He must never waste good money in trying to recover bad debts—or to speak briefly, he must never send good money after bad.

To think Ryle gave these opinions with a degree of detachment would be to misunderstand entirely what he felt at what he called 'the stunning violence of the blow'.

> The immediate consequences were bitter and painful in the extreme, and humiliating to the utmost degree. The creditors naturally, rightly and justly, seized everything and we children were left with nothing but our own personal property and our clothes.

Had Ryle followed his father's offered gift of a home if he married, his resources would have been different. As it was, all he had of his own to sell was two horses, his yeomanry uniform, sword, saddlery, and accoutrements, which raised about £250.

> And the proceeds … were all with which I had to start in the world. This for a young man of 25, about to go into Parliament, a County magistrate, and commonly reckoned to be a son and heir with 1500 [*sic*] a year was rather a fall.

The change at Henbury Hall was immediate. Three of the family's staff had been with them for more than twenty years, but—'man-servants, butler, under-butler, footman, coachman, groom, house-keeper, housemaids, were all at once dismissed, and paid off, and dispersed to the four winds'. There was also a scattering of family, leaving only John Charles and his elder sister, Mary Anne, in the home, to help their father in the winding up of his affairs:

> This occupied about six weeks, I think perhaps about the most trying and miserable six weeks I ever passed in my life. The place was in full beauty in Midsummer but everything seemed as deserted and silent as a tomb. Morning, noon, and night, the crushing feeling was upon me, that we were about to leave the place never to come back again. Worst of all, I had the constant recollection that … I was going to leave my father's house without the least idea what was going to happen, where I was going to live, or what I was going to do. … [I] … as an eldest son, 25, with all the world before me, lost everything, and saw the whole future of my life turned upside down, and thrown into confusion. In short if I had not been a Christian at this time, I do not know if I should not have committed suicide.

Of the August day when he and his sister finally left, he said:

> Nothing I think touched me that morning so much as the face of my old Lyme mastiff 'Caesar', who was excessively fond of me. I remember he looked at me as if he did not understand it, and could not see why he might not go with me too. Poor dog, for a whole month afterwards he made his way into the house every morning as soon as the doors were opened, and went up to my room; there he lay at the door from morning till night, and nothing would induce him to stir.

He was to go to neighbours where he was treated 'as a dog, and not as a friend', and did not live long.

We who read his words today cannot enter into what Ryle's experience meant in a social world so different from our own. The shame of the bankruptcy propelled him down from the equality he had felt with all his peers to a status 'not much better off than their butlers and footmen'. With the exception of a few faithful friends, he felt the best thing he could do was to 'get away from every one I had ever seen, and never see them any more; to bury myself in some distant part of England, and try to form new acquaintances and new friendships'.

Probably the same feeling in his parents led them to remove to a quiet south-coast resort in Hampshire. Thanks to money which Susanna Hurt had brought into her marriage, and which remained her own, Ryle's parents settled in another, far less impressive home, 1 Eastern Terrace, Crescent Road, Anglesey (near Gosport), where they lived for the rest of their lives.[1] Frederic, his brother, stayed in London, while Ryle and his elder sister, Mary Anne, accepted an invitation to stay with old friends of his parents, Colonel William Thornhill, deputy surveyor of the New Forest, who lived with his sister at New Park, Lyndhurst.[2]

* * *

As Ryle paused to consider the previous four years, there were certain things clear to him. He had not become a Christian by his own choice, and God had brought him through a school of trials which had confirmed the meaning of conversion. What he would teach others he had been learning by deeper experience.

> It is easy to be a convert from one party to another party, from one sect to another sect, from one set of opinions to another set of opinions: such conversions save no one's soul. What we all want is a conversion from pride to humility,—from high thoughts of ourselves to lowly thoughts of ourselves,—from self-conceit to self-abasement,—from the mind of the Pharisee to the mind of the publican. A conversion of this kind we must experience, if we hope to be saved. These are the conversions that are wrought by the Holy Ghost.[3]

[1] Alan Munden, who identified this address, tells us their home is now part of Bramley House. *Travel with Ryle*, 30.

[2] Their imposing home is now the New Park Manor Hotel. Munden, *Travel with Ryle*, 34.

[3] *Expository Thoughts: Matthew* (1856; repr. Edinburgh: Banner of Truth Trust, 2015), 177.

And through this change the Christian is brought to understand that the standard of the world and the standard of the Lord Jesus are widely different:

> They are more than different: they are flatly contradictory one to the other. Among the children of this world he is thought the greatest man who has most land, most money, most servants, most rank, and most earthly power: among the children of God he is reckoned the greatest who does most to promote the spiritual and temporal happiness of his fellow-creatures. True greatness consists, not in receiving, but in giving,—not in selfish absorption of good things, but in imparting good to others,—not in being served, but in serving,—not in sitting still, and being ministered to, but in going about and ministering to others.[1]

A chapter of life had closed and greater chapters were about to begin. In December 1841, Charlotte Leycester got news which prompted her to add a postscript to a letter she had written to her cousin, Catherine Marsh:

> John Ryle will be ordained on December 12, and preaches his first sermon on the 19th: would your dear father remember him in prayer?[2]

---

[1] *Ibid.*, 205.
[2] L. E. O'Rorke, *Life and Friendships of Catherine Marsh* (London: Longmans, 1918), 41.

Area around Exbury, Hampshire

5

Peace Disturbed in Hampshire

Top: Exbury Church

Bottom: St Thomas' Church, Winchester

T HE decision Ryle took on his future while in the New Forest had been far from easy. That he needed to take up a profession which would support him was clear enough, but some, such as law, which he might have considered, would not give him any income for four or five years. The only approach made to him was the possibility of the post of private secretary to William Gladstone, who was now a member of Peel's government, but he knew enough of his fellow northerner for it to have no appeal. His father and mother could provide no relief for his anxiety:

> they could suggest nothing, except that they hoped something would turn up. What this something was I do not believe any of them knew, and I soon saw that I must act for myself. … I particularly disliked the idea of becoming a clergyman …

He explained the latter statement by adding that he had 'a strong feeling that God did not intend all Christian men to become clergymen'. But there were other reasons. At this point in his life, Ryle seems to have met few such men that he admired. For many evangelicals, the previous century had seen the office 'seem contemptible' and their persons 'grow cheap'.[1] The early nineteenth century had seen some change, yet the usual successful Oxford or Cambridge man who left the university for a parish went there as a scholar and gentleman not as a preacher.

In this state of indecision Ryle tells us that 'unexpectedly' he received the offer of a curacy. Perhaps at the suggestion of Colonel Thornhill, the invitation came from William Gibson, rector of Fawley

---

[1] The words are those of John Berridge, quoted in my book, *Evangelicals Divided* (Edinburgh: Banner of Truth Trust, 2000), 314.

in the New Forest. By that point, Ryle says, 'I could see nothing whatever before me but to become a clergyman because that brought me in some income at once.' Accordingly,

> I … made up my mind to accept it, though with a very heavy heart. My father and mother neither of them liked it at all, though they were quite unable to suggest to me anything better, and the whole result was that I was ordained by the Bishop of Winchester at Farnham Castle in December 1841.

Ryle would be accused by a later critic of wanting to enter 'the priests' offices' to 'eat a piece of bread' (1 Sam. 2:36). Only someone who never knew him could make such a deduction from his references to money. Money, certainly, occasioned the change in the course of his life in 1841, yet not by his determination but by the hand of God. 'If my father's affairs had prospered, and I had never been ruined … I should never have been a clergyman, never have preached a sermon, written a tract, or a book.' 'Every avenue seemed shut against me', indeed, a whole succession of avenues.

> I never had any particular desire to become a clergyman, and those who fancied that my self-will, and natural tastes were gratified by it, were totally and entirely mistaken. I became a clergyman because I felt shut up to it, and saw no other course of life open to me.

The truth was he was being taught by the Saviour who 'openeth and no man shutteth; and shutteth, and no man openeth' (Rev. 3:7), and who promises, 'I will bring the blind by a way that they knew not; I will lead them in paths that they have not known' (Isa. 42:16). There is nothing unforeseen and unplanned in the lives of God's people.

Yet while recognizing this sovereignty of God in events, Ryle was careful to point out to his children,

> I believe that God never expects us to feel no suffering or pain when it pleases Him to visit us with affliction. There are great mistakes upon this point. Submission to God's will is perfectly compatible with intense and keen suffering under the chastisements of that will.[1]

[1] His suffering was not short-lived. Thirty-two years later he could say, 'I felt most

The underlying principle is *faith*. So Ryle could affirm,

> I have not the least doubt it was all for the best. If my father's affairs
> had prospered, and I had never been ruined, my life of course would
> have been a very different one. I should probably have gone into Par-
> liament very soon, and it is impossible to say what the effect of this
> might have been upon my soul.

* * *

The large triangular parish of Fawley had the Solent (facing the Isle
of Wight) to the south and Southampton Water to the east. For his
curacy Ryle was given entire charge of the chapel of ease and district
of Exbury, an area about three miles wide and two miles broad, with
a population of around 400 people. His first impressions were not
appealing: 'It was a very dreary, desolate, solitary place. This house
and 100£ a year formed my stipend, but as I had to pay the preceding
curate 16£ a year for the furniture, my real remuneration consisted of
84£ and a house.' The surroundings did not improve with inspection.
Instead of the fields, trees and hills of Cheshire, there was low-lying
flat heath and moorland.

> A great number of the people had been brought up as poachers and
> smugglers, and were totally unaccustomed to being looked after or
> spoken to about their souls. … Drunkenness and sin of every kind
> abounded; the Baptists and the Methodists had carried off many of
> the people.

With little preparation for the work before him, Ryle could have
done with advice from his senior colleague. It was not forthcoming.
William Gibson, the rector, was absent in Malta for the greater part
of the time. 'My Rector, when he resided', Ryle commented,

> was extremely kind to me. … But he was eaten up with caution, and
> seemed to me so afraid of doing wrong, that he would hardly do

---

acutely my father's ruin, my exile from Cheshire with the destruction of all my
worldly prospects, and I have never ceased to feel them from that day to this.'

right. I have little doubt too that he was much under the influence of his wife, who always thought me a dangerous extreme man, and struck me as very much inclined to keep in with everybody.

We can be sure that one novelty Ryle introduced raised the eyebrows of Mrs Gibson. Tract distribution was scarcely the work of clergymen but Ryle would obtain supplies of unbound copies from the Religious Tract Society's office in Southampton, bind them up himself in brown paper, and circulate them as widely as possible. He tells us poignantly, 'I was too poor to give any away. I was obliged to lend and change them.'

A cheerful home and surroundings could have mitigated the situation but these were far from congenial. He shared a damp, old house in a nearby hamlet with a dishonest servant maid, 'one boy, one dog, one cat, and one pig. The maid-servant turned out a bad character and though she was 30 years of age she married the boy who was in his 17th year.' His loneliness was occasionally relieved by visits from his sisters Mary Anne and Emma, and by his own visits to the Thornhills and to his parents. With one or two exceptions his parish provided few friends among the better off. A local landowner invited him to dinner, 'as a matter of civility but my opinions were evidently too strong for them', and, when he declined to play cards or to dance with a large party after dinner, he was asked no more.

Perhaps the local cricketers, hearing of his ability on the pitch, might have been allies, but it was too much for them when he spoke against cricket matches continuing until late on Saturday nights, leading one of them to complain to the bishop about the new curate. On reflection Ryle reckoned that, 'On the whole however I think I was regarded as an enthusiastic fanatical mad dog of whom most people were afraid.'

Even so, the church—'a very long mile' from his house—was soon filled. The 'people seemed interested, but the farmers were a rich, dull, stupid set of people, and the labourers had been in the habit of living in such utter neglect of God that it seemed as if nothing could turn them'.

It was among those whom Ryle describes as 'the people' that he was to have the greatest influence. Undoubtedly one reason for it was the amount of time he spent in their homes. 'My regular work', he says,

> was … to visit, confer with, and distribute tracts among 60 families every week. … I kept a regular account of all the families in the parish and was in every house in the parish at least once a month.

This, also, was far from being a normal practice of clergy. The new curate was certainly not acting according to any code book, as the following incident illustrates:

> On one occasion I remember being called in late at night to interfere in a pitched battle between two men on a green not far from my house, where two or three hundred men were present. I remember walking into the ring suddenly between the two combatants and insisting on their stopping. I told them they might do what they liked to me, but I would not have it if I could prevent it; the result was that the fight was stopped. The affair made a great noise at the time, and I do not know that perhaps I acted prudently, but I remember having no feeling about it at the moment but to stop the fight whatever the consequences might be. At any rate it taught me what power one man has against a multitude as long as he has right on his side.

In later years critics of Ryle would accuse him of being a remote, reserved individual, standing aloof from others. That is hardly the impression gained by parishioners at Exbury. 'As for the people I think they would have done anything for me, and I believe the influence I had among them was very great indeed.'

As far as preaching was concerned, as with other new duties, Ryle had to find his own way and it was not easy. He would later say that he was turned fifty before he learned to preach. But in Exbury he made a real start in understanding the difficulties involved in preparing two sermons for Sunday and two expository lectures at cottage meetings on Wednesday and Thursday nights. He found it one thing to fill the time, quite another to make his hearers understand his meaning and hold their attention. He came to believe that it was easier to preach at Oxford or Cambridge, or before Parliament, than to an agricultural congregation on a fine hot summer's afternoon in the month of August. Writing in 'Simplicity in Preaching', he told of one farm labourer who professed to enjoy Sunday more than any day of the week, 'Because', he was reported to say, 'I sit comfortably in church, put up my legs, have nothing to think about, and just go to sleep.' The lesson Ryle started to learn, and would work at for years to come, was that

> it is an extremely difficult thing to write simple, clear, perspicuous, and forcible English. … To use very long words, to seem very learned … is very easy work. But to write what will strike and stick, to speak or write that which at once pleases and is understood, and becomes assimilated with a hearer's mind and a thing never forgotten—that, we may depend upon it, is a very difficult thing and a very rare attainment.[1]

The distinction which Ryle makes between an 'expository lecture' and a sermon should be noted, for a caution he gave on the subject is needed again in our own day. In later years he was to write:

> The value of expository preaching is continually pressed on ministers in the present day, and not without reason … The idea, no doubt, like every good theory, may be easily ridden to death; and I believe that with ignorant, semi-heathen congregations, a short, pithy text often does more good than a long passage expounded.[2]

Ryle was to say, 'The first year of my preaching was a series of experiments.'[3] At least one of his Exbury sermons has survived. The

---

[1] 'Simplicity in Preaching', *Upper Room* (1888; repr. Edinburgh: Banner of Truth Trust, 1977), 36-8.

[2] 'An Estimate of Thomas Manton', *Works of Thomas Manton*, vol. 2 (London: Nisbet, 1871; repr. Edinburgh: Banner of Truth Trust, 1993), xvii-xviii.

[3] 'Simplicity in Preaching', *Upper Room*, 54.

warmth is still on its pages. He told his hearers plainly, 'He that has no zeal about the souls of others can have but little about his own', and he did not flatter them:

> Think you there would be much religion in Exbury, if all the places of worship were pulled down, if all the ministers were withdrawn, and each was left to the care of his own soul? In a very few years sin would abound, and God would be almost forgotten.[1]

But at this stage there was not the same close questioning of his hearers as in later years, when personal pronouns were prominent—not '*our* Savour' but '*my* Saviour', not '*we* must repent but '*you* must repent'.

He felt the burden of sermon preparation. 'Perhaps you may think I have nothing to do but to open my Bible, take the first text that meets the eye, and write off a sermon in two or three hours. But it is far otherwise.' Nor did the demands on his time stop with the more expected parish duties. 'I was always at work', he tells us, and part of that work was of a medical kind. The locality, with much undrained land, was very unhealthy, the habitat of snakes, vipers and adders: 'I never knew a time when ague, scarlet fever, and typhus were not to be found in the district.' 'Ignorant young man' though he considered himself to be, he took seriously the need for supplying medical help:

> I cured many ague cases by administering first an Emetic of Ipecac and Syrup, and afterwards Tincture of Quinine. I saved many lives in Scarlet fever by supplying them with large quantities of very strong Beef Tea, made from concentrated essence, and insisted on their swallowing it, as long as their throats kept open. However 10 per cent of the population had the Scarlet fever and 10 per cent died, chiefly children.[2]

For typhus fever he urged port wine, and for viper bites olive oil, 'but

[1] *The Christian Race and other Sermons* (London: Hodder & Stoughton, 1900), 227.
[2] For Ryle's views of the necessity for treating bodily and spiritual ills, see his sermon 'Luke, the Beloved Physician' preached at the Annual Conference of the British Medical Association in 1883, *Upper Room*, 35-4.

I think the people had more faith in ointment made of viper fat'. It is little wonder that after nearly two years with little relaxation, no home life, and the oppression of memories of better days, he needed a doctor himself, finding himself with 'constant headache, indigestion, and disturbance of the heart'. He had no option but to resign and to seek the help of the celebrated Dr Henry Jephson at Leamington Spa for a month. The recommendation had come to him from a well-to-do Christian couple who lived at Leamington whom he had got to know when they visited the Exbury area for sailing on the Solent. 'Being as poor as a rat, I was too happy to avail myself of the kindness of the Bradleys, who lived at Leamington, and insisted on my staying with them for a whole month.' Meanwhile the bishop of Winchester offered him the rectory of St Thomas, Winchester, serving some 3,000 people, with an income of £100 p.a. This he accepted and began work early in December 1843 in 'a very cold pinching winter'.

* * *

The ancient city of Winchester, once the metropolis of England, had recently been linked by rail with London and Southampton at the time of Ryle's settlement. From the railway station its appearance was described as 'a wide extended mass of old brick houses, grey church towers, and red tiled roofs'. The cathedral, built between 980 and 1200, was the most dominant feature, and crowded around it within the comparatively small city boundaries were no fewer than nine parish churches, of which St Thomas was one. The 'tumble-down' state of its building gave Ryle an impression which was confirmed by an early visit to the previous rector of the church: 'when I called upon him, [I] found him in slippers and dressing gown in the middle of the day. I made up my mind that I should find that little had been done in the parish.' The one exception was a middle-aged lady, Miss Althea Wickham, 'who really appeared to be the life of the whole place, and the mainspring of anything good'.

The house awaiting him was small, though 'a tolerably good one'. It was furnished by two or three of his father's friends, and for additional occupants he had 'one elderly woman servant, one boy, and one dog'. The congregation, he discovered, was of town average, containing a good many respectable people and a good many poor. There was a morning and evening service on Sundays, and the absence of a meeting mid-week he at once remedied by beginning an 'Expository lecture in the Infant school room'. If this was not well attended from the start it soon was, for his manner of speaking 'was quite new at Winchester'. He would look back on it as youthful and inexperienced preaching, but it caused something of a sensation by its contrast with the prevailing religious conditions. 'The whole place struck me as being in a very dead state like most Cathedral towns. The influence of the Cathedral body was as bad as possible, and worldliness reigned supreme in the Close' (the homes of clergy around the cathedral). Most of the other parishes were occupied by 'unsatisfactory incumbents, while those who were Evangelical, were cautious proper men, who were dreadfully afraid of going into extremes'.

Of his own preaching he commented:

> there was not that amount of deep thought, and matter, and illustration in them which I afterwards found valuable. Nevertheless, they were all thoroughly Evangelical, and being well composed, and read with a good deal of earnestness and fire, I have no doubt they sounded very fine and very effective, but I should not care to preach them now.

As in Exbury, he gave priority to personal contact. He found a district visitors' society already in operation, which he had to supervise, but he led by example, and 'every day of the week' was personally busy visiting. This was far from being the common practice of the clergy at the time.[1]

---

[1] Dr James Milnor, rector of St George's Church, New York, noted this on a visit to England in 1830: 'This I found to be a frequent complaint among the laity. Where

Given what Ryle says of the clergy of the city, it is not surprising that the loneliness he felt at Exbury continued. How little he had in common with most of them is illustrated by his contacts with Samuel Wilberforce, one of the family he had first met at Oxford. Since then the third son of the evangelical leader had been a successful high-flyer. In 1840 he had been made a canon at Winchester and the rector of St Mary's, Alverstoke. The latter was a parish between Gosport and Portsmouth, within which lay the coastal resort of Anglesey where John Ryle Sr and his wife now had their home. The influence of Wilberforce's charm and intellect soon entered that family, and the more so when he invited Frederic, Susanna Ryle's 'favourite in the family', to be his curate. 'I fear that this made a little coolness between us', John Charles was to say of his brother. 'Not that there was ever anything like a quarrel or division, though it was impossible to feel thorough oneness of heart when we manifestly did not agree as to what was true religion.' Speaking of his connection with Wilberforce he wrote:

> To me when I visited Anglesey he [Wilberforce] was always studiously civil, though I suspect he secretly disliked me, and was a little bit afraid of me as a dangerous person; but he always asked me to preach whenever I was there on a Sunday, and tried to talk as if we were all agreed in the main. … Manning his brother-in-law, and Henry Wilberforce his brother (both of them since perverts to Rome) were frequently visitors at his house; and the whole result was such a tide and currant [sic] in the direction of Ritualism as fairly carried most of the people in the Parish off their legs. It could not be wondered that unestablished and uninformed Church people, who had never seen zeal and earnestness before, were completely carried away by it, and the harm done in the whole district round Gosport was immense. As for myself, I thoroughly distrusted and disliked the

---

they are perfectly satisfied with the public services of their ministers, they charge them with remissness in visiting, and express regret that they have so little religious intercourse with their pastors.' John S. Stone, *A Memoir of the Life of James Milnor D.D.* (New York: American Tract Soc., 1849), 306.

whole set and their system, and they knew it and did not much trust me … My poor brother, my eldest sister and Emma in my belief, all suffered greatly from it.[1]

Not long after his settlement in Winchester, Ryle had a visit from Canon Wilberforce which was memorable. 'He showed me great kindness', Ryle records,

occasionally attended my Church, and tried hard to get an influence over me. This lasted till one memorable night when he had a long discussion with me till a late hour about Baptismal Regeneration, in which he tried hard to turn me from Evangelical views on that subject; but it had no effect.

While Ryle could hold his own in any male company, he was by no means so secure with the opposite sex. In relation to his medical work at Exbury he noted, 'I did not pretend to touch the women's cases, and left them alone', and in Winchester, 'I studiously avoided all young ladies in company.' It was not that he had no interest in marriage; on the contrary, he was conscious that his position as 'a young unmarried Rector in a town like Winchester' was extremely awkward, 'but I saw no remedy for it; and this made me constantly anxious and uncomfortable'. He was also, no doubt, conscious that a family home would be more beneficial for his health, about which he had to be careful, with a regimen which included a three-mile walk before breakfast in the dark on winter's mornings. The problem was money. He was certain he could not think of getting married until he had an income of £500 p.a. as well as a house to offer anyone.

It was while such thoughts weighed on his mind that, unexpectedly, the offer of the rectory of Helmingham, in Suffolk, came to him with an annual income of over £500:

[1] Frederic Ryle died in May 1845 and was buried in the church of Elson, where he had been appointed first incumbent. 'We all felt his death very much; it was the first gap in our family. The grave is at the east end of the Churchyard under the Chancel window; and my mother [died 1852] lies by him.'

> This turned the scale. ... I went very unwillingly, and of all the steps I ever took in my life, to this day I feel doubts whether the move was right or not. I sometimes think that it was want of faith to go, and I ought to have stayed. Certain it is, that as soon as my going was announced, the inhabitants of St Thomas', Winchester, offered to raise my income to 300£ a year, and to build a new Church. This of course would not do at all, and the offer came too late.

All who have felt a similar crisis over guidance can surely have sympathy with Ryle. Wondering whether he had been right or not to leave Winchester after only five months, the decision would, he says, afflict his spirits for two or three years. 'I only know that my chief desire was to set my father free from any charge on my account, and so I tried to hope it was all right.' If any are disposed to criticize him for allowing the financial factor to play this part in his decision, there is something else which he did not tell his children and which only became generally known after his death. James Bardsley, an evangelical of Ryle's generation, told Alfred Christopher of Oxford

> that for many years, when Mr Ryle was Rector of Helmingham, he wore threadbare clothes, and denied himself many things, in order to pay off, so far as was possible, the small depositors at his father's bank. He was not himself a partner in the bank, and was not legally liable for anything.

Christopher tells us that he checked the accuracy of these words with Ryle: 'I asked him if Canon Bardsley's story was in all respects correct, and he was obliged to acknowledge that it was.'[1]

While Ryle was not without real encouragements in his first two parishes, one major lesson had been confirmation of a truth that he was often to preach:

---

[1] *The Record*, 15 June 1900, 572. We do not know the date of Bardsley's report. It clearly referred to a period before Ryle left Helmingham. Christopher also commented, 'When Bishop Ryle and I have both fallen asleep some of the self-denying good works of a great preacher of Justification by Faith without the works of the Law, will come to be known.' J. S. Reynolds, *Canon Christopher* (Abingdon: Abbey Press, 1967), 144.

Who does not know that spiritual religion never brings a man the world's praise? It never has done, and it never does. It entails the world's disapprobation, the world's persecution, the world's ridicule, the world's sneers. The world will let a man go to hell quietly, and never try to stop him. The world will never let a man go to heaven quietly—they will do all they can to turn him back. Who has not heard of nicknames in plenty bestowed on all who faithfully follow Christ?—Pietist, Methodist, saint, fanatic, enthusiast, righteous overmuch, and many more. … Let a young person go to every ball and theatre and race-course, and utterly neglect his soul, and no one interferes … But let him begin to read his Bible and be diligent in prayers, let him decline worldly amusement and be particular in his employment of time, let him seek an evangelical ministry and live as if he had an immortal soul,—let him do this, and the probability is all his relations and friends will be up in arms. 'You are going too far', 'You need not be so very good', 'You are taking up extreme lines,'—this is the least that he will hear. … If a man will become a decided evangelical Christian he must make up his mind to lose the world's favours; he must be content to be thought by many a perfect fool.[1]

[1] 'The Second Advent (Ten Virgins)', *The Christian Race*, 210-11.

67

The Protestantism of the Thirty-nine Articles: Extracts

Article VI: Holy Scripture containeth all things necessary to salvation: so that whatsoever is not read therein, nor may be proved thereby, is not to be required of any man, that it should be believed as an article of the Faith.

Article XIX: As the Church of Jerusalem, Alexandria and Antioch, have erred; so also the Church of Rome hath erred, not only in their living and manner of Ceremonies, but also in matters of Faith.

Article XXII: The Romish doctrine concerning Purgatory, Pardons, Worshipping and Adoration, as well of Images as of Reliques, and also invocation of Saints, is a fond thing vainly invented, and grounded upon no warrant of Scripture, but rather repugnant to the Word of God.

Article XXIV: It is a thing plainly repugnant to the Word of God, and the custom of the Primitive Church, to have public Prayer in the Church, or to minister the Sacraments in a tongue not understood of the people.

Article XXV: Confirmation, Penance, Orders, Matrimony, and extreme Unction, are not to be counted for Sacraments of the Gospel.

Article XXVIII: Transubstantiation (or the change of the substance of Bread and Wine) in the Supper of the Lord, cannot be proved by holy Writ; but is repugnant to the plain words of Scripture, overthroweth the nature of a Sacrament, and hath given occasion to many superstitions … the mean whereby the Body of Christ is received and eaten in the Supper is Faith.

Article XXX: The sacrifices of Masses, in which it was commonly said, that the Priest did offer Christ for the quick [living] and the dead, to have remission of pain or guilt, were blasphemous fables and dangerous deceits.

Article XXXII: Bishops, Priests and Deacons, are not commanded by God's Law, either to vow the estate of single life, or to abstain from marriage.

6

Rural Suffolk: Stepping-Stone to the World

Top: St Mary's Church, Helmingham

Bottom: The church from the park

AT THE age of twenty-seven, when he went to Helmingham, Ryle was already a man of settled convictions, with assured foundations for his future ministry. In reference to his time at Winchester he could say:

> the story of my life has been such, that I really cared nothing for anyone's opinion, and resolved not to consider one jot who was offended and who was not offended by anything I did. I saw no one whose opinion I cared for in the place, and I resolved to ask nobody's counsel, in the work of my Parish, or as to the matter or manner of my preaching, but just to do what I thought the Lord Jesus Christ would like, and not to care one jot for the face of man.

Other young preachers have thought in this way in their twenties, only to find they had arrived at their certainties prematurely. But though Ryle had much more to learn, the main lines of his thought would undergo no change. If this was not the result of his own ability, how is it to be explained?

First, the Bible which had been so little in his hands before he was twenty, had since then been his constant companion. He had joined the company of those who could say, 'The law of thy mouth is better unto me than thousands of gold and silver' (Psa. 119:72). And Scripture had become his only rule. It was there he heard the voice of Christ. Yet to deduce from his independence of others, which he resolved at Winchester, that other reading had little part in the formation of his understanding, would be entirely wrong. Authors who put Scripture first were his choice, and at their head the Reformers of the Church of England who had compiled the Thirty-nine Articles. He had studied those Articles in order to pass exams at school and university and, once he became spiritually alive, he saw their statements as the interconnected parts of gospel doctrine. 'I shall always feel thankful', he said,

> for the Articles and I think it an immense pity that young people are not taught them more systematically than they are. In my own case they enabled me to regard the arguments with which I was often plied by the adversaries of Evangelical religion among my relatives, and especially by my cousin Canon Wood who was horrified at my change, with perfect indifference. I found that whatever they might say they could not prove that my views were not those of the 39 Articles.

But as a young Christian he also looked for contemporary books to help him. In the process, he tells us, he 'made sad blunders', for want of an adviser, before he was led to the six significant titles which 'helped most'. They were William Wilberforce's *Practical View of Christianity* (1797), John Angell James's *Christian Professor* (1837), John Newton's *Cardiphonia* (1781), Thomas Scott's *Reply to Bishop Tomline* (1811), Joseph Milner's *Church History* (1812[1]), and Edward Bickersteth's *Christian Student* (1829). 'I always feel respect for these books, for I really believe they were useful to me.' They might not be the first choice for every young believer but they were what Ryle needed.

Wilberforce had startled the religious world with his *Practical View* which went through four editions in the year of its publication. He demonstrated from Scripture that Christianity was something very different from much current religion; the new birth was not just a church doctrine, it was the indispensable entrance into personal fellowship with Christ. John Newton, from slave-trader to curate at Olney, and later rector of St Mary Woolnoth, London, was an example of that experience, and his Letters (of which *Cardiphonia* was one volume) would remain a store of wisdom on the life of the

---

[1] I give the date of the fourth edition, 'revised and corrected' by Isaac Milner.

Christian. James's title enforced the difference between 'profession' and 'possession'. He challenged contemporary ministers with a 'too ready admission of persons to the church', thus being accessory to their self-deception, and confessed, 'Though I have been more strict than many of my brethren, there are many, very many, that I now wish I had rejected.'[1]

Such convictions became part of Ryle's ministry. The other three titles had a particular significance for him. Milner's monumental *History* showed, as few had done before, that a spiritual understanding of church history produces a narrative very different from the dull titles which too commonly profess to teach it. Milner struck a different path, and one which Ryle would follow.

Ryle must have picked up the three volumes of Thomas Scott's *Reply to Bishop Tomline* with more than a little interest. More accurately, the title read *Remarks on the Refutation of Calvinism by George Tomline.* Bishop Tomline, who left the Winchester diocese in the state which Ryle had seen under his successor, had become alarmed at the increase of evangelical clergy in the Church of England, and took a very different view of the Church than that of evangelicals. Joseph Milner, for instance, believed that from the time of Charles II, when the Puritans had been silenced or ejected (1662), until the Evangelical Revival, the Church was 'full of party, faction and animosities, and love of the world, yet in its public ministrations adorned with learning, and abounding in external morality'.[2] Tomline, on the contrary, was persuaded it was not worldliness but Calvinists who were the danger to the Church, and argued that no true Church of England man should be a Calvinist. Helped by Scott to come to the opposite conclusion, Ryle would later write:

> Whether men like it or not, it is an acknowledged fact, that the first
> five Archbishops of Canterbury [after the Reformation]—Cranmer,

[1] R. W. Dale, *Life and Letters of John Angell James* (London: Nisbet, 1861), 329.
[2] Milner, *History of the Church of Christ*, vol. 1, 501.

Parker, Grindal, Whitgift, and Abbott—were decidedly Calvinistic in sentiment, and discouraged all kind of teaching which was opposed to the Calvinistic school.[1]

Scott believed it was not so much the Genevan Reformer that Tomline meant to attack as contemporary evangelical clergy whom he regarded as Calvin's disciples. 'Within the writer's remembrance', Scott wrote in the Preface to his *Remarks*, 'the Calvinists, especially the evangelical clergy, were so inconsiderable and neglected a company, that, except a declamation now and then in a visitation sermon, little public notice was taken of them.' He was encouraged that the bishop now thought of them in terms of growing numbers needing to be put down.

The amount of Calvinistic belief in the Church of England at the beginning of the nineteenth century is hard to estimate. John Scott, son of Thomas, was of the opinion that there was only one 'avowedly Calvinist preacher in London' around 1800. But the qualification of 'avowedly' is significant. There were certainly more clergy of Calvinistic belief in the capital at that date, but they were hesitant about using the word and not without reason. A controversy between Calvinists and evangelical Arminians in the 1770s, in which Augustus Toplady was prominent, had not always been edifying. Thereafter some who were over-eager and too poorly prepared to defend Calvinism had fostered further dissension by unbalanced teaching. But the main reason for the trepidation of clergy to use the name was that for over one hundred years the belief that Calvinists and Puritans do not belong in the Church of England had been firmly promoted. There was no question in the controversy between Scott and Tomline which position had the majority support. While the bishop's *Refutation of Calvinism*, published in 1803, was in an eighth edition by 1823, Scott's answer appears to have had no second printing. The common opinion was that only the anti-Church Dissenters—'Puritans'—were Calvinists.

[1] Ryle, *The Bishop, the Pastor, and the Preacher* (Ipswich: Hunt, 1854), 31.

In consequence even such evangelical leaders as Charles Simeon and Richard Cecil, at the beginning of the nineteenth century, were very chary of seeming to support Calvinistic belief and the older Puritan authors. While their profession of sympathy with the evangelical clergy of the eighteenth century was open, the idea gained credence that the Puritans were not to be thought of as evangelicals. So Eugene Stock, writing as a Church of England evangelical, could assert, 'The Evangelicals, properly so-called, are but a small body, within the Church … and totally distinct from the old Puritans of the seventeenth century.'[1] As proof for the distinction he quoted the words of the church historian J. H. Overton:

> The typical Puritan was gloomy and austere; the typical Evangelical was bright and genial. The Puritan would not be kept within the pale of the National Church; the Evangelical would not be kept out of it.[2]

This representation, which has continued to the present time, Ryle came to reject.[3] He referred to the 2,000 men silenced by 'the unhappy Act of Uniformity' of 1662 (thereafter to be called 'Dissenters' by the Church) as containing

> many of the ablest preachers, and the most learned, holy ministers of the time. Such were Owen, Manton, Baxter, Calamy, Philip Henry, Poole, Brooks, and Watson. Not a few of them might have been kept

---

[1] Eugene Stock, *History of the Church Missionary Society* (London: Church Missionary Society, 1899), vol. 1, 38.

[2] *English Church in the Eighteenth Century*, ch. ix.

[3] Hence the recent series of volumes under the general title, *A History of Evangelicalism*, began with the eighteenth century, Mark Noll, *The Rise of Evangelicalism* (Leicester: IVP, 2004), yet the evidence is incontrovertible that the gospel recovered in the eighteenth century was in direct succession to that of the Puritans. Whitefield was happy to report the words of 'a good old Puritan' who declared, 'this is *Puritanismus redivivus*'. George Whitefield's place in the revival of the eighteenth century is well documented in Ryle, *Christian Leaders of the Eighteenth Century* (1885; repr. Edinburgh: Banner of Truth Trust, 2002). J. I. Packer, endorsing the understanding of Whitefield and Ryle, has written, 'The truth is that evangelicals, so-called, yesterday and today, should be seen as Puritanism continuing.' *Faithfulness and Holiness*, 82.

within our pale by some reasonable concessions. But the ruling party showed no desire to keep them: they were all Evangelical men![1]

It was in addressing the idea that loyalty to the Church of England was not consistent with Calvinistic belief that Scott's response to Tomline was important. He showed that what the bishop was attacking, far from being opposed to the Christian faith, were the very truths to be found in the Articles, and recovered at the Reformation. They should not be tiptoed around but openly owned and defended. Ryle would represent a generation ready to speak more plainly for Calvinistic belief and Puritan theology, and it is significant that he should name Scott's *Remarks* on Tomline as one of the titles which 'helped me most'.[2] It was part of the preparation that fitted him to take a lead among those who would be reproached as being 'more like Dissenters than Churchmen,—that thay are narrow Calvinists'.[3]

The last title among the six listed by Ryle, Bickersteth's *Christian Student*, could well have been the one to which he most repeatedly referred in his early ministry. As well as covering material which Charles Bridges would also later cover, Bickersteth had nearly a hundred pages on 'The Minister's Library' which could well have been the means of introducing Ryle to the track of reading he was to follow. Apart from Bunyan's *Pilgrim's Progress* there is no indication that he had a prior knowledge or interest in Puritan authors. They were certainly not praised in the circles in which he had grown up.

---

[1] Ryle, *Light from Old Times* (1890; repr. Edinburgh: Banner of Truth Trust, 2015), xxii.

[2] The three volumes of Scott's *Remarks* have outlived their usefulness, being made up largely of word for word comment on Tomline's text. Scott himself wanted to 'remodel' his work but I do not know whether he ever did so. Scott may have influenced Ryle in believing that Calvinistic belief does not include a denial of what has been called 'the double reference theory of the atonement', i.e. the definite redemption of the elect, and a hypothetical general redemption for all, sometimes expressed as 'the *sufficient* for all, the *efficient* for the believer'. But it is the person of Christ crucified, not the number of the redeemed, that is to be preached to lost sinners.

[3] *Light from Old Times*, xxiii.

Bickersteth, however, in his extensive listing of works of Protestant divines, expressed high esteem for Puritan authors such as Baxter, Brooks, Burroughs, Bunyan, Charnock, Flavel, Howe, Manton, Owen, Perkins, Sibbes, and Traill.[1] All these names would reappear often in Ryle's ministry.

* * *

Ryle's assertion, then, that he 'cared nothing for anyone's opinion', is only true in a limited sense. Nor were books the only influence on his thinking. His personal contact with contemporary Christians was another factor. As already mentioned, when he still lived in Cheshire he had been 'mightily helped' by the counsel and friendship of older Christians whom, in a future world, he hoped to thank 'for what they did for me'. But he tells us little of contemporary preachers who helped him. One of them was probably Hugh McNeile, a rising leader among evangelicals in the Church of England. Ryle, as a young man, heard him preach in Liverpool 'and formed an opinion of him that I never altered from that time'. He would later describe him as the 'grand old Protestant champion'. An American heard McNeile in London in 1830, and described him as 'a fine-looking man, and a remarkably fluent and powerful speaker'. But he was somewhat surprised that McNeile urged 'the high doctrines of Calvin as among the purest principles of the Reformation'.[2] In later years Ryle and McNeile would share in many meetings.

A clergyman who is known to have been an early friend of Ryle's was William Marsh, the man whose prayers Charlotte Leycester sought at the time of Ryle's ordination in 1841. Marsh is one of the remarkable figures of Christian history almost forgotten today. Born

---

[1] Edward Bickersteth, *The Christian Student: Designed to Assist Christians in General in Acquiring Religious Knowledge* (London: Seeley, 1829), 480-3.
[2] John S. Stone, *A Memoir of the Life of James Milnor D.D.* (New York: American Tract Society, 1849).

in 1775, a student at Oxford, he became a minister of the gospel at a time when, in the words of his daughter and biographer, Catherine Marsh, 'The position of an evangelical clergyman … was not an enviable one in the eyes of the world.'[1] At the height of his strength, he ministered to a congregation of about 2,200 in Birmingham from 1829 to 1839. Poor health then required a quieter role at Leamington, yet even at the age of eighty-three he was ready to take up another parish at Beddington, Surrey, where he died in 1864.

It was at Marsh's home, Lansdowne House, at Leamington, that Ryle came to know him. This was the same spa town where he had gone from Exbury for his health in November 1843. Catherine Marsh says that his relationship with her father had begun earlier: 'John Ryle had been a frequent visitor at Lansdowne House, and a lifelong friendship began with him then.'[2] There was much in Marsh that appealed to the younger man—his concentration on the person of Christ, his cheerfulness, his belief that the Reformation battle had to be fought again, his insistence on being ready for Christ's coming, and, not least, his memorable sayings in conversation. Marsh could express much sound theology in one sentence, for instance: 'We are justified freely, by grace; meritoriously, by Christ; instrumentally, by faith; evidentially, by good works.'[3]

Among the older Christians who helped Ryle after his conversion, the name of Georgina Tollemache has been mentioned above. Until 1840 she lived with her husband, John, in Cheshire, where they owned 26,000 acres as well as another 7,000 acres in Suffolk. Although John Tollemache would be Tory Member of Parliament for South Cheshire from 1841 to 1868, on the death of a great aunt, he and his wife moved into Helmingham Hall in 1840, and it is there that Ryle would meet them again.

[1] *Life of William Marsh, by His Daughter* [Catherine Marsh] (London: Hatchard & Nisbet, 1867), 206.
[2] O'Rorke, *Catherine Marsh*, 41.
[3] *Life of William Marsh*, 206.

* * *

The *Parliamentary Gazetteer of England and Wales* for 1843 reported under 'Helmingham':

> Helmingham Hall, built in the reign of Henry VIII, is a quad-rangular building, surrounded by a moat, having two drawbridges. It is situated in a beautiful park, comprehending 400 acres, and has been the principal seat of the Tollemache family from the period of its erection.

On one corner of that park was the parish church of St Mary's of which the Lord Chancellor, Lord Lyndhurst, was the patron. While the invitation to Ryle to go to Helmingham came in a letter from this patron, it is probable that the instigators were John, and perhaps especially Georgina Tollemache, his wife, whom Ryle would describe as 'the brightest example of a Christian woman I ever saw'. There were also other Christian friends from Cheshire days, namely, Admirals Harcourt and Hope, friends of the Tollemaches,[1] who could have spoken for Ryle to the Lord Chancellor. However the invitation came, it was in the Tollemaches' home that Ryle was settled by Easter 1844.

Residence in Helmingham Hall was not his personal choice. During the long incumbency of the previous rector, both church (dating from the late thirteenth century) and rectory close by, had become dilapidated. The restoration work on the church had been completed before Ryle's arrival but the rectory was another story. In the course of time it had seen many occupants. One of them, over forty years earlier, was the landscape painter, John Constable, whose work included *Dell in Helmingham Park*. Ryle may have noticed that another of his paintings, *The Lock*, sold in the 1830s for £131 10s. He could never have imagined that the same painting would sell at auction for £22.4 million in 2012! The new rector found the house 'in

---

[1] The father of John Tollemache had also been an admiral in the Napoleonic Wars.

a miserable condition and it cost me a great deal of money to put it into decent order, which I was ill able to afford'.

So for about a year the Hall had to be his home. It was not the start he would have desired, but it compelled him to be mixing again with the high society he had been avoiding. It was John Tollemache's practice 'to have his house continually full of visitors, chiefly from London and Cheshire, and a continual stream was passing through the house of individuals and families who came for a week or ten days'. 'Some of them', Ryle continues, 'were very thorough Christians chiefly brought there by Mrs Tollemache's influence.' This number included the Harcourt and Hope families whom he now met again. But other guests who arrived 'were very worldly, one or two about the loosest, most unsatisfactory characters that I ever met'. All had to hear Ryle, the acting chaplain, conduct family prayers, morning and evening—sometimes for at least forty people—and preach on Sundays.

John Tollemache moved in evangelical circles, and was a supporter of such agencies as the Protestant Reformation Society. Another member of that circle was John Plumptre, MP for East Kent, member of the Committee of the Church Missionary Society, and a collaborator with Tollemache in Parliament for upholding laws for the public maintenance of the Fourth Commandment.

Ryle was now able to give more serious thought to marriage but he came to the conclusion that eligible and 'really attractive Christian ladies' in the surrounding society 'were not to be met with'. Eligible, in his terms, meant 'a woman who was a real Christian, who was a real lady, and who was not a fool'. Probably it was when the Plumptre family were guests at Helmingham Hall that Ryle met their younger daughter, Matilda. Before long he had decided that she was the bride for whom he had been waiting and they were married on 29 October 1845.[1] She was twenty-one and he twenty-nine.

[1] In a lapse of memory Ryle gave the date in his short autobiography as October 1844; this led him to mistake the time of other family events down to 1847. Correct dates can be confirmed from other sources.

Before that date Ryle had moved into the rectory although the renovation was still unfinished. Even now, and after his marriage, money was still tight, 'as we had barely 700£ a year between us'. How that comparatively high figure still required some frugality he does not explain. It cannot have been the cost of servants, of which there were only three, a cook, a housemaid, and one labouring man who looked after the garden, and Ryle's one horse. The comment of Eric Russell looks correct: 'We can only suppose that out of his stipend he was making a considerable contribution to reducing his father's debts.'[1]

Marriage made little change to Ryle's routine; the main change was the company he enjoyed, both Matilda's, and, through her, acquaintance 'with several very Christian people of a gentler kind than I had seen before among men'. 'I shall always be thankful for having known my wife's father, and his two brothers Charles and Western. They were certainly three of the most amiable men I ever knew.' These friends were together bereaved by the sudden death of Georgina Tollemache. A plaque in the church at Helmingham recorded how she

> After a Life Devoted to the Service of Her God and Saviour,
> and to the Promotion of the Temporal and
> Spiritual Welfare of Those Around Her
> Entered upon a Blessed Immortality
> the 18th of July, 1846
> Aged 37 Years

Of this 'great blow' Ryle was to say:

> To her husband it was an irreparable loss, and he never was the same man again in religion. To myself it was an enormous loss, she was always most kind and friendly to me, and I believe really delighted in my ministry; ... Her loss to my wife was also very great, she was

[1] Russell, *Man of Granite*, 64.

a wise and most kind adviser to young women and just such an one my wife needed.

When the first Ryle baby was born at the rectory on 13 March 1847 the parents' shared affection for their late friend meant that she was baptized 'Georgina Matilda'. But the happiness at her birth was short-lived. Within ten days the mother was 'extremely ill' and post-natal depression also developed. For a time 'her intellect seemed like that of a little child and not of a grown up woman'. Slowly her mind recovered and Ryle could say that in September/October 1847 'she was really happier than ever she had been before'. Then a deterioration of her physical condition prompted him to take her to London for better medical opinion. Lung disease was diagnosed, and when the advice was that she should go immediately to a resort on the south coast, Ryle decided on Ventnor, near his parents at Anglesey. There they went together, 'about the middle of December, without my wife ever returning home'. Matilda's condition slowly worsened, and when various changes of environment made no difference, they settled at Fredville Manor, her parents' home in East Kent, where she died 25 June 1848. A blood vessel had given way in a lung.[1]

Through the dark months of his wife's suffering, Ryle records, 'Mr Plumptre was kindness itself all the way through. Mrs Plumptre never believed her illness was dangerous, and always said it was only a cough.' Ryle took three months to recover sufficiently to go back to Helmingham in October 1848. He left Georgina at Fredville, 'as it seemed the only natural course to take. To have her alone at Helmingham was of course out of the question.' He would visit her for five days once a month. The resumption of life in the now empty rectory 'was indeed a solitary, dreary, miserable period, and I often felt as if everything was going wrong, and as if everything I touched must come to no good'.

[1] She was buried in the Plumptre family vault in the church of St Mary the Virgin, at Nonington, Kent, where her daughter was also buried in 1915, 'waiting', says the memorial, 'for the redemption of our body'. Munden, *Travel with Ryle*, 59.

* * *

Events are no guide to the believer's condition. Jacob said, 'All these things are against me' (Gen. 42:36), when in reality they were working for good. It was no mistake that Ryle was deep in rural Suffolk, in a small work, with his patroness gone, and now bereft of his wife after only two years. It was an extremity in which God did not fail him, and his roots went down deeper in Scripture and in prayer. Maybe at the time he could not repeat a testimony which William Marsh liked to quote: 'It is all for the best. I am in the hands of a sovereign God', but he would later see that all along, 'God was fitting me for an after-work in a way I did not know.'

An essential part of that fitting, we may believe, was the part which private prayer played increasingly in his life. In the summer of his bereavement in 1848, he had spent three weeks in Scotland with John Plumptre and one of the Cootes. A common interest in the ministry of Robert Murray M'Cheyne had taken them to the scene of his ministry in Dundee, where he had died in 1843 at the age of twenty-nine. Ryle was impressed with the words of one of his hearers who told them that it was not simply M'Cheyne's words and teaching that were the cause of his influence: 'You must have seen the man, and heard him, and known him, and have been in company with him, to know what a man of God he was.' Ryle would not speak of his own experience of fellowship with God but he would underline to others the part which prayer must play in an effective ministry:

It was said by an old writer that Luther's habits of private prayer, and John Bradford's habits of private prayer, were things more talked of than practised and imitated. Private prayer is one grand secret of the strength of the ministry. It is here that the roots of the ministry, practically speaking, are to be found. The ministry of a man that has gifts, however great, but who does not give the closet the principal place, must sooner or later become jejune and ineffective.[1]

[1] 'What Is Our Position?', *Home Truths*, seventh series (Ipswich: William Hunt,

* * *

Ryle had not planned what his chief usefulness would be. He had not gone to Suffolk to be a writer. He meant writing to be no more than an accessory and it began in an almost accidental manner. On his arrival at Helmingham his first sermon took its title from Christ's words in Luke 7:40, 'I have somewhat to say unto thee.' Tradition says that 'with his own hands' he had it printed for private circulation.[1] It was an inauspicious beginning. The next year something happened to open a much wider door. It was occasioned by a tragedy at the port of Great Yarmouth, in the neighbouring county, on 2 May 1845. The day was one for special entertainment at which a circus clown promised to sit in a tub, drawn by four geese, across the North River and under a newly built suspension bridge. All went well until the clown drew near the bridge, and the crowd above him all rushed to one side for a closer view. The chains holding the bridge could not hold the weight and a mass of people were thrown into the water below where seventy-nine would drown.

While the thought of everyone in the eastern counties engaged with what had happened, an anonymous gospel tract appeared, and gained wide attention. No one doubted the ability of the writer and, when it was known to be the rector of Helmingham, the owners of the *Evangelical Magazine* sought him as their editor. He declined but proposed a series of 'Ipswich Tracts', 'if his brethren in the ministry would contribute their aid'. The aid was not forthcoming but Ryle went ahead on his own, with a ready publisher in William Hunt of Ipswich. At least three tracts were printed under his name in 1846, five in 1849, and thereafter there was no year until 1861 in which new items did not appear.

1859), 261. The words were addressed to clergy at Weston-super-Mare in 1859. The previous year Ryle had told the same conference the words quoted above about M'Cheyne.

[1] It was reprinted, with some revision, in *Home Truths*, third series.

The term 'tract' would mislead us if we visualized a few slight pages. Ryle used the word in the broader sense he had seen exemplified in the literature of the Religious Tract Society. Their tracts, which we noted him using from the outset of his ministry in Exbury, were commonly several pages long.[1] At least at the outset, the RTS subsidized their publications to keep their prices low. For the widest distribution, some of Ryle's tracts were only of one or two pages, while others were much more extensive. His tract, *Do You Pray?*, which sold over 130,000 copies, ran to forty-five small pages when printed in *Home Truths*.[2] A single tract on *Regeneration* ran to 104 pages. A catalogue of the tracts, printed in the back of *Home Truths*, shows the extent of what was available. *Expository Tracts* were eight-page items, available at six pence per dozen. *Plain Speaking* were 'forty short large-type tracts' available at one shilling in a packet. *Seed Corn* were a hundred one-page 'handbills, containing 48 sorts', price 8 pence. The seven volumes of *Home Truths* (1851–59) contained 'Addresses and Tracts' which had been previously published separately. An eighth volume in the series was to be added in 1871. They were of matching size of around 300 pages, and cost three shillings and sixpence. One has to admire both the confidence and ingenuity of Ryle's publisher, William Hunt, of Tavern Street, Ipswich. It cannot have been of Ryle's planning that copies of *Home Truths* were available in cloth binding, or in 'Morocco, Russia, and other elegant bindings, for presents'.

* * *

Ryle's first book was entitled *Spiritual Songs* in 1849. It was not, however, from his pen but 'A selection of Hymns, not to be found in many of the Hymn Books commonly used'. It is significant he

[1] The Society, formed in 1799, produced a first bound volume of 27 tracts in 1800, entitled, *The Publications of the Religious Tract Society*. They believed 'a wide field opens'. 'St Paul wrote tracts,' Ryle affirmed.

[2] Also published in *Home Truths*, second series, 3rd ed. (1855).

would early give attention to this. Hymns and public worship would be of abiding importance in his ministry: 'I strongly hold that holy thoughts often abide for ever in men's memories under the form of poetry, which pass away and are forgotten under the form of prose.' A second hymn book followed in 1850, then the first book title of his own composition in 1854, *The Bishop, the Pastor, and the Preacher*, covering the lives of Hugh Latimer, Richard Baxter, and George Whitefield, with forty-eight pages of introduction on 'What Is Wanted? Being Thoughts and Suggestions on Some of the Wants of the Church of England in the Present Day.'

Then followed in succession the series which would become his best-known works, *Expository Thoughts on the Gospel, Matthew* in 1856, *Mark* 1857, and *Luke* in two volumes, 1858–59. All these works came from Hunt's busy steam press.

How a Christian could write as much, mostly within twenty years of his conversion, illustrates to us that he was a man doing what he was called to do. Certainly it was not without constant hard work. There is a touch of autobiography in what he said to clergy in warning them of the danger of 'ministerial indolence', and of 'how easy it is for a watchman of souls to go back from his "first love"'. He believed that men in rural areas were in special danger: 'I speak feelingly on this point. It is my own position. I am persuaded we have certain peculiar temptations, from which our brethren in towns are very much exempt. The rector or vicar of a rural parish has frequently a sufficient income—a good house, a small population.' With few demands necessitating intellectual work, a man's mind can insensibly begin to rust.

> Many a clergyman who, at one time, did run well, … winds up … being nothing more than a clerical farmer, gardener, musician, or painter. I implore my rural brethren to remember this. I feel the approach of this plague often myself.[1]

[1] 'Neglect not the Gift', address to clergy at Weston-super-Mare, 5 July 1853, *Home Truths*, sixth series (Ipswich: Hunt, 1858), 237-8.

The significance of Ryle's writings needs to be appreciated in their wider historical context. At the beginning of the nineteenth century there were few popular writers in the Church of England. One of them was William Wilberforce, whose *Practical View of Christianity* was the means of the conversion of a young clergyman in the Isle of Wight by the name of Legh Richmond. Richmond then followed the example of Hannah More in writing tracts, and on discovering that the teaching of the English Reformers coincided with the Scriptures, he succeeded, it seems single-handed, in producing extensive selections from their works, in eight handsome leather-bound volumes, entitled, *The Fathers of the English Church*.[1] Among the evangelicals in the Eclectic Society there was also a recognition that the press was going to be a vital agency in the recovery of evangelical Christianity, and Josiah Pratt Sr had the works of Bishop Joseph Hall (10 vols) and Bishop Hopkins (4 vols) reprinted in 1808 and 1809. But it seemed as though the time was not ripe for a wide readership of such authors. Legh Richmond, personally responsible for the cost of *Fathers of the Church*, found himself as a result in debt to the extent of £2,000, and with no means of payment other than the unsold volumes. Only when friends discovered the reason for his uncharacteristic depression did they come forward to his aid.

Legh Richmond died in 1827 at the age of fifty-five. A fellow minister who visited him near the end reported that, in speaking to the dying preacher, he had commented on 'the immense value and importance of our principles', at which, 'he raised himself upright in his chair, and with great solemnity of manner, said, "Brother, we are only half-awake—we are none of us more than half-awake."[2]

---

[1] London: Hatchard, 1807–12. His interest in the Reformers had been awakened by a leaf of Bishop Jewel's *Apology* which a grocer had used to wrap something he had bought. Richmond went back to the shop to ask if there were any more such pages. He got the reply, 'O yes, Sir, here they are, and I have a whole hogshead of these worthies; they are much at your service, for two pence a pound.' T. S. Grimshawe, *Memoir of Legh Richmond* (London: Seeley, 1828), 133.

[2] *Memoir of Legh Richmond*, 577. Ryle, in quoting Richmond's dying words, said

* * *

If evangelicals were only 'half-awake' to the importance of literature in Legh Richmond's lifetime, a change was coming, and part of
that change was prompted by those of contrary belief as the Tractarians took to the press. 'The tracts have been selling so well,' Newman could report in 1837. But that was far from all. In the early
1840s a whole 'Anglo-Catholic Library' was launched, being a series
of volumes containing seventeenth-century theologians, from Laud
onwards, who had opposed the Puritans or secured their ejection
from the Church of England. The intention was to change the whole
climate of opinion and to discredit both Puritan and evangelical.

The evangelical response showed a degree of awakening that had
not been evident thirty years earlier. Edward Bickersteth (who traced
his conversion to a tract by Hannah More) was now leading evangelicals in the Church of England. From him and George Stokes came
the proposal for the largest publishing venture of the century. They
formed the Parker Society, 'to re-publish the entire mass of the printed
works of the leading divines of our reformed church, who flourished
in the age when the Roman yoke, which pressed so grievously upon
our forefathers, was broken.'[1] With the aid of Bickersteth's friend,
Anthony Ashley Cooper (the future Lord Shaftesbury), and a whole
group of clergy who acted as editors, the series began with the works
of Nicholas Ridley and Edwin Sandys in 1841. Supported by 7,000
subscribers, the Society went on to publish fifty-four volumes, the
last, a *General Index*, in 1855.[2]

---

of him, 'Few believers were ever more useful in their day and generation.' *Coming
Events and Present Duties* (London: Hunt, 1879), 40.

[1] 'Thirteenth and Final Report', prefixed to *General Index to the Publications of the
Parker Society* (Cambridge: University Press, 1855). The Society was named after Matthew Parker, the Elizabethan archbishop.

[2] The complete list of titles will be found in the *General Index*. There was no
attempt to publish in order of importance; they probably came out in the order
that the research and editorial work was completed. Five of the volumes (*Works of*

Among the Council of the Parker Society were individual authors who also wrote forcefully to the defence of the truths at stake. Perhaps the ablest of them was William Goode who, in two massive volumes, answered the Anglo-Catholic attempt to coordinate tradition with Scripture.[1]

This literature, comprehensive and invaluable for the serious reader, was the 'heavy guns' of a campaign, but something more popular was no less wanted and Ryle's writings were to be pre-eminent in meeting that need. England's leading newspaper, *The Times* (11 June 1880), was to observe that Ryle gained a 'niche for himself as a pamphleteer. As a weapon dropped from the hands of the Oxford School of Tractarians, Canon Ryle picked it up and tempered it to a new and very different use of his own.' The statement is hardly accurate. As noted above, evangelicals were writing tracts before the 1840s, but it is true that no one was to make a wider use of them than the rector of Helmingham.

From his first tract at Helmingham in 1844, the primary intention was evangelistic and pastoral. But contemporary Church issues, and response to the teaching of the Anglo-Catholics, also produced some of the most telling of his early tracts. His horizons were not set by the needs of rural Suffolk. As he wrote in 1858:

> These are not times in which men ought to get into their little parishes, and say they care not what goes on outside that ditch, or that wall, or that lane, which is the boundary of their parish. We must have public feelings, and do our duty, and take our part against the common foes by which the Church of England is in danger of being assailed. … We must not suppose that anything will do except fighting,—not fighting with carnal weapons, but with the sword of the Spirit.[2]

William Tyndale and *Writings of John Bradford*) were republished by the Banner of Truth Trust in 2010 and 1979 respectively.

[1] *The Divine Rule of Faith and Practice*, 2 vols (London: Hatchard, 1842).

[2] 'What Is Our Position?' an address to clergy in 1858, *Home Truths*, seventh series (1859), 266-7.

But even Ryle's extended vision could not have begun to antici-pate where that written ministry, begun quietly after Christmas 1844, would lead. His tracts, and then his books, would go round the world wherever English was spoken. Marcus Loane, his Austral-ian biographer, comments on how his forebears in Tasmania, at the other end of the world, read what began in Suffolk. Nor did language barriers hinder circulation. He was translated into Welsh, Gaelic, French, German, Dutch, Danish, Norwegian, Swedish, Portuguese, Italian, Russian, Hindustani, and Chinese. Had a record of the influ-ence been preserved it would have made marvellous reading. We can catch a glimpse of how God used what was written in a recollection of his friend James Bardsley. Spanish was not mentioned in the above list. Bardsley refers to one of Ryle's tracts, *Are You Free?*,[1] as one of forty translated into that language. A copy was given to a Dominican friar, Manuel Aguas, in Mexico. When he received the tract in the place where he had been sent to erase Protestant witness, 'The scales fell from his eyes while reading it, and, like St Paul, though sent to persecute, he began to build up the Church.'[2] A Mexican Reformed Church was to grow to 7,000 adherents, and another of its leaders, Bishop Riley, was to speak of how he was 'much indebted' to Ryle's tract *Are You Forgiven?*

In his lifetime Ryle would witness only a small part of the fruits of what he had written in faith. But he believed in the multiply-ing power of the gospel and in the God who said, 'A little one shall become a thousand, and a small one a strong nation' (Isa. 60:22).

---

[1] The tract was translated into Spanish by Bishop Henry Chauncey Riley and published under the title *True Liberty*.

[2] Machray, *First Bishop*, 44.

7

Puritans at Helmingham Rectory

Interior of Helmingham Church

R YLE'S years at Helmingham are the last on which there is comment in his short autobiography. There is much we would like to know about this period of which he tells us nothing. On his short years at Exbury we know how many services he had every Sunday, and how many cottage meetings he took mid-week. No such record exists for Helmingham. Nor do we know anything of how the congregation fared in the many months of his absence, 1847–48. Did another man, under John Tollemache's super-vision, fill the temporary vacancy? We do not know. The same prob-lem was to be repeated in the 1850s, and once again ill health in the family would be the cause.

On 21 February 1850, at Torquay, Ryle was remarried. The lady was Jessy Elizabeth Walker, daughter of a London merchant, then living in Torquay but a Scot, who came from Crawfordton House, near Moniaive, Dumfriesshire. Jessy was not a new acquaintance. She had been a friend of Georgina Tollemache, and of Ryle's first wife, of whose child she had been the godmother. Like Matilda Ryle, she was a committed Christian, but for her also, the happiness of marriage was soon to be overshadowed. In the words of her husband, 'We had not been married six months before she became very unwell, and from that time till she died, a period of nearly ten years, she really never was well more than three months together.'

There were to be five pregnancies. First, Jessy Isabelle (1851),[1] as a sister for four-year-old Georgina; another girl followed who died soon after birth (1853);[2] then Reginald (1854), Herbert (1856), and

---

[1] Usually known as Isabelle.
[2] For this knowledge we are indebted to Munden, *Travel with Ryle*, 59.

Arthur (1857). Such was the state of the mother's health that all five confinements necessitated their being in London for never less than two months. Twice they had to take a house there for the duration of their stay, once from December to May; at other times they lodged with friends.

> How much discomfort, inconvenience, and expense all this occasioned, I cannot pretend to describe; in fact, without Mr Walker's kind assistance we could not possibly have managed to get through. But he was the most unselfish, generous man I ever met with, and was always helping us.

One might suppose from such extended times of absence from his pastorate that the work at Helmingham was not a priority in his thinking. That would be an entire mistake. His firm principle was, 'A minister's sermons should be incomparably the first thing in his thoughts. He is not ordained to be a schoolmaster, a relieving officer, or a doctor, but to preach the Word.'[1] His pastoral care for his people was real, and he turned down invitations to stay in London half a dozen times. 'When my wife got well enough, we always returned to Helmingham, and there work went on much as before, with the addition of more writing.' The time that the people lost of his presence he seriously sought to make up, and could say, 'As to holidays, rest or recreation, in the year I never had any at all.'

How he got through the work that he did, he did not himself understand. No doubt much that was in his tracts came straight from his preaching, and his published addresses commonly had their origins from public occasions. Similarly some of his teaching Sundays or mid-week must have gone into his *Expository Thoughts*, but unlike numbers of preachers today he did not treat expository lectures as the standard for preaching. He commonly took individual texts. He did the same when he preached to children, and when—as was often the case—he accepted mid-week invitations to preach elsewhere. The

---

[1] *Bishop, Pastor and Preacher*, 38-9.

latter, with rare exceptions, he would do only if he could be back home that same night, to be present if his wife needed anything. 'I have frequently', he recalled,

> in the depth of winter driven distances of 12, 15, 20, or even 30 miles in an open carriage to speak or preach, and then returned home the same distance immediately afterwards, rather than sleep away from my own house.

One of the few letters of Ryle's which have survived is on this subject. To a request for his help he replied on 11 July 1857:

> Dear Sir,
>
> I feel that I had better decline your invitation to lecture at Newport.
>
> With a delicate wife, and not always very well myself, my movements are so uncertain that I am very unwilling to make distant engagements.
>
> I have frequently found that, when the time draws near, I have been unable to keep engagements and this always gives me much annoyance.
>
> Yours faithfully,
>
> J. C. Ryle

It is curious that the above letter was written on black-edged paper. Perhaps what was usually used for occasions of bereavement was the only paper he had to hand. The period was certainly one about which he could say, 'death made great gaps in the circle of those that I knew'. The number included his mother, his unnamed baby daughter, his sister Caroline, and his wife's parents.

That he was now in demand as a preacher is clear. On their necessary visits to London he preached 'in no less than 60 church pulpits'. Despite the small populations in Helmingham, a visitor one Sunday found the church crowded and counted 160 people who heard Ryle preach at length seemingly without notes.[1]

His 'worst trial' was his wife's continued ill health. Before Jessy died at the age of thirty-eight on 19 May 1860, Ryle noted:

[1] *Suffolk Chronicle* (23 March 1858), quoted in Toon and Smout, *Evangelical Bishop.*

> For four or five years, she had painfully little enjoyment of life, and was neither able to fill her position as a mother or as a mistress, to her own great sorrow … the whole business of entertaining and amusing the three little boys in an evening, devolved entirely upon me.

It was part of his grief that had there been an earlier diagnosis of her lingering illness (Bright's disease, a malfunction of the kidneys) she might have lived longer.

> She was buried in Helmingham Churchyard, at the North side of the Church, and I was once more left a widower with five children, the eldest only just 13; and altogether more disconsolate and helpless than ever.

All that her second son, Herbert, was to remember of Helmingham was 'being held up by his nurse at the attic window in the rectory to see his mother's funeral'.[1]

During the last three years of Jessy Ryle's life there had come a new burden for her husband. Perhaps an estrangement had been growing over the years, but of these years Ryle was to speak of an uncomfortable 'breach between myself and Mr Tollemache, and a complete suspension of all friendly relations between us'. What had caused it he does not record, save to repeat of his patron, 'he never was the same man after he lost his first wife'. That John Tollemache was imperious is not to be doubted. He was distinguished by arriving in the courtyard at the Great White Horse at Ipswich in his coach and four, and, even on Sunday mornings, he needed his carriage and attendants to convey him—who had once beaten the champion sprinter of England over 100 yards—the 600 yards across the park to the church. He was 'Old Lord John' before he was formally made a baronet in 1876, and he expected Ryle to recognize it. When he built and maintained a new school on his estate in 1853 it seems he wanted some limitations

---

[1] Maurice H. Fitzgerald, *Memoir of Herbert Edward Ryle* (London: Macmillan, 1928), 11.

on the religious instruction for which Ryle was responsible. If he judged Ryle's sermon was too long, it is rumoured he was known to stand up in his pew, holding up his watch conspicuously in his hand. Ryle was not a man to be treated as one of Tollemache's many employees. 'The people were not interesting', he would later tell his children, 'living in a state of servile subjection to Mr Tollemache, who owned every acre of the Parish, and not daring to have an opinion of their own about anything.' That Ryle was free of all blame is more than can be asserted. There are indications that Tollemache was a good employer and provider for his people. The preacher was perhaps unwise when, on a Sunday in March 1858, while speaking of the fleeting nature of treasures upon earth, he asked the congregation, 'Will Mr Tollemache take Peckforton Castle or Helmingham Castle or his fine house in St James when he dies?' If the gentleman was not in his pew that day, he would have read the words in the *Suffolk Chronicle* (23 March 1858). Peckforton Castle was another home which Tollemache had built for himself near Tarporley, Cheshire, in the years 1844–50. As a magnificent replica of a medieval castle, it must have been a common talking point.[1]

Wherever all the faults lay, we can understand Ryle saying that the breakdown in the relationship 'made our position at Helmingham extremely uncomfortable, and decided me to leave whenever an opening should offer'. 'In fact, the whole state of things', he was to say of the time of his second wife's death, 'was a heavy strain upon me both in body and mind, and I often wonder how I lived through it.'

The twelve months after Jessy Ryle's death in May 1860 must have been particularly difficult ones. In referring to a parallel instance in the life of Henry Venn, Ryle was to write, 'There are anxieties in such cases which no one knows but he who has gone through them; anxieties which can crush the strongest spirit.'[2] It would seem that the

---

[1] This impressive structure remains today as a hotel.
[2] *Christian Leaders*, 280.

financial pressure had at least reduced by this date, for an item he put in the *Ipswich Journal* for 22 December 1860 advertised for 'A good plain cook to act as housekeeper, in a clergyman's family, containing, FIVE children and SIX servants.' His household help had clearly doubled. The census for 1861 shows that two sisters-in-law were also resident in the rectory.

* * *

I have already mentioned the extent of Ryle's written output in his years at Helmingham. That he could produce so much of enduring value, and that in the midst of many trials, is indication enough that he was himself being fed from rich sources. Certainly, he was constantly reading, and would later say of his early years in Suffolk, 'I had more time for reading and thinking and storing my mind than I have ever had before or since.' With respect to the nature of that reading the guidance which he had found in Bickersteth's *Christian Student* took effect. He made himself familiar with the English Reformers through the volumes of the Parker Society, then appearing, and their influence on him would be lifelong.

But it was from the Puritans, in particular, that he gained most for his own ministry. What he read in Bickersteth he proved for himself. There he had read concerning the Puritans: 'All Thomas Manton's Works are worth having'; of John Flavel, 'Few more practical, popular and edifying'; of Thomas Brooks, 'A popular, lively, and practical writer'; of Richard Sibbes, 'very tender and striking'; of John Owen, 'an invaluable treasure of divinity'. That this school of authors became his regular companions in these years is clear. His tract on *Assurance* of 1849 was not only the old divinity in fresh language; it was backed up with some fifteen extracts from Puritan authors taken from various of their works.[1]

---

[1] The quotes occupied some nine pages when the tract was reprinted in *Home Truths*, first series (1860). This was not their first appearance as my edition of the

His Suffolk location played a part in deepening the same inter-
est. Fifteen miles away from Helmingham, the Reformer Rowland
Taylor, had been burned to death at Hadleigh; nine miles away, the
Puritan preachers Samuel Ward and Stephen Marshall had stirred
Ipswich; further to the west, William Gurnall had ministered at
Lavenham from 1644 to 1679, and many others, including Samuel
Fairclough and Mathew Lawrence, gave Ryle good reason to write
'Some of the most eminent Puritans were Suffolk ministers.' 'From
the day I was translated into the Eastern Counties, and became a
Suffolk incumbent, I have made it my business to study the lives of
eminent Suffolk divines.'[1] He was proud to call himself 'A Suffolk
minister, and a thorough lover of Puritan theology.'[2]

With respect to reading Ryle practised what he said to others.
Every true minister, he urged, should be always reading:

> Men must read, if their ministry is not to become threadbare, thin,
> and a mere repetition of hackneyed commonplaces. Always taking
> out of their minds and never putting in, they must naturally come to
> the bottom. Reading alone will make a full man.[3]

Ryle's reading of Puritan authors put light and strength into his
ministry. He saw their spirituality and warmth as characteristics of
the best evangelical teaching. From them he learned that the Christian life is primarily a life of faith, and he was passing on to others
what he had first preached to himself when he said,

> You read the lives of eminent Christians … And you are disposed
> to say, 'What wonderful gifts and graces these men had!' I answer,

---

first series volume is the sixth, nor do I know if they were attached to the original
tract. They will also be found in *Holiness* (Edinburgh: Banner of Truth Trust, 2014),
168-79.

[1] *Light from Old Times* (Edinburgh: Banner of Truth Trust, 2015), 299.

[2] 'Memoir of Samuel Ward', in *Sermons and Treatises by Samuel Ward* (Edinburgh:
Nichol, 1862; repr. Edinburgh: Banner of Truth Trust, 1996), v. The Memoir was
reprinted, with slight editing, in *Light from Old Times*.

[3] 'Neglect Not the Gift', *Home Truths,* sixth series, 239.

you should rather give honour to the mother-grace which God puts forward in the eleventh chapter of the Epistle to the Hebrews—you should give honour to their faith. Depend on it, faith was the mainspring of the character of each and all.[1]

Ryle early saw the value of calling attention to the lives of eminent Christians as a means of awakening interest in what they stood for. With that in view he spoke on 'George Whitefield' to the Church of England's Young Mens' Society in London in 1852. The next year he followed this with another London lecture on 'Baxter and His Times'. It was immediately printed and marked his first challenge to the assessment which had long been prevalent in the Church of England. Disparagement of the Puritans was commonplace, and protest at Ryle's attempt to reverse the accepted opinion was inevitable. Probably the longest critical response to his lecture came in the form of a thirty-two-page letter published by 'A Clergyman of the Diocese of Exeter, in Reply to the Lecture "Baxter and His Times"' (London: Rivingtons, 1853). While written for the most part in moderate tones, the writer expressed his alarm that this address was from one whose other writings come 'from the press by tens of thousands and for their general excellence [have] been extensively read'. It was detrimental to the Church to which Ryle belonged, and the reviewer told the author he hoped to 'counteract, if not to prevent, the injurious consequences which that work of yours tends too strongly to promote'. Ryle ought to remember

that your popularity as a tract writer has involved you in great responsibility. Never were Bulls of Popes, or Decrees of General Councils, received by Romanists with stronger belief in their infallibility, than are your books by a certain class of readers.

The comment was double-edged and it would appear the critic was not an admirer of the 'class of readers' to which he refers.

---

[1] 'Moses—An Example', *Holiness*, 198.

In general this clerical reviewer believed that history was a subject Ryle should have left alone. His treatment of the Puritans was one-sided, disloyal, and very incomplete. With the aid of various authors unsympathetic to the Puritans, the critic argued that

> the Puritans were a restless, revolutionary body, desirous, not only of personal liberty but also of liberty *to do with other men and systems as they pleased*, which, on the downfall of the Church and Throne, they lamentably proved … These unscriptural principles having once been started by men professing godliness, it was no wonder, as a consequence of their spread, to see a martyred King and Archbishop [Laud].'

The reviewer was particularly indignant at Ryle's statement:

> Settle it down in your minds, that for sound doctrine, spirituality and learning combined, the Puritans stand at the head of English divines. Settle it down in your minds that with all their faults, weaknesses and defects, they alone kept the lamp of pure evangelical religion burning in this country in the time of the Stuarts.

To give such a classification to men who were opponents of 'the Church', he told Ryle, was to show 'you are unfaithful to your own Church'.

This critique raised some matters of history to which Ryle gave no attention. The reviewer was right to see the Elizabethan era, as well as the time of Laud, as necessary to the Puritan story, but the underlying key to the difference between the two men was not over history, but theology. Ryle's words to his hearers, 'I love the Church, of which I am a minister', drew this response: 'In your own words I may ask you: Do you "mean the building where you worship on a Sunday"; or "the Clergy", or "the Christians who are governed by bishops?"' The words quoted from Ryle were taken from his tract, *What Is the Church?*, which he characterized as 'a work containing a deal of valuable truth, but alas! not unmixed with serious and palpable error *touching the duty of visible unity*'. Ryle did not believe that the authenticity of a Church is to be determined by its belonging to an observable line from the first century. His critic, on the other hand, meant by 'Church' the body which through its bishops had come down in visible succession from the time of the apostles, and he was shocked that Ryle should warn his readers against that understanding:

> You will often hear some semi-popish stripling fresh from Oxford, puffed up with new-fledged views of what he calls 'Apostolical Succession', and proud of a little official authority, depreciating and sneering at the Puritans, as men alike destitute of learning and true religion. While, in reality, he is scarcely worthy to sit at their feet and carry their books.

On these words, his reviewer asked,

> In thus holding up to obloquy and contempt your younger brethren in the ministry, who can estimate the injury done to that Church, whose honour you profess to have so warmly at heart? Give me leave to remind you, that what you are pleased to denominate 'new-fledged views of Apostolical succession', are held by men as old, as wise, as holy as yourself; and that your own Church holds them also. Why are converted Romish priests allowed to minister in our Churches without re-ordination, while Presbyterians and dissenters are required to receive 'the laying on of hands' by a Bishop, according to Apostolical usage?

There can be little doubt that Ryle read this *Letter* and he made a few revisions when he reprinted his lecture in later years, but the substance and the theology was not only preserved but repeated and enlarged.

Appreciations of other Puritans were to follow, notably accounts of Samuel Ward, William Gurnall, and Thomas Manton.[1] His

---

[1] For Manton, see *Works of Thomas Manton*, vol. 2, ix-xix; for Baxter and Gurnall, *Light from Old Times*. His account of Gurnall first appeared in the 1864 edition of the Puritan's *Christian in Complete Armour* (repr. Edinburgh: Banner of Truth Trust, 2013), xv-xliii.

'Estimate of Manton' appeared in 1870 in volume 2 of the twenty-two volumes of *Manton's Complete Works*, which formed the capstone of a remarkable decade of Puritan reprints by the publisher James Nisbet. Ryle shared in the promotion of the Puritan sets and told his readers,

> Few things need reviving more than a taste for such books as these …
> But the more I read, the less I admire modern theology. The more I
> study the productions of the new school of theological teachers, the
> more I marvel that men and women can be satisfied with such writing. … In matters of theology the old is better.[1]

In more than one way the influence which came through Ryle would reach millions. It was all planned in heaven. If the words of Ephesians 2:8 explain Ryle's conversion, the truth which stands out two verses further on gives the right understanding of his life: 'For we are his workmanship, created in Christ Jesus unto good works, which God hath before ordained that we should walk in them.'

I conclude this chapter with Ryle's mature and final word on why he worked (and suffered reproach) for a recovery of the Puritans:

'With regard to the Puritans … I believe that they deserve almost as much attention … as the Reformers. I want to promote acquaintance with them in the minds of all students of English church history. Never, I believe, were men so little understood and so absurdly maligned as the Puritans. On no subject perhaps are English Churchmen so much in the dark, and require such thorough enlightening. …

'The common impression of most English Churchmen about the Puritans is, that they were ignorant, fanatical dissenters, who troubled England in the seventeenth century,—that they hated the monarchical form of government, and cut off Charles I's head,—that they hated the Church of England, and caused its destruction,—

---

[1] *Light from Old Times*, 351.

and that they were unlearned enthusiasts who despised knowledge and study, and regarded all forms of worship as Popery. There are some ecclesiastical orators of high rank and brilliant reputation, who are never weary of flinging the epithet "Puritanical" at Evangelical Churchmen, as the hardest word of scorn that they can employ. … The Puritans were not faultless, I freely admit. They said, did, and wrote many things which cannot be commended. Some of them, no doubt, were violent, fierce, narrow-minded sectarians. Yet, even then, great allowance ought to be made for the trying circumstances in which they were placed, and the incessant irritating persecution to which they were exposed. It is written that "oppression maketh a wise man mad" (Eccles. 7:7). With all their faults, the leaders of the party were great and good men. With all their defects, the Puritans, as a body, were not the men that certain writers and orators in the present day are fond of representing them to have been.

'(*a*) The Puritans were *not enemies to the monarchy.* It is simply false to say that they were. The great majority of them protested strongly against the execution of Charles I, and were active agents in bringing back Charles II to England, and placing the crown on his head after Oliver Cromwell's death. The base ingratitude with which they were treated in 1662, by the very monarch whom they helped to restore, is one of the most shameful pages in the history of the Stuarts.

'(*b*) The Puritans were *not enemies to the Church of England.* They would gladly have seen her government and ceremonial improved, and more liberty allowed to her ministers in the conduct of public worship. And they were quite right! But the bulk of them were originally ordained by bishops, and had no special objection either to episcopacy or a liturgy. …

'(*c*) The Puritans were *not unlearned and ignorant men.* The great majority of them were Oxford and Cambridge graduates, many of them Fellows of colleges, some of them heads and principals of the best houses in the two universities. In knowledge of Hebrew, Greek, and Latin,—in power as preachers, expositors, writers and critics,—the Puritans in their day were second to none. Their works will speak for them on the shelves of every well-furnished theological library. Those who hold them up to scorn in the present day, as shallow, illiterate men, are only exhibiting their own lamentable shallowness, their own ignorance of historical facts, and the extremely superficial character of their own reading.

'The Puritans as a body, have done more to elevate the national character than any class of Englishmen that ever lived. Mighty at the council board, and no less mighty in the battlefield,—feared abroad throughout Europe, and invincible at home while united,—great with their pens, and great with their swords,—they were a generation of men who have never received from their countrymen the honour that they deserve. The body of which Milton, Selden, Blake, Cromwell, Owen, Manton, Baxter, and Charnock were members, is a body of which no well-informed Englishman should ever speak with disrespect … Unhappily, when they passed away, they were followed by a generation of profligates, triflers, and sceptics and their reputations have suffered accordingly, in passing through prejudiced hands. But, judged with "righteous judgment", they will be found men "of whom the world was not worthy". The more they are really known, the more they will be esteemed.

'For myself, I can say only, that the very reason why many in this day dislike the Puritans is the very reason why I love them, and delight to do honour to their names. They deserve honour, in my opinion, on account of their bold and outspoken *Protestantism*. They deserve honour on account of their clear, sharply-cut, distinct *Evangelicalism*. I want to see their writings more widely read, and their conduct more fairly judged and duly appreciated by English Churchmen. …

'For the length of the attempt I have made in this introduction to defend the Reformers and Puritans, I have no apology to make. I have defended them because they have numerous enemies and few friends in this day, and many Englishmen seem to know nothing about them. ... As long as I live, I hope I shall never be ashamed to stand up for them, and to vindicate their claim to respect.'[1]

[1] Abridged from 'Introduction' to *Light from Old Times*, xviii-xxi.

8

Stradbroke: Twenty Fruitful Years

Top: Stradbroke School

Bottom: Street scene in Stradbroke

Both photographs taken by Henrietta Ryle

THE release Ryle needed from the circumstances in Helmingham came in the form of an invitation from John Pelham, bishop of Norwich, which offered him the living at Stradbroke. Ryle accepted and became vicar there in September 1861. The next month this new stage of his life was completed on his marriage to Henrietta Clowes of Broughton Old Hall, near Manchester. In the words of Marcus Loane, 'Ryle had emerged from the shadows of deep sorrow and care into a world of sunlight and joy.' With Henrietta at his right hand, they were to enjoy long years of happiness together, and she was ideally suited to the role before her. The home circle needed a wife, a mother, a nurse, a teacher, and musician. She would meet all these, plus she had another gift, too modern for its absence to be unnoticed: Henrietta Ryle would be the village photographer, and leave us permanent windows into some Stradbroke scenes which the world would not otherwise have had.

In a note prefixed to a continuation of his *Expository Thoughts* on John, written in 1869, Ryle explained the delay in the series in terms of the changes taking place in his life:

> the delay has been unavoidable, and has arisen from circumstances entirely beyond my own control. Deaths, domestic anxieties, illness, and change from one residence to another, have had much to do with it. The principal cause has been my removal to my present parish. The work was begun in a little quiet parish of 300 people. It has been resumed in a widely-scattered parish of 1400 people, requiring almost the whole of my attention. ... I cannot create time. It is not one of the primary duties of a parochial clergyman's office to write commentaries.[1]

[1] *Expository Thoughts: John,* vol. 1 (1865; repr. Edinburgh: Banner of Truth Trust,

Although no more than fifteen miles from Helmingham, Stradbroke was a contrast to his former charge in many respects. With a few hundred houses, some clustered round the church, it was one of the largest and busiest villages in Suffolk. Ryle would describe about 400 of the neighbourhood as 'farmers, tradesmen and professional persons', and the remainder were chiefly agricultural labourers. Twice a month there was a corn market, and there was an annual market of livestock. 'There were butchers, grocers, and tradesmen such as boot and shoe makers, tailors, milliners, joiners, blacksmiths, saddlers and watchmakers. There was also a police station with two resident policemen.'[1]

In after years Ryle would speak of Stradbroke's 'total absence of urban temptations' but it had not been without the problems which make a police station necessary. It was recorded in 1875:

> Some twenty or thirty years ago Stradbroke was one of the worst places in the neighbourhood. A respectable person could hardly ride through without being insulted or very likely his hat would be knocked off his head.

For Ryle the greatest contrast with Helmingham was probably the relief that there was no landlord ruling the area and its people. At the same time, that added to his role, as he soon found out. If repair and rebuilding had to be done the responsibility fell on him. An immediate need was for a replacement of the old school building to house 250 children. One who answered his appeal for help was his old friend William Marsh; not without humour as his life drew to a close, he wrote on October 20 1863:

2015), xiii-xiv. This volume covered John chapters 1-6. Chapters 1-4 had been published earlier. A third edition was in print by 1877. He advised his readers, 'Use commentaries; but be a slave of none. Call no man master … Men read many books, and yet neglect "the one Book"' (Preface, vol. 3; 1873). 'If I can make the Bible more plain and interesting to any man's soul, I shall be abundantly content' (Preface, vol. 2; 1869).

[1] Munden, *Travel with Ryle*, 69.

My Dear Ryle,—If I should ever visit you, I should like a 'sitting' in your new schoolroom; so I pay for it in advance, £1—I only wish it were £100. I am so glad to hear of the movement at Ipswich. The great enemy is awake and astir; if we sleep, the land will be sown with tares. May truth conquer among our Suffolk brethren, and the wheat they sow produce an abundant harvest. Controversy, 'with meekness and wisdom', in the present day is a bounden duty; silence would be too like neutrality, and *neutrality is treason.* Yours most truly,

William Marsh

Work on the vicarage had to follow the new schoolroom, leading to the major project of the repair of the church itself, which would take eight years and more than £4,000. Such funds were far beyond the local resources, and Ryle appealed to his readers in a letter printed inside the cover of a tract entitled *Are You Fighting?*:

After standing probably four hundred and fifty years, almost every part of this noble fabric requires more or less repair and renovation … It is quite impossible for the inhabitants of Stradbroke to raise such a sum as £2,700. Stradbroke is a large straddling parish on clay soil and seven miles from a railway station. There are no resident landlords or gentry and the population is made up of farmers, labourers, and three professional men. It is quite evident that without help from kind friends unconnected with the parish the work cannot possibly be done … I am bold to express a hope that many unknown friends in Britain and Ireland, who have for twenty years read and approved the writings of the Vicar of Stradbroke, will kindly remember the church in which he preaches and generously aid him in the heavy work he has undertaken.

Such was the response that by December 1871 only a further £250 was needed. By the next year the work on the main body of the church was complete, but more work and cost was necessary on the chancel and in another appeal Ryle gave an added reason why it was needed:

Time is short and uncertain. Before the connection of the present Vicar of Stradbroke with his parish is ended he is anxious to leave every part of the church in such complete order that no fair excuse may be left to any succeeding Vicar for introducing ornaments or fittings of an un-Protestant character.

What he meant by that was illustrated by the new east window. Instead of a stained-glass figure, supposedly of Christ or the apostles, it showed the whole armour of God which the Christian wears. Ryle kept his eye on details, including not only a new pulpit but the text he wanted on its desk. To be seen by every preacher, the words were carved, 'Woe is unto me if I preach not the Gospel', with a deep groove under the word 'not' cut by his own hand. He contributed to the costs, including £500 for a new roof. The renovated chancel was dedicated in memory of his father who had died in 1862.

Stradbroke certainly involved Ryle in a great deal more public work. As well as three services on Sunday, there was the supervision of three weekly 'house meetings', the school and a flourishing Sunday School. The same writer who spoke on the former condition of the village observed how much changed during Ryle's ministry:

> In parish work he was practical and thorough, taking great interest in the temporal as well as the spiritual welfare of his parishioners. Services well attended, bright and hearty congregational singing, plain and forcible, rarely concluded without some words to boys and girls in the congregation. Ryle urged parents to bring young children. Now a quieter and more orderly parish is hardly to be found.[1]

Ryle could now afford the aid of curates. One can only regret that none of them left any record of their time with him. For more personal glimpses we are largely dependent on a modicum of information contained in the biography of his son Herbert, who was seventeen in 1873 when his father gave the family the autobiographical narrative which only went as far as 1860. The vicarage was evidently a lively household, with the father the stimulus for much that

[1] An article in *Public Men of Ipswich and Suffolk* (1875), quoted in Russell, *Man of Granite*, 74.

went on, whether carpentry, cricket for the boys, or country walks. Other children in the village had his attention. Meeting a group of children on their way home from school he was liable to organize them in competitions for jumping or running, with sweets as the prizes. 'He used to say that he ruled the parish through the sweets he carried about with him for such occasions.' Doing nothing was the one thing not to be tolerated in children. Seeing young fellows lounging at the corner of a street, he was heard to tell them, 'Don't stand there *idle*: it would be better if you went and got into mischief.'

A glimpse inside the Ryles' home comes from the memory of one who stayed with them as schoolboy:

> Mr Ryle, with his gigantic figure and stentorian voice, was per-
> haps rather formidable to a youthful visitor, but he was very kind
> and hearty, and I soon felt at home. The boys, each in his way, were
> delightful companions. The atmosphere of the house was, like that of
> my own home, devotional: daily Bible readings, somewhat lengthy
> family prayers, and a good deal of religious talk. But all was quite
> wholesome and unpretentious, and I don't think any of us were bored,
> much less inclined to cavil at the régime, at any rate at that time.[1]

In the family happiness Henrietta Ryle may have played the major part. She was loved by her step-children, was a correspond-ent for the boys when the time came for them to be away at school, and we do not hear of her being incapacitated by poor health. She was the organist for the church, taught Sunday School and used her photography to keep a visual record of the restoration of the church.

Only one letter from Ryle to her appears to have survived in print. It was written to her from Eton in July 1868 when he had taken Herbert there for an entrance examination. Anticipating the letter would be read aloud to everyone at home, before 'Dearest Love' came a caution, '*Read privately first.*' Probably the reason for the caution related to the words which have also been removed from the copy

---

[1] Fitzgerald, *Memoir of H. E. Ryle*, 11.

which has survived:

> I write out of doors sitting by the river, with Windsor Castle in front of me.
>
> Very hot last night.
>
> It is painful work to see the crowd of anxious fathers and mothers bringing boys for examination, and watching them into the room!
>
> I see many that I just know or that claim acquaintance with me. But I see none of God's people. …
>
> The boys are a wonderfully fine handsome set! I fancy you could not find 860 such boys together anywhere else in the world.
>
> Also I observe just ten times as many young (real) ladies walking about, and at their ease, as in my time. So I suppose their appearance does not cause so much excitement as it did 34 years ago.[1]

* * *

While Ryle's name was well known in evangelical circles in the 1850s it was in the next decade, when he was in his forties, that he rose to leadership among the evangelical agencies. It would seem that Henry Law (1797–1884), archdeacon of Wells, who became dean of Gloucester in 1862, was one of the first to bring Ryle to the fore. Law was the incumbent at Weston-super-Mare (1849–62) where he started a conference for clergy. Ryle was introduced into its circle, and gave two addresses there in 1853 from which we have quoted above. After that point he seems to have been in regular attendance. At the 1856 conference he shared in a significant conversation with his friends Henry Law, Hugh McNeile, and John C. Miller (1814–80) who was rector of St Martin's, Birmingham. The outcome of their discussion was a decision to promote special evangelistic services, for five or six successive nights, with the object of reaching non-churchgoers. The first of such a series was held in Miller's huge church in November 1856 and was said to have reached 2,000 of the working classes.

---

[1] *Ibid.*, 21-2. Either Herbert Ryle or his biographer would have been responsible for the words cut from the fourth paragraph of the letter as quoted above.

A local newspaper reported that the services, in which Ryle and McNeile shared the preaching with Miller, 'were simple and solemn'. 'In spite of many a prediction of failure,' Ryle believed, 'it was clearly proved that when you go out of your routine path to meet the working classes, they will come and meet you.'[1]

This was evangelism with doctrinal content. Like Ryle, Miller urged the republication of the Puritan works, with their 'massive theology baptized with all the rich unction of Christian experience'. It was Miller who wrote the General Preface to the twelve volumes of the *Works of Thomas Goodwin*, reprinted in James Nichol's series, convinced that if preaching were to become what it ought to be, 'ministers must be, as were Puritan giants, students. Less public work. Fewer committees. Less serving of tables.' The alternative would be 'a disastrous state of malady—an ill-stored, unlearned, untheological clergy'.[2]

Such special services as took place in Birmingham were to multiply in the years which followed and Ryle shared in them whenever possible. He wanted to be 'ready to go anywhere or any distance to speak or preach for Christ'. In 1860 he was introduced as a speaker for the first time to the oldest of the evangelical gatherings, the Islington Clerical Conference. In 1862 he was asked to preach the annual sermon of the Church Missionary Society at St Bride's Church in London, 'an honour described by Magee as the "blue ribbon of the evangelical pulpit"'.[3] On both of these occasions Ryle took subjects which were at the heart of his ministry. At Islington it was the need for revival and more effective preaching; at St Bride's, from the text of Paul at Athens (Acts 17:16-17), the uselessness of human reason in finding God. The most learned and cultured city in the world stood in absolute need of divine revelation. Far from giving any support to

[1] 'What Is Our Position?', *Home Truths*, seventh series, 254.
[2] *Works of Thomas Goodwin*, vol. 1 (Edinburgh: James Nichol, 1861), xx.
[3] Toon and Smout, *Evangelical Bishop*, 67.

'natural theology', which he called 'an impudent assertion', there was no answer for a city 'full of idols' except that of Paul: 'he preached unto them Jesus and the resurrection'.[1]

In the CMS sermon Ryle spoke strongly on those in the Church who did not hold Scripture as God-given revelation. That same year 1862 there was a widely-noted example of such unbelief in a publication by John Colenso, Church of England bishop of Natal, *The Pentateuch and the Book of Joshua Critically Examined.* The following year Ryle provided a Preface to 'A Detailed Reply' to Colenso by William Wickes, entitled *Moses, or the Zulu?* In that Preface he wrote, 'I never could have believed it possible that any Bishop of the Church of England could put forth such a book, and yet retain office a single day as a minister of the Church of England, much less a Bishop.'[2]

Eugene Stock speaks of Ryle in the 1870s as 'perhaps the most prominent and honoured of the Evangelical leaders'.[3] At this period he was also heard by students at both Oxford and Cambridge. He preached at the latter in 1873 and 1874, and at Oxford five times between 1874 and 1880. For the sermon in 1880 he used largely the same material on 'Athens' as at the CMS annual service in 1862. The 'heads' were: 1. What St Paul *saw* at Athens; 2. What St Paul *felt* at Athens; 3. What St Paul *did* at Athens. But there was difference in the application.[4]

Twenty-eight years had passed before Ryle had first gone back to Oxford. The occasion was an invitation from Alfred Christopher, rector of St Aldate's in 1865. In the 1870s, Dr Liddell, Ryle's former tutor at Christ Church and now the Vice-Chancellor, nominated him to preach at St Mary's before the university. But he had to follow the

[1] Stock, *History of the Church Missionary Society*, vol. 2, 342.

[2] *Moses, or the Zulu?* (London: Wertheim, 1863), vii. The title of the book came from the words of a Zulu, whose incredulity over the Flood narrative in Genesis Colenso justified.

[3] Stock, *History of the Church Missionary Society*, vol. 3, 8.

[4] The 'Athens' sermon, as preached in Oxford, will be found in *Upper Room*, 154.

invitation the next day with the comment, 'I find you are only a B.A.' University regulations required clergymen to have taken the M.A. degree before exercising such a function. Hearing what had happened, Christopher urged him to come and take the M.A., and on his doing so in 1871, he commented, 'It was curious to see this stalwart veteran of fifty-five among the young M.A.'s taking his hitherto avoided M.A. degree.'[1]

In this same period the leading evangelical societies within the Church of England—the Church Missionary Society, the Church Pastoral Aid Society (founded in 1836), the Irish Church Missions— were growing in influence and Ryle had become one of their regular speakers.

In 1865 a new society was formed within the Church of England named the Church Association and from the outset Ryle was present at its meetings and gave it his full support. The stated objectives were:

> to uphold the doctrine, principles and order of the United Church of England and Ireland, and to counteract the efforts now being made to pervert her teaching on essential points of the Christian faith, or assimilate her services to those of the Church of Rome, and further to encourage concerted action for the advancement and progress of spiritual religion.

Ryle became a main speaker at the Association's Conference, spoke regularly at the Annual Meetings, and was elected a Vice-President in 1870. He spoke on deputation for its work at various times and places. One of his best-known addresses, 'What Do We Owe to the Reformation?', was delivered on behalf of the Association, and in printed form sold 88,000 copies in one year.

Part of the Association's work was to challenge in court the legality of numbers of changes in services which Anglo-Catholics were

---

[1] 'Canon Christopher's Reminiscences', *The Record*, 15 June 1900. Four sermons of Ryle's before the University of Oxford are published in *Upper Room*, chs. 4, 9, 10, and 11.

steadily introducing. The latter claimed that the law was on their side, and the Association had repeated successes in obtaining decisions which showed the claim to be false. This appeal to the law was taken up by opponents and employed to claim that a policy of persecution was being followed. In the House of Lords, the bishop of Peterborough wanted the Church Association designated as a 'Persecution Society, Limited'. Ryle's voice was heard in refutation as he called on men to support the Association:

> It is too often regarded as a mischievous, intolerant, persecuting body. I hear such charges with perfect indifference. I remember that poachers do not like gamekeepers, and burglars do not like watchdogs, and thieves do not like police, and Ahab did not like Elijah, and I cannot expect Ritualists to like the Church Association. But when Bishops, a few years ago, would or could do nothing, when Popery was coming in on our Church like a flood, I challenge any man to tell me what better thing could have been done than to form the Church Association, for defence not defiance, for conservation of the Church, not for persecution.[1]

Ryle supported appeals to the law.

> Our simple aim in suits has been not to persecute persons, but to establish principles. After all what saith the Scripture? Would St Paul have gone to law? I reply by another question, Would St Paul have tolerated false teachers and not recommended discipline? Would he recommend us not to interfere with heretics?[2]

This is not to say that Ryle regarded the legal procedure as dependable. When Colenso had been deposed for heresy in South Africa, the judicial committee of the Privy Council in England had overruled the

---

[1] *Church Association Monthly Intelligencer*, XI, 1877, 163.

[2] *Ibid.*, XIV, 1880, 22. I am indebted to Derek Scales for drawing my attention to the importance of Ryle's connection with the Church Association and for my quotations from their *Monthly Intelligencer*. Ryle did not discount the importance of the vestments issue. In an address on 'Distinctive Vestments' (*ibid.*, 1874, VIII) Dr Scales notes, Ryle 'explained what they were, listed twelve historical facts about them, and finished with seven reasons why all who love the Church of England should use every effort to prevent their use being sanctioned'.

decision. Nor did Ryle regard legal procedure as the most desirable. The adverse publicity given to the decisions of courts of law on such ceremonial points as the clothing worn by priests gave opportunity to represent the Association as concerned with mere secondary things, ignoring the fact that unauthorized vestments were being used to inculcate doctrine contrary to gospel and Protestant belief. The priority for the Association and Ryle was with spiritual truth as expressed in his words: 'Christ rightly known, Christ truly believed, and Christ heartily loved, is the true preservative against Ritualism, Romanism, and every form of idolatry.'[1]

Ryle was also a supporter of the various Clerical and Lay Associations of evangelicals in the Church of England which grew up in various parts of the country from the late 1850s, for the purpose of mutual counsel and support. But tension arose among evangelicals over their participation in Church gatherings not specifically evangelical, and, particularly, whether attendance at the annual three-day Church Congresses was consistent with their convictions. The Congresses, begun in 1861, stipulated no doctrinal emphasis, being intended to bring together clergy of different views. In 1866 Bishop Pelham asked Ryle to attend the Congress at Norwich and to give his impressions of its value. Ryle's judgment proved to be controversial among his evangelical colleagues. He was not surprised to find few men of his convictions present, but he concluded that for evangelicals to absent themselves was to leave all leadership to others, and to miss influencing those who could gain a better understanding of evangelical belief. He reminded his fellow evangelicals that, 'Great is the power of the face, the voice, the eye', and that it was possible to like a man without agreeing with him.

In an indirect reference to this thinking, he wrote concerning the attendance of Nicodemus in the Sanhedrin:

[1] *Knots Untied: Being Plain Statements on Disputed Points in Religion, from the Standpoint of an Evangelical Churchman* (1874; repr. London: Hunt, 1885, tenth ed.), 421.

> In large assemblies of men convened to consider ecclesiastical and
> religious questions, we may confidently assume that there are always
> some present whose hearts are right, and who are willing to sup-
> port the truth, even though they sit in bad company, and are for the
> present silent and overawed. There is no warrant for staying away
> from assemblies and councils merely because we happen to be in a
> minority.[1]

From being a listener at Norwich, Ryle rose to be a speaker in 1868,
and thereafter was active in another twelve Congresses until 1880,
giving one final address at Hull in 1890.

There was an argument for taking his view, and he put it to fellow evangelicals in a tract *Shall We Go?* Some other leaders, as Hugh
McNeile and Francis Close of Cheltenham, said 'No.' Dean Close,
after attending one Congress, believed 'he had no business to be in
that atmosphere of cloudy, confused, misty compromise' and never
attended again.[2] To this subject we will return below.

This same period saw Ryle undertaking a larger part in diocesan
affairs. In 1869, John Pelham, the evangelical bishop of Norwich,
had made him a rural dean of Hoxne which involved a measure of
oversight for twenty-five other parishes, and in February 1872 he was
made an honorary canon of Norwich.

Certainly Ryle's commitments beyond Stradbroke were enough to
keep his coachman busy, and like his employer he was not expected
to favour a slow pace. For meetings away from home, trains had commonly to be caught at Diss or Harleston, eight or nine miles distant.
We are told:

> Often he was pressed for time. 'Garnham, we shall lose the train',
> he would call out through the carriage window. 'I can't go faster, Sir,
> unless the horses gallop.' 'Then make them gallop', would be the
> reply, and through the main street of Harleston the horses would

---

[1] *Expository Thoughts: John,* vol. 2, 173.
[2] Chadwick, *Victorian Church, Part II* (London: Adam & Black, 1970), 363.

dash at a pace that brought people running to their doors to see 'old
Ryle late again'.[1]

* * *

While tracts and addresses had been Ryle's main written output
at Helmingham it was books which received his main attention at
Stradbroke. In a Preface to one of them, he wrote in 1877,

> Experience has taught me, at last, that the peculiar tastes of all classes
> of society must be consulted, if good is to be done by the press. I am
> convinced that there are thousands of people in England who are
> willing to read a *volume*, but will never look at anything in the form
> of a *tract*.[2]

I have already mentioned the publication of volume 1 of *Expository Thoughts* on John in 1865. He had written on John chapters 1-4
nearly five years before; now, with chapter 5 and 6 added, they made
up the first of what would be a three-volume set. Volume 2 came out
in 1869 (fourteen years after he 'first began writing on the Gospels'),
and volume 3 in 1873, with regret expressed in the Preface that the
completion had been so delayed:

> The work was first begun in a little quiet parish … and then brought
> to a standstill by heavy domestic affliction. It has been resumed and
> carried on, amidst many interruptions … In the face of these difficul-
> ties and distractions, I can only wonder that I have been enabled to
> finish my work on St John at all.[3]

The three volumes came to some 1,400 pages, the size being due
to a change of procedure on his part. Whereas the earlier *Expository
Thoughts* had only selected leading thoughts from a passage, the work

---

[1] Fitzgerald, *Memoir of H. E. Ryle*, 13. He adds, 'This must have been in the earlier
days, for when his sons were at university he cheerfully gave up horses and carriage
to maintain them.'
[2] *Old Paths* (1877; repr. Edinburgh: Banner of Truth Trust, 2015), x.
[3] *Expository Thoughts: John*, vol. 3, ix.

on John was to include comment on every verse, in either Ryle's words or those of 'about seventy commentators, both ancient and modern, of almost every Church and theological school in Christendom'.[1] His evaluation of these different commentators, in the Preface to the third volume, will be of special interest to students.[2] He was perfectly at home with the Greek text, and conceded short-comings in the translation of the Authorized Version, but wrote, 'I doubt much whether we should gain much by throwing it aside. Taking it for all in all, the authorized English version is an admirable translation. I am quite content to "let well alone".'[3]

Despite the value which he placed on commentaries, he is ready to confess of his own work, 'I am sensible that I have often failed to hit the mark', and cautions his younger readers to remember that commentators 'are good helps, but they are not infallible. Use your own judgment prayerfully and diligently. Use commentaries; but be a slave to none.'

From the outset *Expository Thoughts* had an extensive sale; volume 2 on John, for instance, was in a ninth edition within ten years of its first publication, and today his readers are to be found across the earth. William Marsh said of the series, 'I know nothing of the kind likely to be more useful. It is clear as light.'[4] George Moore, a

---

[1] *Ibid.*, v.

[2] He says on Matthew Poole that his 'Annotations are sound, clear, and sensible; and taking him all in all, I place him at the head of English Commentators on the whole Bible'. Matthew Poole, *Commentary on the Holy Bible*, 3 vols (Edinburgh: Banner of Truth Trust, 1979).

[3] Preface to *Expository Thoughts: John*, vol. 1, xii-xiii. The Preface also contains a valuable treatment of the full inspiration of all Scripture: 'A partially inspired Bible is little better than no Bible at all. … I thoroughly distrust these new theologians, however learned and plausible they may be … I believe that the want of our age is not more "free" handling of the Bible, but more "reverent" handling, more humility, more patient study, and more prayer' (viii, ix).

[4] *Life of Marsh*, 503. His daughter adds, 'Mr Ryle's tracts were those which he gave away most widely, excepting only the series entitled *Christ Is All* by his beloved friend, Archdeacon Law.'

successful Christian business man and friend of Ryle's, gave away 2,500 copies of *Expository Thoughts*, inscribed, 'on condition that a portion of this book is read every day'. 'We prize these volumes,' Spurgeon wrote of the series; 'Mr Ryle has evidently studied all previous writers on the Gospels.'[1]

Despite such a mountain of literary work, the commentaries were by no means all his written work in the Stradbroke years. In 1866 and 1867 he supplied what he called 'biographical papers' for the popular monthly, *The Family Treasury*. 'Its chapters were written from month to month in the midst of many ministerial engagements.'[2] They consisted of the twelve evangelical leaders of the eighteenth-century revival, beginning with Whitefield and Wesley, and were ultimately published as *Christian Leaders of the Last Century*. When the title was chosen it was never envisaged that the book would continue to be published two centuries later. In the opinion of W. F. Machray, this title 'was probably the best known' of his books in 1900.[3] Few had attempted to cover that history in the same way. The same year as *Christian Leaders* was published, 1868, another volume of biographical history came out with the title, *Bishops and Clergy of Other Days*.

Further volumes were to appear regularly, generally made up of material already published, sometimes as items in the *Family Treasury* or *The Record*, or as tracts, sermons, or lectures. These he might revise and enlarge, with a new introductory chapter. Thus when *Knots Untied: Being Plain Statements on Disputed Points in Religion* was published in 1874, he wrote in the Preface that those who had been reading him for twenty-five years, 'will not find much that is new to them. They will find some of their old acquaintances, but

[1] C. H. Spurgeon, *Lectures to My Students* (Edinburgh: Banner of Truth Trust, 2008), 844.

[2] *Christian Leaders of England in the Eighteenth Century* (Edinburgh: Banner of Truth Trust, 2002), iv.

[3] Machray, *First Bishop*, 44. Ryle's reading for this title had begun by the early 1850s.

altered, remodelled, recast, and partially divested of their direct and familiar style.'[1]

Most of his books came about in the same way: *Holiness* in 1877,[2] *Old Paths* in 1878, *Practical Religion* in 1879, *Coming Events and Present Duties* in 1879. All brought together material previously published as separate tracts. The most singular example of how a work could develop and expand across the years is probably *Bishops and Clergy of Other Days*. With the exception of the pages on George Whitefield (to be used in *Christian Leaders*), this title of 1868 was an enlargement of *The Bishop, the Pastor, and the Preacher* (1854). It reappeared, with additions, in 1882, as *Facts and Men: Being Pages from Church History, 1553–1683*,[3] and with yet another title in 1890, *Light from Old Times, or, Protestant Facts and Men*, when the only addition was a chapter on John Wycliffe.

New tracts also continued to appear during these years. When a list of 100 was made in 1876, presumably by the printer, the total printed exceeded 8.5 million. By 1888 it is said that between 200 and 300 tracts of various lengths had been published, with over 12 million issued.

The great aim of all he wrote was to lead readers to respond to the words of the Lord Jesus Christ, 'Come unto me, all ye that labour and are heavy laden, and I will give you rest.' 'This is the end for which I desire to write and preach; and it is of little use or value to write and preach for anything else.'[4]

* * *

---

[1] *Knots Untied*. This was Ryle's leading work in defence of the evangelicalism of the Church of England. It was in a tenth edition by 1885.

[2] *Holiness* was in a fifth edition by 1900, with probably the last Preface he ever wrote.

[3] *Facts and Men* (London: Hunt, 1882).

[4] *Principles for Churchmen: A Manual of Positive Statements on Doubtful, or Disputed Points* (London: Hunt, 1884), 149.

When Ryle had been fifteen years at Stradbroke the following interesting comment appeared in a short report of his life in 1876:

Whether from considerations of health or otherwise, Mr Ryle has preferred to labour in the country. Repeated offers have been made to him to fill town charges of importance—such as St John's, Derby; St John's, Bedford Row, London; St George's, Southwark; and St Martin's, Birmingham. These offers he has, however, declined. Suffolk still continues the sphere of his pulpit ministrations and the centre of his spiritual influence, which is as widespread as it is wholesome.

'Mr Ryle', says a writer, 'is one of the messengers of the good news sent to the fallen races of mankind, and he simply applies himself to the work of his commission. In this work he is strong and eloquent. To this he devotes himself absolutely. He meddles with nothing else. He has great gifts for the task. He is known to every Low Church congregation, and on every Evangelical platform in England. His voice everywhere revives the flagging attention. There is a healthy force about the man that wakens people up, and his power is greater than his mere words would seem to imply.'

His name has been sometimes mentioned in connection with higher preferments, and surprise expressed that he has so long been passed over.[1]

Ryle was sixty-three and continuing his ministry as usual in Stradbroke when on 21 February 1880 he received from the Prime Minister, Lord Beaconsfield (better known as Benjamin Disraeli), the startling offer of the Crown appointment of the deanery of Salisbury Cathedral. 'I did not like it,' Ryle commented. 'I went to Salisbury and the more I looked at it, the less I liked it.'[2] But friends gave him a contrary opinion about the offer, and, after much hesitation, he accepted. The next Sunday he preached from John 13:7, 'What I do thou knowest not now; but thou shalt know hereafter.' Many of his people were said to be in tears as they heard of his departure and his

---

[1] *Sunday at Home*, 1876, 106.
[2] Quoted by Russell, *Man of Granite*, 132, from A. R. M. Finlayson, *Life of Canon Fleming* (1909), 178.

words that he never expected to be as happy anywhere else as he had been in Stradbroke. They noted his forlorn looks, and his feelings cannot have been improved by a telegram he received early the next week, to which he replied as follows on 5 March:

> My Dear Friend,
> Very many thanks for your kind telegram.
> It is true that last Saturday week Ld. Beaconsfield offered me the Deanery of Salisbury.
> It is also true that last Friday after a week of much doubt, conflict and prayer, I accepted.
> Since then I have had no further communication but I suppose it is all correct. Flesh and blood were utterly against it. But *almost* every one of 16 whom I consulted said, 'you ought to go for the sake of Christ's cause in the Ch. of E.' So who was I that I could withstand? I had prayed for light and signs of God's will and this was all I got. If three men had said 'refuse' I would have refused. Cathedral music is not *congenial* to me. I go into a nest of hornets and shall stand alone.
> Moving at my age is a very treacherous and expensive business. Old trees transplant badly.
> I have little heart for any move except into heaven. The last twenty years have swept away nearly all I knew and loved best, and I feel sadly alone.
> But after all the time is short. I am a soldier. The Captain of my salvation seems to say, 'these are your marching orders'. I have nothing to do but to *obey.*
> Pray for me. My heart is very heavy.
> Ever yours affectionately in Christ
>
> J. C. Ryle[1]

Public comment followed the news of his appointment. *The Times* (6 March) thought that such appointments were usually reserved for 'extinct volcanoes' and did not consider that to be Ryle's condition. A correspondent in the same paper wondered how 'the eager and

---

[1] Most of this letter is printed in Packer, *Faithfulness and Holiness*, 251. The original is in the possession of the Rev. Simon Manchester of Sydney, to whom I am indebted. He obtained it in a London shop selling manuscripts.

restless temperament of the controversialist will reconcile itself to becoming the central figure of a pre-arranged pageant' (13 March). The *Church Times* professed an inability to understand 'why Mr Ryle should have thrust himself into it'. It could not be for money:

> for he will receive rather less as Dean of Salisbury. It would be insulting to say he coveted the title 'Very Reverend'. It cannot be that he craved for a larger audience when he preached, and so we arrive at the only possible solution—either he is after all a Ritualist at heart, or he wanted to get into Convocation, and despaired of finding a constituency where he would have the least chance of being elected (12 March 1880).[1]

Before any move to Salisbury was possible, reflections and criticisms were cut short by a still greater surprise for Ryle. On 16 April 1880, while still at Stradbroke, Ryle received a letter summoning him to meet the Prime Minister, Benjamin Disraeli. On arrival in London he was met by Viscount Sandon, an evangelical Tory MP for Liverpool, and, on asking the reason for the call, he was stunned by the answer: 'We have sent for you for one purpose, to ask you to accept the Bishopric of Liverpool.' 'You strike me all of a heap', was his response; 'I don't know what to say.' Further conversation with Sandon followed, and Ryle heard the gist of a letter that Disraeli had written to Queen Victoria on 10 April which told her,

> The people of Liverpool are very anxious about their new Bishop. The Tories subscribed the whole of the endowment and bought the palace … The whole city is most anxious that your Majesty should appoint the present Dean of Salisbury, Canon Ryle.

Ryle may not have heard the whole of the letter to the Queen. It had included the sentence, 'Lord Sandon says his seat for Liverpool depends upon the appointment being made by your Majesty's present adviser.'[2] The background, necessary to understanding what

---

[1] Russell, *Man of Granite*, 132.
[2] The words are as reported by Ryle in 1897 by which time Dudley Ryder, Viscount

was happening, was that the Prime Minister and his Tory (Conservative) party had been defeated in the recent February General Election by their old Liberal opponent William Gladstone. They were to leave office on the Monday after the interview with Ryle. From that day Gladstone, an Anglo-Catholic, would become responsible for appointment to the diocese of Liverpool, if still vacant. But Gladstone had fallen out of favour with the Queen, Disraeli had no love for ritualists, and, for one reason or another, Sandon thought that holding his parliamentary seat in what was Gladstone's old city, or re-appointment to it, would depend on Ryle's presence in the city. Ryle was not a Tory, but the unexpected participant in a situation to which the Queen had given her blessing.[1]

'It takes me all unawares; it is a very serious matter,' Ryle told Viscount Sandon. Sandon urged, 'You must give us your answer as soon as you possibly can. You see, if you don't make up your mind, we will lose the Bishopric of Liverpool.' 'But', Ryle rejoined, 'remember how old I am, and I am not a rich man.' 'We know, that is all right,' said Sandon, and then 'jumped in the air' when Ryle said, 'Well, if you want to know whether I'll come or not, I'll come.' He was then shown in to Disraeli, who expressed his pleasure at their not being kept waiting, and brushed aside another reference from Ryle to his age with the words, 'I think you have a pretty good constitution, and I think you will live a few years yet.'[2] Later Ryle would say, 'Salisbury took a week to think about, but to be Bishop of Liverpool did not take five minutes. I thought it was a clear, plain call of duty.' Letters patent confirming the appointment were issued on 19 April, the same

Sandon, had succeeded to the peerage. He was an MP for Liverpool from 1868 to 1882.

[1] Ryle did not enter into politics, but Gladstone's high church beliefs and his Church policy for Ireland, had his opposition. While opposing Gladstone over his policy for the Church in Ireland, he said in 1868, 'Tory Politics were not my reason. I am not a Tory and never was; if I have any politics I am a Liberal.' Toon and Smout, *Evangelical Bishop*, 63. Neither the Queen nor Disraeli normally favoured evangelicals but they were not averse to thwarting Gladstone in his own city of Liverpool.

[2] Machray, *First Bishop*, 14.

date Liverpool became a city; hitherto, without that status, it had been part of the diocese of Chester.

Ryle arrived back home that night to tell his wife, 'I am Bishop of Liverpool.' It was the first time for many years that an evangelical who was already a national figure had been made a bishop. Stradbroke village hung out flags and rejoiced, and Richard Hobson, one of Liverpool's clergy, believed that the appointment 'was hailed with delight by every evangelical clergyman throughout the world'.[1]

On 20 June 1880, Ryle said farewell to his people at Stradbroke, calling on them, 'Pray I might be a true Bishop of the Reformed Church of England.' It was a crowded congregation on a wet day, and he had the heartfelt sympathy of many as they heard his farewell:

> 'The old street down which I walked so often, the school which I so often visited, the shops to which I have so often gone, the fields over which I have so often walked, the road with every yard of which I was so thoroughly acquainted, my own little garden in which I had meditation and prayer, my own little field shut out from the world, where I have had quiet walks and communion with God, my own beautiful little church in which I have often seen so many faces—all these things I am about to leave and leave forever. I go, called by God, to the noise, bustle, smoke and confusion of a great sea port town.' His final word in the sermon was a request for prayer: 'Pray for me, name me before the throne of grace and say, "Lord God, bless Bishop Ryle."'[2]

Fitzgerald, biographer of Herbert Ryle, was to write in 1928, 'Even today, nearly fifty years after he left Stradbroke, J. C. Ryle is vividly remembered there. Some of his pithy sayings, such as "If the cap fits, wear it", are still repeated.' Other well-known sayings of Ryle were: 'What we weave in time we wear in eternity', 'It matters little how we die, but it matters much how we live', and 'It is hard for an empty bag to stand upright.' Those who wanted Ryle in Liverpool knew that he would be no 'empty bag'.

[1] *Hobson of Liverpool*, 139.
[2] Toon and Smout, *Evangelical Bishop*, 58.

Top: Stradbroke Vicarage, as rebuilt in time of Ryle

Bottom: Ryle, when Vicar of Stradbroke

9

The Teacher

Ryle preaching to emigrants leaving Liverpool

A FTER Ryle left Stradbroke at the age of sixty-three there would be no change in the substance of his beliefs for the remaining twenty years of his life, nor had there been at any significant point in his preceding ministry. At the age of eighty-one, when most men had finished their work, he would be still teaching the same message he delivered in his first pastorate, only with greater fullness. This, then, is a suitable point to pause in the narrative of his life, to comment on abiding emphases in his teaching.

In the first place, the gospel itself was ever the most important part of whatever he spoke or wrote, and the gospel meant the person and work of the Lord Jesus Christ. Whether he was addressing Members of Parliament, or a rural congregation, whether university undergraduates or children, the primary intention was evangelistic—presenting Christ to both the unbeliever and the Christian, as with Paul, 'Whom we preach, warning every man and teaching every man, in all wisdom; that we may present every man perfect in Christ Jesus' (Col. 1:28). We are useful, he believed, and the church is useful, 'so long as we exalt the great object of faith, but useful no further'. 'What the sun is in the firmament of heaven, that Christ is in true Christianity.' Nothing is to be added to Christ in salvation, nothing is to be joined with him in honour, nothing can satisfy apart from him. 'Christ is all'—'All building without him is on sand, which will surely fall. All working without him is in the fire, where it will be consumed. All riches without him have wings and will fly away.'

> There are only too many baptized men and women who practically know nothing at all about Christ. ... What experimental acquaintance have they with His offices and work, His blood, His righteousness,

His mediation, His priesthood, His intercession? None, none at all! Ask them about a saving faith,—ask them about being born again of the Spirit,—ask them about being sanctified in Christ Jesus. What answer do you get? You are a barbarian to them.[1]

No one could preach with this emphasis for the greater part of a lifetime without living in Christ. The heart will determine the message. 'Out of the abundance of the heart the mouth speaketh' (Matt. 12:34).

It was the priority which Ryle gave to the gospel and to the salvation of men and women which made him thankful for the good which could be done by the earnest testimony and speaking of men not set aside in the ministerial office. That there was such an office, and a calling to it, he was well convinced, yet without the slightest sympathy for the idea that others should be stopped from public speaking for Christ lest Church regulations be overthrown. Such men as Henry Varley evangelizing in Stradbroke, and D. L. Moody in Liverpool, would have his support. He believed with Whitefield that 'it was far better for men to be uncanonically saved than canonically damned'.[2]

A fellow servant with Ryle in Liverpool was 'Happy Ned', Edward Sunners, who had been a town missioner in the city since 1838. He took outdoor services at such places as 'the Big Lamp in Lime Street' and worked among 'sweeps, tinkers, carters, cab-drivers, fish-women, shoe-blacks, policemen, soldiers, sailors, prostitutes, thieves, and drunkards'. Before his conversion when he learned to read by spelling out the verses of John's Gospel word for word, he had belonged to such company himself. He worked most closely with cabmen, which led Ryle to say on one occasion that when he first came to the city 'he was not aware of the number of bishops Liverpool possessed. There was a Roman bishop, a Protestant bishop and, he believed, a cab-

---

[1] 'All in All', *Home Truths*, third series, 247.
[2] 'George Whitefield', *Home Truths*, second series (Ipswich: Hunt, 1854), 300.

men's bishop.' Ian Farley tells us that 'Ryle regularly supplied Sunners with tracts and leaflets … was well acquainted with him, thought highly of him and urged that imitation of him would promote the cause of the gospel.'[1]

This was characteristic of Ryle's thankfulness to help those who were spreading the gospel. On this subject he wrote:

> It is high time that the old tradition that the clergy alone ought to teach and spread religious knowledge should be exploded and cast aside for ever. To do good and diffuse light is a duty for which all members of Christ's church are responsible … Christians ought to tell others that they have found medicine for their souls, if they see them ignorant and dying for want of it. What saith the Apostle Peter? 'As every man hath received the gift, even so minister the same one to another' (1 Pet. 4:10). They will be happy days for the church when that text is obeyed.[2]

In the second place, there is much to be learned from Ryle's teaching with respect to keeping a right proportion in the presentation of the truth. It is no small thing both to state biblical truth and to keep it in a right relationship with other collateral truths. One doctrine magnified out of proportion to other truths will limit the usefulness of any ministry. Similarly, a secondary truth constantly delivered as though it was a main truth will produce unbalanced Christians. Truth needs to be stated with the right degree of emphasis in relation to other biblical teaching.

No teacher is perfect in this area, but Ryle is a valuable example. A young Christian taking up Ryle is not going to be diverted into any hobby-horse. Ryle will not be found pressing a subject which was only of special interest and significance at that date. The study of unfulfilled prophecy is a case in point. In Ryle's youth numbers of

---

[1] Farley, *J. C. Ryle, First Bishop of Liverpool*, 117, who gives as his source, S. Johnson, *Edward Sunners* (1886).

[2] *Expository Thoughts on the Gospels: Mark* (Edinburgh: Banner of Truth Trust, 2015), 55.

evangelicals changed their belief on this subject. The gradual spread and ultimate success of the gospel around the world, leading to a millennium of peace and blessing, had been the common expectation. This expectation was now challenged by those who believed that Christ must come *before* there is any such millennium. It was a case which had many notable and able spokesmen. Ryle himself, it seems, from the start of his ministry, belonged to this pre-millennial school of thought, which also believed in a future for Israel in the kingdom of God. But while many would harp on the subject, lecture, and publish repeatedly about it, Ryle was guarded. Certainly it was his 'deep conviction that the second advent of Christ is one of the leading truths of Christianity'. He constantly preached the need for Christians to live in that expectation, yet he avoided such fanciful details of interpretation as would ultimately endanger the second advent keeping the place it ought to have in evangelical thinking. He would not be called by the epithet given to his friend William Marsh, nicknamed 'Millennium Marsh'. He was shocked in 1847 when, with his dying wife at Ventnor, along with numbers of other sick people, he listened to the clergyman,

> a worthy evangelical man who thought it his duty to preach to the invalids in the morning expository sermons on the book of Revelation or expatiate by the hour to poor dying creatures about seals, vials and trumpets. A more deplorable instance of want of common sense I never saw in my life.[1]

Among instances where the proportion of truth is often lost is teaching on the respective place of faith and duty. In Ryle's time there developed a view in evangelical circles that to preach the duty of obedience to the law of God to the unregenerate was a mistake. It was faith alone which they needed to hear. How this was consistent with our Lord's words to the unconverted was not explained, except by dispensationalists who treated such passages as the Sermon on the

---

[1] *Coming Events* was Ryle's one title on this subject. The Preface gives a good summary of his understanding.

Mount as belonging to the Old Testament 'legal' dispensation. Ryle complained, 'I sometimes fear if Christ was on earth now, there are not a few who would think his preaching legal ... But let us remember that the Lord Jesus *did* speak the Sermon on the Mount.'[1] I will refer to this again below; all I mean to draw attention to here is the way both obligation and faith, law and gospel, were rightly present in Ryle's preaching without any contradiction. Sinners are both to 'strive to enter in at the strait gate' and to 'believe on the Lord Jesus Christ'.

The place of duty and faith in the life of the Christian became, in Ryle's lifetime, no less controversial. The possibility of sanctification by one decisive step of faith suddenly became popular teaching in the 1870s, inspired by the visit of Robert and Hannah Pearsall Smith from the United States. Special meetings were held to promote the teaching and it brought the Keswick Convention into being in 1875. Keswick had become a favourite holiday location for Ryle, and he would preach for Thomas Harford-Battersby, vicar of St John's, Keswick, and one of the Convention's first chairmen, but he never appeared or spoke at the annual summer convention. He believed that by focusing on faith alone in sanctification, and by making the 'victorious life' rest on one act of faith, the New Testament was being distorted. Certainly faith plays a vital part in sanctification, but it is an ongoing, not once-for-all, part, and not the only part. Faith is alone in justification, and justification is an act, not a process; but sanctification is a process, and one in which the believer's obedience, discipline, and duty are conjoined with faith. Thus Ryle quotes the words of Samuel Rutherford, 'The way that crieth down duties is not the way of grace. Believing and doing are blood friends.' For a clear statement of Ryle's thinking, see the seven 'Cautions for the times on the subject of holiness', in his Introduction to *Holiness*.[2]

[1] 'Are You Holy?', *Home Truths*, first series (Ipswich: Hunt, 1860), 148.
[2] *Holiness* (Edinburgh: Banner of Truth Trust, 2014). See also on the Pearsall Smiths, my book, *Evangelical Holiness* (Edinburgh: Banner of Truth Trust, 2013), 9-10.

No less important was it for Ryle that truths expressing the sovereignty of the grace of God in salvation should not be preached in isolation from other truths which show that those who remain unsaved under the hearing of the gospel do not do so because the Saviour has no interest in them. On the contrary, he believed that 'God loves all mankind with a love of pity and compassion' and that it is fully expressed in the gospel. 'He is not willing that any should perish, but that all should come to repentance.' He has 'no pleasure in the death of him that dieth'. After quoting these verses, Ryle says, 'In this sense our Lord Jesus tells us, "God so loved the world, that he gave his only begotten Son, that whosoever believeth in him should not perish, but have everlasting life" (2 Pet. 3:9; Ezek. 18:32; John 3:16).'[1] He did not hesitate to preach, 'In my Master's name I offer you complete salvation if you will believe; free salvation if you will believe; everlasting life if you will believe.'

But at the same time Ryle in no way passed over, or sought to moderate, those truths which assert the certainty of the salvation of an elect number, chosen before the foundation of the world, and loved with a special and efficacious love. Because numbers have thought that the consistency of both sets of statements cannot be explained, they settle to preach one or the other, in the unscriptural presentation of Arminianism or Hyper-Calvinism. Ryle, however, did not seek to explain but preached both truths and exemplified how being an evangelist and a Calvinist ought to belong together.

There was another conjunction of truths in Ryle's ministry which was being downgraded in the nineteenth century. 'Behold the goodness and severity of God', we are commanded in Scripture. But increasingly it was the 'goodness' alone which was heard from pulpits, love but not wrath, heaven but not hell. Yet no one spoke more often and plainly of hell than the Lord Jesus Christ. We have become so sensitive about the very word today that it can be startling how it

---

[1] *Coming Events*, 203.

occurs in Ryle's teaching in unexpected places. For instance, in speaking of marriage, he says,

> But marriage is a state of life which has the greatest effect on the souls of those who enter into it. It helps them upwards or downwards. It leads them nearer to heaven or nearer to hell. We all depend much on the company we keep.[1]

Is that less scriptural than our too common silence?

Ryle viewed with dismay how too many were condoning the omission of plain, New Testament language, and never warned their hearers:

> Beware of manufacturing a God of your own,—a God who is all mercy, but not just,—a God who is all love, but not holy,—a God who has a heaven for everybody, but a hell for none,—a God who can allow good and bad to be side by side in time, but will make no distinction between good and bad in eternity.[2]

In yet another area, Ryle saw a loss of biblical balance. He believed in both practical, vigorous action, *and* in prayer for revival. The church has both the promise of Christ to be with her always, whatever the situation, but also the knowledge that the measure in which Christ gives the Holy Spirit is not static, and that sometimes, he grants such an outpouring of grace that the whole scene is dramatically changed. Ryle's consciousness of what happened at the time of the Evangelical Awakening of the eighteenth century never left him. At a time when believers began to ask 'shall the enemy blaspheme thy name for ever?' (Psa. 74:10), England saw again the power which changes whole communities.

I turn to note another feature which is marked in Ryle's teaching. He believed that the teacher had to be both positive and negative.

---

[1] *Expository Thoughts on the Gospels: Luke*, vol. 1 (Edinburgh: Banner of Truth Trust, 2015), 61.

[2] *Practical Religion: Being Plain Papers on the Daily Duties, Experience, Dangers, and Privileges of Professing Christians* (1878; repr. Edinburgh: Banner of Truth Trust, 2013), 434.

In stating what is true, there is often the need to show what is not true. It is not enough to refer to the converted and the unconverted; a preacher must bring home to his hearers the difference between the living and the dead. 'See now how important it is that we ministers should divide our congregations in preaching to them. ... I know well some do not like it.'[1]

Ryle took in the advice of his early mentor, Edward Bickersteth, who wrote:

> there is a prevalent notion among those to whom we may justly give the blessed title of *peacemakers*, that the simple statement of truth is a sufficient confutation of error. Such forget the advantage that error has against truth in its falling in with the natural principles of the heart. Exposure of error and false statement, in a controversial form, is a prominent part of the Epistles to the unsettled churches.[2]

This does not mean that a teacher should be always controversial; that would be the way to build a company of contentious Christians. But the clear difference between grace and no grace, truth and error, is commonly not grasped until it is precisely stated. It was not for nothing that our Lord likened error to 'leaven' in dough, which spreads insensibly, and demands the warning, 'Take heed and beware of the leaven of the Pharisees and of the Sadducees' (Matt. 16:6).

To the absence of discrimination Ryle traced one of the greatest dangers:

> It is not Atheism I fear so much in the present times as Pantheism. It is not the system which says nothing is true, so much as the system which says *everything is true*. It is the system which is so liberal, that it dares not say anything is false. It is the system which is so charitable, that it will allow everything to be true. It is the system which is so scrupulous about the feelings of others that we are never to say they are wrong ... What is it but a bowing down before a great idol

[1] *Christian Race*, 200.
[2] Edward Bickersteth, *The Christian Student* (London: Seeley and Burnside, 1829), 113.

speciously called liberality? What is it all but a sacrificing of truth upon the altar of a caricature of charity? Beware of it if you believe the Bible.[1]

Before leaving the subject of the preacher as a teacher, there is an addition which Ryle saw as indispensable. However eloquent or apparently knowledgeable a preacher may be, there will be something seriously lacking in the man who is not to be found in the homes of his people. Sermons which come *only* from the study are not likely to be messages which bind speaker and hearers together in a common bond of affection and sympathy. A preacher *must* be a visitor and be ready to preach everywhere.[2] Few circumstances can justify the omission. If the excuse be offered that there is too much public work to do, to give time to the private, then the priorities are wrong. He deplored

> a growing disposition throughout the land, among the clergy, to devote *an exaggerated amount of attention to what I must call the public work of the ministry*, and to give comparatively too little attention to pastoral visitation and personal dealing with individual souls.[3]

Perhaps Ryle's urgency on this subject was related to the remembrance of having never seen a clergyman visiting his own home. Certainly from the start of his ministry in Exbury his own practice was not of that more usual kind. An anonymous writer, who had personal knowledge of Ryle, referring to his first charge, spoke of 'the way he went in and out of the cottage homes. During the two years of his seclusion there he acquired, it can be stated, an entire pastoral knowledge of every man, woman, and child, under his charge.'[4]

[1] 'Only One Way', *Home Truths*, first series (Ipswich: Hunt, 1860), 174-5.
[2] The preachers of the Evangelical Awakening, Ryle pointed out, treated no place amiss for preaching: 'In the field or by the road-side, on the village green or in a market-place, in cellars or in garrets, on a tub or on a table, on a bench or on a horse-block, wherever hearers could be gathered.' *Christian Leaders*, 24.
[3] Ryle, *Charges and Addresses* (1903; repr. Edinburgh: Banner of Truth Trust, 1978), 95.
[4] 'John Charles Ryle' in *The Christian Portrait Gallery* (London: Marshall, Morgan

In his last extended pastorate in Liverpool the point occurs repeatedly in his charges to the clergy. They must take time to sit by the firesides of their people, hear their thoughts, and 'speak boldly and faithfully about the things of God'. He believed that a man who only speaks of Christ from behind a pulpit should not be surprised at having small usefulness. Real love for people will take a preacher into their homes, and it will affect the way these same people hear him in public. Preaching confined to churches is not New Testament Christianity. 'Give me a clergyman', he would say,

> who can preach in a street without a surplice, as well as in a pulpit; a man who will go in and out of every alley in his district and talk simple Gospel to half-a-dozen ragged folks in a dirty cellar as heartily as to five hundred well-dressed people in a church; a man of fire, and love, and sympathy, and tact, and patience, and sanctified common sense.[1]

He envisaged an ideal parish of 5,000 people, in which only a third might belong to the Church of England, and argued that his men should visit 105 homes every week.[2]

* * *

There is another area of Ryle's teaching which also calls for comment here. Although not to be taught alongside Scripture, he believed that church history gives mighty confirmation to the truths of revelation, and that Christians need to know its lessons. I have already noted how the appeal made by the Tractarians to history was used to awaken Ryle and others to the need to bring the facts of church history before people. He was himself personally thrilled by

---

and Scott, n.d.) 319.

[1] *Charges and Addresses*, 238. He also urged occasional visiting on others besides clergy. Heads in the manufacturing and colliery districts would do more good than fifty Acts of Parliament if they visited 'those long, dreary, monotonous lines of cottages, to shake hands with the dwellers, and sit down and exhibit a kindly interest in the births and deaths and marriages and sorrows and joys of the family' (295).

[2] Farley, *J. C. Ryle, First Bishop of Liverpool*, 107.

what he studied of the subject in the 1840s, and was ready to speak in London on George Whitefield in 1852. He could tell his hearers at the conference of clergy at Weston-super-Mare in 1858:

> I have been lately studying the lives and private habits of those men whom God raised up to be the revivers of the Church of England in the last century. ... We should do well to consider whether we are living as near to God as they did.[1]

Such reading had a profound effect on his own life and ministry. As already seen, part of his lifelong work was to help Christians enjoy this heritage as he had done. There was no lack of critics busy in disparaging evangelical Christianity; they needed to be answered from history as well as Scripture. Did men profess to regret what the Reformation did to the Church in England? Then let them hear the spiritual conditions which pre-existed that revival. Was John Foxe's account of the 275 martyrs in the reign of Mary Tudor the work of 'a mendacious partisan'? Let them listen to the truth![2] Did the Puritans deserve to be set aside? On the contrary, it must be shown that 'as a body, they have done more to elevate the national character than any class of Englishmen that ever lived'.[3] Might the Methodist preachers of the eighteenth century be despised and ignored? Far from it, Ryle spoke of 'The blind stupidity with which John Wesley was treated as a disaster to our Church', and gave the world a true account of the eighteenth-century leaders who 'began a mighty spiritual revolution without the patronage of Church or State'.[4]

In his conference address to his clergy and laity in Liverpool in 1898 Ryle urged the importance of history for the last time:

[1] 'What Is Our Position?', *Home Truths*, seventh series, 261-2.
[2] It was Ryle's opinion that Foxe's work, usually given the title, *The Book of Martyrs*, 'has been assailed and abused more violently by the advocates of Popery than any uninspired book that ever was printed'. *Light from Old Times*, xv.
[3] See above, 105.
[4] The Index references to Wesley and Whitefield in his *Charges and Addresses* are all worth turning up.

> I should like the leading events in the history of our Church during the last three centuries to be made quite familiar to our people … It is time to awake out of sleep. … But systematic pulpit instruction is only part of what is needed in order to meet the ignorance of the times. We ought to organize a supply of information about English Church history. We ought to provide a qualified body of lecturers whose whole business shall be to visit every diocese, and tell people what the story of the Church of England really is.[1]

Ryle could have mentioned the aid in sermon illustrations which he found in history and biography. Who could not pay attention when, for example, he illustrated the certainty of Christ building his church by reference to the sneering Emperor Julian. '"What is the carpenter's son doing now?"' Julian demanded to know, only to hear an aged Christian answer, '"He is making a coffin for Julian himself." But a few months passed away', the preacher added, 'when Julian, with all his pomp and power, died in battle. Where was Christ when the fires of Smithfield were lighted, and when Latimer and Ridley were burnt at the stake? What was Christ doing then? He was still carrying on His work of building. That work will ever go on. Even in troublous times.'[2]

What Ryle taught on church history contributed to the hostility he encountered. There are very different opinions on his books which deal with history and biography. Canon Christopher of Oxford had the highest regard for them. For thirty years he took Ryle's *Christian Leaders* with him on his summer holidays, and in a Preface to a new edition spoke of his prayer that the Spirit of God would so

---

[1] *Charges and Addresses*, 356. More recently, David Wells has warned: 'The anti-theological mood that now grips the evangelical world is changing its internal configuration, its effectiveness and its relation to the past.' *No Place for Truth* (Grand Rapids: Eerdmans, 1993), 96. A. A. Hodge wrote: 'The history of Christendom, especially the history of the English-speaking races, and the philosophy of history in general, will prove an utterly insoluble riddle to all who attempt to read it in any non-theistic, religiously indifferent sense.' *Evangelical Theology* (1890; repr. Edinburgh: Banner of Truth Trust, 1990), 243.

[2] 'The True Church', *Home Truths*, seventh series, 225.

accompany the reading of it by young men that many of them would be encouraged 'to devote themselves to the service of the Lord Jesus Christ for the work His Gospel at home or abroad'.

In similar language Christopher recommended Ryle's *Light from Old Times* in *The Record* in May 1902. His commendation received no approval from Dr William Sanday, Lady Margaret Professor of Divinity at Oxford. Sanday wrote in the same journal of his regret that Christopher, who 'usually associated with good causes', had not done so on this occasion. The rector of St Aldate's, also an honorary Canon of Christ Church Cathedral, was not intimidated. In a personal letter of reply to Sanday he suggested

> that before publicly condemning *Light from Old Times* and the faithful bishop who has finished his work, it would have been more fair to him and more conducive to truth if he had *read* his book instead of condemning it and its deceased author after only reading the extracts which I gave.

The distinguished professor's complaint was that Ryle had not learned the scientific manner in which history should be written. Christopher believed that the real offence was not that at all. Sanday was a high churchman who became a modernist.[1]

Among the six authors who had been such a help to him in his youth, Ryle had learned from Joseph Milner a different approach to history from that of the academic. That which deserved the name of 'Church history', Milner wrote in the Introduction to his eight volumes, is writing which shows that 'in every age there have been REAL followers of Christ'. The objective of the Christian historian is 'To see and trace the goodness of God taking care of His church in every age by His providence'. In so doing, 'The honour of Christianity will be supported; the value of its essential doctrines will be

---

[1] *Canon Christopher*, 314-5. Christopher, notes the same author, 'remained unmoved, offering a copy of *Light from Old Times* to any undergraduate who cared to call at the rectory and was prepared to read it during the long vacation'.

ascertained; and we shall have frequent occasion to state what the Gospel is and what it is not.'[1]

Such was also Ryle's view of how church history should be studied. At the same time it is important to say that history does not determine the rule of faith. There is necessarily an element of uncertainty commonly belonging to the interpretation of history which distinguishes it from statements which rest on the revelation in Scripture.

* * *

This leads to comment on a subject where, at times, Ryle's judgment is open to question. We noted above the clergyman from Exeter who challenged him with the words, 'Why are converted Romish priests allowed to minister in our Churches without re-ordination, while Presbyterians and dissenters are required to receive "the laying on of hands" by a Bishop, according to Apostolic usage?'

The question was intended to confirm the Anglo-Catholic belief that the Church of England traces the authority of her bishops to the same line of apostolic succession as the Church of Rome. It was grounded on the words of the Prayer Book, in its Preface to the Form of Ordaining, 'It is evident unto all men … that from the Apostles' time there have been these Orders of Ministers in Christ's Church: Bishops, Priests and Deacons.' This statement, the questioner believed, was the reason why ministers not belonging to that line of succession needed to be re-ordained, whereas for Roman priests entering the Church of England there was no such requirement.

The appeal to history on which this argument was based is false. In the apostolic churches there were no three 'orders' (or 'offices') in the churches but only two, namely, *episcopoi / presbyteroi* (different names for the *same* office) and deacons. The *episcopoi* ('overseers', 'bishops') of the New Testament differed radically from the post-apostolic men who separated that office from that of presbyters and slowly received

---

[1] *History of the Church of Christ*, vol. 1, vi.

distinct powers. Whereas in the New Testament there could be many bishops in *one* congregation, in later times the title was given to a man exercising authority over a whole region of churches, and with prerogatives which belonged to the apostles.[1] The subsequent Roman hierarchy was built on this development and it makes the name of 'bishop' much more than a difference over a word.

With the idea that the true 'Church' is to be recognized by a visible succession of bishops from the apostles, came a different view of the way of salvation. For Rome, followed by Anglo-Catholics, salvation comes to the individual through the instrumentality of sacramental grace administered by priests lawfully authorized by 'the Church'. Protestant belief in salvation by grace, through faith, without churches as the necessary intermediary, was incompatible with that teaching, hence the violence with which it was opposed by the Church of Rome. For evangelicals, sacraments do not *convey* saving grace; they are signs and seals to strengthen the faith of believers. In this connection, at the reformation in England, controversy raged over the meaning of the Lord's Supper; later, it would turn to what baptism accomplished, and, as baptism was near universal in Protestant countries, the focus was on infant baptism. The Articles of Edward VI (1553), while briefly commending the baptism of infants, made clear that the sacraments only have 'wholesome effect and operation' for those who 'rightly use them', that is, with faith in Christ, 'not that of the work wrought, as some men speak'.[2] This was a rejection of the traditional belief that the sacraments in themselves convey benefit, *ex opere operato*.

These words from the Articles of 1553 would appear to rebut the Roman and Anglo-Catholic claim that in their baptism infants are

[1] Among those prerogatives, the declaration of bishops when placing their hands on the heads of those being ordained to the priesthood, 'Receive the Holy Ghost: whose sins though dost forgive, they are forgiven: and whose sins thou dost retain, they are retained.'

[2] 'Of the Sacraments', *The Two Liturgies in the Reign of Edward VI* (Cambridge: Parker Soc., 1844), 533.

born again and the original sin of their birth is removed. But interminable controversy has ensued because the language of the Prayer Book, as distinct from the Articles, says nothing of how baptism is 'rightly received' by an infant, and speaks only in terms of the baptized being brought into a state of salvation: 'Then shall the priest say, Seeing now, dearly beloved, that these children be regenerate and grafted into the body of Christ: let us give thanks …'[1]

Ryle, of course, did not accept the teaching of apostolic succession. He pointed out that, for years after the reformation in England, the validity of ministers not ordained by bishops was not disputed. He also agreed with Bishop Lightfoot that in the New Testament bishops and presbyters were one and the same office.[2] The words of the Ordinal on 'from the Apostles' time' were not therefore to be taken in the strictest sense. But with the Prayer Book's words on 'these children be regenerate' Ryle had more difficulty and he addressed it at some length.[3] His conclusion was that the compilers of the liturgy spoke of 'regenerate' only as 'a judgment of charity'. They were not teaching that a saving change takes place at the time of baptism; the words were conditional on the hoped-for existence of a later faith.

But there is a serious obstacle in the way of an acceptance of this interpretation. It is the problem to which Baptist Wriothesley Noel was referring when he wrote, 'I once laboured hard to convince myself that our Reformers did not and could not mean that infants are regenerated by baptism.'[4] The problem, however, does not lie simply in *one* sentence of the Edwardian Prayer Book. The same thought is both continued and amplified in the Prayer Book

[1] *Ibid.*, 289.
[2] J. B. Lightfoot, *Saint Paul's Epistle to the Philippians* (London: Macmillan, 1891), 95, with whom Ryle agreed on the New Testament understanding of *episcopus*, *Principles for Churchmen*, 152.
[3] See chapter 7 of *Knots Untied*, 'Prayer-Book Statements about Regeneration', and, in more popular form, *Upper Room*, 'Questions about Regeneration'.
[4] *Essay on the Union of Church and State* (London: Nisbet, 1848), 439.

revisions of 1559 and 1662. Before administering baptism to children, 'the priest shall say … Almighty and immortal God, we call upon thee for these infants, that they, coming to thy holy Baptism, may receive the remission of their sins by spiritual regeneration.' In conclusion the congregation is to be assured that the prayer has been answered, 'it hath pleased thee to regenerate this infant'.[1] The Catechism for Children, 1559, asserts, 'It is certain by God's word, that children, being baptized, have all things necessary for their salvation, and be undoubtedly saved.' Thus, in answer to the first questions in that Catechism, 'What is your name?' and 'Who gave you this name?' the answer is, 'My Godfathers and Godmothers in my Baptism, wherein I was made a member of Christ, and child of God, and an inheritor of the kingdom of heaven'.[2] These words all convey one impression: the work of the Holy Spirit in regeneration takes place at baptism. The unregenerate are brought to the font; they leave it regenerate. After that nothing need delay their confirmation by a bishop apart from the ability to say 'the Articles of faith, the Lord's prayer, and the ten commandments: and be further instructed in the Catechism'. Over all the baptized, at death, the declaration shall be, 'it hath pleased Almighty God of his great mercy to take unto himself the soul of our dear brother departed … in sure and certain hope of the Resurrection to eternal life'.[3]

Ryle resolutely denied this Anglo-Catholic interpretation of the Prayer Book: 'there is not one text in Scripture which says distinctly and expressly that we are born again in baptism, and that every baptized person is necessarily regenerate!'[4] He argued that the Prayer Book could not be teaching what was claimed, because it would

---

[1] 'Public Baptism', *Liturgical Services in the Reign of Queen Elizabeth* (Cambridge: Parker Soc., 1847), 200, 204.

[2] *Ibid.*, 210-11.

[3] The rubric which prefaces 'The Order for the Burial of the Dead' (1662) excludes from the service only the 'unbaptized', the 'excommunicate', and suicides.

[4] *Knots Untied* (1885), 133.

contradict what was clearly taught in other services and formularies of the Church. It would be to deny what is said in the Articles on the necessity of faith and to suppose grace inherent in the sacraments, an idea which the Articles reject. So which is likely to be the true interpretation of the words in dispute? The one which understands them in terms of 'a charitable supposition' and consistent with the Prayer Book and Articles as a whole, or the one which insists on a literal meaning which cannot be reconciled with the teaching of the whole? Is it likely that the Reformers would have allowed the inconsistency of the second in their formularies?

These questions, however, leave out another explanation which I find convincing. The compilers of the Prayer Book of 1552 were not using the word 'regenerate' in the charitable hope of the future experience of every infant baptized, neither were they expressing the Roman teaching on the certain communication of grace by the sacrament; rather they were allowing wording which *could be* assumed to mean that regeneration occurs at baptism. That is to say, they left a deliberate avoidance of clarification. Both the 1552 Book and the earlier Prayer Book of 1549 had been drawn up chiefly under the direction of Archbishop Thomas Cranmer and that policy had been still more evident in the formulation of the 1549 Book. At the time the 1549 Book was prepared, Cranmer, in private, had given up the belief that the bread and wine in the mass *become* the body and blood of Christ, yet the Book allowed the traditional teaching to stand. 'No doubt this was part of the continuing effort in 1549 to keep conservative bishops and theologically aware laity from all-out rebellion.'[1] Between 1549 and 1552 there was definite advance by Cranmer and the Reformers in the openness of their evangelical beliefs. The *ex opere operato* teaching of the mass was rejected, but there was not yet the same agreement on baptism. Not only was an evangelical understanding contrary to the traditional belief still held by the

---

[1] Diarmaid MacCulloch, *Thomas Cranmer* (New Haven: Yale, 1996), 462.

large majority of priests, but Peter Martyr, close associate of Cranmer, wrote to Henry Bullinger in Switzerland on 14 June 1552 that the effects of baptism had not yet been clarified among themselves: 'Many will have it, and those not otherwise unlearned nor evil, that grace is conferred, as they say, in the sacraments.' One reason was that this had been the teaching of Augustine, whose name, for other reasons, carried weight with Protestants. So Martyr continued, 'If our doctrine had been approved by public authority, then, say they, Augustine would most manifestly have been condemned.'[1]

The consequence was that the 1552 Prayer Book avoided clarification on the issue with respect to the baptism of infants and it was left to worshippers to put what sense they wished to the word 'regenerate'. That this same policy was followed by the Reformers in dealing with other questions of vocabulary is confirmed by the contemporary John Whitgift, future archbishop of Canterbury, who answered the Puritan objection to the continued use of the word 'priest' by saying that the word was not to be taken in the traditional sense: 'As heretofore use hath made it to be taken for a sacrificer, so will use now alter that signification, and make it to be taken for a minister of the gospel.'[2]

William Goode, a strong nineteenth-century defender of an evangelical understanding of infant baptism, did not accuse Anglo-Catholics of dishonesty for upholding their understanding of the Prayer Book, and he accounts for the difference in interpretation in these words:

> The circumstances in which our Reformers found themselves placed, when they had to draw up Formularies for a nation, a large proportion of whom were opposed to their doctrine, and were bound by law

---

[1] The letter is in *Writings of John Bradford* (Parker Soc., 1853; repr. Edinburgh: Banner of Truth, 1979), 405. By 'our doctrine' Martyr is referring to the Swiss and Reformed teaching, for which see Calvin, *Institutes*, IV xvi:21. On Augustine, see B. B. Warfield, *Studies in Tertullian and Augustine* (New York: OUP, 1930), 121-3.

[2] *Works of John Whitgift* (Cambridge: Parker Soc., 1853), 351.

to worship according to the prescribed National Ritual, necessarily produced an effect upon their labours. They retained all which it was possible to retain of the old Ritual, where the words could be interpreted in what they considered an orthodox sense, though bearing with the Romanists another sense.[1]

Whether or not expedience was justifiable in such circumstances, its outcome was to give support to deviations from Scripture for centuries to come. Instead of the reformation in the reign of Edward VI being, as the Reformers hoped, a stage towards further reformation, its documents were the high-water mark of evangelical statements. On the point of infant baptism the subsequent Prayer Books of 1559 and 1662 strengthened rather than weakened or removed ideas of baptismal regeneration.

A warning against expediency given to his colleagues by John Knox in the 1550s proved justified. He believed that if nests were left, birds could return to them. The later observation of the evangelical Archbishop James Usher is relevant. He recalled with regret the policy of kings and queens which left some things in church services familiar to Roman Catholics, in the hope

> to win and gain them, by yielding as far as they might in their own way: but the experience of many years hath shewed that this condescension hath rather hardened them in their errors than brought them to a liking of our religion; this being their usual saying, 'If our flesh be not good, why do you drink of our broth?'[2]

While Ryle did not concede as much as Goode (as in the quotation from Goode given above), he thought the compliers of the

---

[1] William Goode, *The Doctrine of the Church of England as to the Effects of Infant Baptism in the Case of Infants* (London: Hatchard, 1850).

[2] Usher, *Of the Ceremonies*, 209. Quoted by John Flavel, *Works*, vol. 4 (1820; repr. Edinburgh: Banner of Truth Trust, 2015), 565. 'The Prayer-book … [was] written at a time when a large proportion of the people were inclined to Romanism, and at the same time compelled to attend the services of the national Churches,—and consequently carefully drawn up, so as to give as little offence as possible to Romish prejudices.' William Goode, quoted by Ryle. *Principles for Churchmen*, 8-9n.

14 13 21	John George Smyth.		Feb 5	12
3 13 21	Charles Spencer March Phillipps.		Feb 28	12
13 12 24	Charles Whittingham.		Septr 23	11
30 15 24	Frederick Freeman		Jany 2	13
13 12 29	Walter Wandesford Butler (D)		Jany 14	14
1 14 29	Paulet Henry St John Mildmay		Octr 26	73
3 14 30	Charles William Henry Steward		march 30	11
9 15 30	Richard Luce		Febr 3	15
11 31	Frederick William Chitt Villiers (Mr)		July 20	12
11 31	Stephen Algernon Chichester (D)		Decr 18	13
12 7	John Charles Ryle.		May 10	11
12 4	John Eustace Grubbe		June 14	12
13 15	Robert Ellue		Jany 1	12
12 17	Osbert Fishlake Cundy		July 17	10
12 20	Michael Watts Russell		April 28	12

Prayer Book 'undoubtedly used some expressions liable to be misunderstood, which have been fruitful causes of division and evil'.[1] 'Blots were left on the face of our Church', because 'Queen Elizabeth prevented their [the Reformers] perfecting the work of the English Reformation.' But he did not believe it was allowable for baptismal regeneration to be upheld from the Prayer Book, and treated the assumption of children regenerate at baptism as 'dangerous' because it led clergy to treat their congregations 'as regenerate, or possessors of grace'. He was certain that the teaching was unscriptural. He held it as a fundamental principle, 'that the nearer a Church can get to Scripture the better she is, and the farther she gets away from it the worse'.[2] This was the voice of the Puritan. It was not a principle *consistently* followed in 1552. It was certainly not the voice of the followers of Archbishop Laud who framed the Act of Uniformity in 1662, and who did not believe in evangelizing those already 'Christian' by baptism.

Life would have been easier for Ryle had he gone along with a Church ready to embrace both the evangelical and the Anglo-Catholic understandings of baptism. Whether or not, at this point, his appeal to history was sound, it was Scripture he wanted to determine his practice. He saw the two belief systems, the evangelical and the sacramental, in inevitable conflict, and that there was no room here for compromise. That he was loved, and is loved, by numbers who would disagree with his defence of the language of the Prayer Book on baptism, is proof enough that the gospel itself is the great message of his writings. Spurgeon differed from Ryle over what I have just discussed, but he had no hesitation in stating what made Ryle

---

[1] *Bishop, Pastor and Preacher*, 27-28. Ryle did not tie the words specifically to the subject of baptism. When the subject of baptismal regeneration was raised at the Eclectic Society (an exclusive meeting of Anglican evangelical clergy) in 1803, the Rev. H. Foster said that 'because the expressions have stumbled thousands, I wish them altered'. *Thought of the Evangelical Leaders*, 297.

[2] *Ibid.*, 326.

the leader that he was. In a review of Ryle's book *Practical Religion*, the Baptist preacher wrote:

> Little more needs to be said of this volume than that it sustains the author's well-earned reputation for evangelical simplicity and power. Mr Ryle is looked upon as a typical representative of evangelical churchmanship, but in reality he ascends far higher. While with all her faults he loves the Church of England still, he loves the souls of men much more, and most of all the gospel of their salvation. This, too, is a gospel to be loved, the gentleness of which has made him great, and the experience of which has led to the earnest desire that it may do for others what it has done for him. … Men's ideas of the wrath to come may be judged of by the earnestness with which they exhort others to fly from it.[1]

---

[1] *The Sword and the Trowel*, 1879, 392. For criticism of Ryle's churchmanship in the same volume, see 237.

10

Liverpool

*The floating Landing Stage, Liverpool (1912),
scene of his almost daily walk*

I N MOVING to Liverpool Ryle was returning to the region he loved. While the city was in Lancashire, his home county of Cheshire was less than a mile away across the Mersey. Much had happened on that river since the days Ryle remembered when the first two steamships sailed from Liverpool to New York in twenty days. The port he had known in the 1830s had become, in his words, a 'giant city'. Comparing it with the situation fifty years earlier, he said in 1887:

> the population in 1837 was only 246,000. It is now, including sub-urbs, 700,000. ... The number of ships entering was 15,038. It is now 21,529. ... In 1837, Liverpool had nine docks, with a frontage of two miles and a half to the river. There are now fifty docks and basins with a frontage of six miles. ... We have bridged the Atlantic with our steamers, and brought our English-speaking cousins within a week of our shores ... We have covered the land with a network of railways, making journeys possible in a few hours, which formerly occupied days. We have opened communication with every part of the world by electric telegraph ...[1]

The 1860s and '70s had seen the erection of several great buildings, including St George's Hall, regarded as one of the finest of classical style in Europe. But the city's economic progress was by no means shared by all. A Commission on conditions in Liverpool in the 1880s reported 75,000 people in 'constant grinding poverty', and receiving less than fifteen shillings per week. Another 35,000 'were either paupers or on the verge of pauperism'.[2] Thousands lived in cellars

---

[1] *Upper Room*, 464-5.
[2] Farley, *J. C. Ryle, First Bishop of Liverpool*, 191, 187.

which never saw sunlight. Out of 200,000 British seamen, many from Liverpool, it was found that on average 'more than 4,000 annually die abroad', leaving destitute wives and children. Ryle would not have walked far in the city before he saw 'ill-fed, ill-clothed, ill-clad little boys and girls'.

But though social problems were the most visible, it was at the moral level that the greatest need existed. With good reason, the evangelist D. L. Moody called Liverpool 'the black spot on the Mersey'. In an allusion to the most critical battle of the Napoleonic Wars, the Rev. Charles Garret, Wesleyan Methodist leader in the city, believed that Liverpool was 'the moral Waterloo of the nation, where good and evil were engaged in hand-to-hand struggle. In no place was evil stronger, more active and more determined.'[1] An estimate of alcohol consumed daily gave the figure as £10,000.

The contrast with the conditions which Ryle had known during his thirty-six years in Suffolk was enormous. This was an age when the unemployed, the destitute, the sick, the orphans, and the handicapped were not the responsibility of governments. It was rather to the national Church that the needy might look for help, and bishops were expected to take the lead in raising funds for the many charitable agencies. Ryle had administered help of that kind in Stradbroke but in Liverpool one street might house more people than the whole population of that village.

Further, while a bishop in the south of England could often draw on considerable help from affluent parishioners within his diocese, this was not the case in Liverpool. Although the city was said to be 'staunchly Protestant', a local census of the 1880s showed that 'only one third at the most attended a church', and of that number well below half belonged to the Church of England.[2] Presbyterians,

---

[1] Quoted by Farley, *J. C. Ryle, First Bishop of Liverpool*, 146. I am indebted to Farley for other information on Ryle's attention to moral and social problems.

[2] Toon and Smout, *Evangelical Bishop*, 81. While the total figure for church attendance was 165,000 in 1891, Church of England attendance was 66,000.

Methodists, Welsh Baptists and Calvinistic Methodists were commonly people who 'knew not' bishops. One contemporary noted, 'The princely merchants of the great city, who could spare their thousands as common men do guineas, are mostly from beyond the Tweed where they have known "presbyters" only. A bishop, therefore, is sorely straitened for means and countenance.'[1]

Ryle might have had more help in this area had he known the full support of the press. Inevitably such Anglo-Catholic sympathizers as the *Church Times* (2 July 1880) condemned him for not 'holding his tongue', and for being 'ready to thrust himself at a moment's notice into the most difficult of all sees—excepting perhaps London'. The same writer sarcastically concluded, 'We wish the Evangelical brethren joy in their champion.' In the opinion of Dean Church, 'The Bishop of Liverpool is as obnoxious to all High Churchmen as the Bishop of Lincoln can be to any Low.' *The Times* of London (12 April 1880) was accurate in predicting of Ryle, 'Like many bishops he will have his professed champions, and like many he will have his serious antagonists.'

The antagonists did not lack representatives among the journalists of Lancashire and Liverpool. The city's outspoken and blunt daily press had not all been among the 'most anxious' for Ryle's appointment (Disraeli's words to the Queen). One section would have preferred a high church appointee of Gladstone's and were ready to call the beliefs of Liverpool's first bishop 'hideous'. Ryle was used to opposition, and the occasional criticism or gossip in the columns of the Suffolk press, but the Liverpool daily newspapers on his doorstep were to make life more akin to living in a goldfish bowl. It is well he could say, 'When a man gets to sixty-four years of age, his skin gets thick.'

* * *

[1] 'Ryle', in *Christian Portrait Gallery*, 321.

Faced with difficulties of many kinds, Ryle had no doubt where his priority lay: 'my first and foremost business, as Bishop of a new Diocese, is to provide for preaching of the Gospel to souls now entirely neglected'.[1] Under God, he believed that the success would depend on the quality of the clergy who manned the parishes of the diocese which extended far beyond the boundaries of the city. His responsibility was to lead by word and example but he was well aware that much would turn on how many of his clergy wanted his leadership. From the time of his conversion he had believed that nominal Christianity—'churchianity' without personal experience of Christ—was 'the grand defect of the Christianity of our times':

> How many go to church and chapel merely as a form! How few are really in earnest about the salvation of their souls! … Go to the most godly, quiet, and orderly parish in our land at this moment. Ask any well-informed child of God residing in it, how many true Christians it contains, and what is the proportion of the converted to the unconverted. Mark well the answer he will give. I doubt if you will find a parish in Great Britain where one third of the people are converted.[2]

Elsewhere he said, 'Many congregations might say, like one of old, "We have not so much heard whether there is any Holy Ghost."'

How many of his clergy would endorse such convictions he could not know. He was, of course, aware that he would face differences. He had decided many years earlier how best to respond. If men were 'loyal to the Church of England', that is, obedient to the Prayer Book and Thirty-nine Articles, he would count them as brethren, irrespective of what name they used, or what position they took on such things as vestments, gestures and church ornaments. He could disagree with the views of others on such points, and not make his opinion their rule. Thus at his 'consecration' at York Minster, and his subsequent 'enthronement' at Liverpool's provisional cathedral of St

[1] *Charges and Addresses*, 14.
[2] 'What Time Is It?' *Home Truths*, fourth series (Ipswich: Hunt, 1857), 87-8.

Peter's, he did not wear the embroidered cope and mitre offered him, and declined to carry a pastoral staff: 'If you send me a staff I shall lock it in a cupboard and never see it again. A Bishop wants a Bible and no staff.'[1] Similarly, during those initial services, when the choir and clergy turned east to say the Creed, Ryle bent forward so that it might be better seen that he did not turn. Yet at the same time he made it known that he found 'no fault with bishops who were happier with their staffs and croziers, but he was happier without them'.[2]

Even so, from the outset Ryle did not disguise his own preferences. A large house had been settled as the bishop's residence at 19 Abercromby Square. The location was nearly opposite the parish church of St Catherine, convenient for them to make their place of worship, but for Ryle, his wife and daughter, its services were too 'ceremonial' for their choice.

For some evangelicals, the latitude which Ryle allowed to himself and others was incompatible with their convictions. As already mentioned, this had led some to disagree with his involvement in Church Congress meetings where men of evangelical belief were in a minority. Ryle's response to such disagreement was clear. First, he laid down what were for him the five leading features of evangelical Christianity:

1. The absolute supremacy of Holy Scripture as the only rule of faith and practice.

2. The depth and prominence it assigns to the doctrine of human sinfulness and corruption.

3. The paramount importance it attaches to the work and office of the Lord Jesus Christ.

4. The high place it assigns to the inward work of the Holy Spirit in the heart of man.

[1] Russell, *Man of Granite*, 143, quoting the *Liverpool Courier*, 15 February 1900. For his dress he wore the white episcopal surplice known as a rochet, and was heard to tell a friend afterwards, 'I have changed my clothes, but I have not changed my coat nor my principles.'
[2] *Liverpool Courier*, 15 February 1900.

5. The importance it attaches to the outward and visible work of the Holy Ghost in the life of man. True grace will always make itself manifest in conduct.[1]

These evangelical truths, far from being different from the creed of the Church of England, were all to be found in the Thirty-nine Articles. To those Articles every clergyman had to assent at the beginning of his public ministry. When instituted to a living he was to read them 'publicly and openly, in the presence of the congregation' and again declare his assent. However, Ryle did not believe that only professed evangelicals should be counted as true Churchmen. A man might believe the Articles, but fail to present their truths in the right proportion. He might put first things second, and second things first. Such weakness, he argued, was no grounds for rejecting a man's Christianity. 'Different shades of statement', and 'different schools of thought' on some subjects, do not justify divisions. Unity, as well as correct belief, is the mark of a church, and that cannot be without a degree of toleration. He believed that there was a comprehensiveness consistent with Scripture and, on such grounds, called on other evangelical clergy 'to remember that it is unwise to keep aloof from Diocesan Conferences, Church Congresses, and other machinery which is being brought into use in this age'.[2]

Ryle's 'first charge to the New Diocese' spelt out clearly where he stood on comprehensiveness.

> I came to the position I occupy as Bishop of Liverpool with a settled resolution to be just and fair and kind to clergymen of every school of thought, whether High or Low or Broad, or no party. … Whenever I see in a clergyman hearty working, consistent living, and loyal Churchmanship, I shall be thankful, and ready to help him, though things may be said in his pulpit and done in his parish with which I do not entirely agree.[3]

---

[1] 'Evangelical Religion', *Knots Untied* (1885), 3-7. See the same points forcefully expounded in 'Thoughts on the Ministry', *Principles for Churchmen*, 167-72.

[2] *Principles for Churchmen*, 62.

[3] *Charges and Addresses*, 28.

With a concern to strengthen that same unity he was to establish an annual Diocesan Conference at which 'brotherly love, kindness, courtesy and respect' would be urged.

In this understanding of churchmanship Ryle made an important distinction between churchmen who favoured modest ceremonial and committed Anglo-Catholics who put themselves outside the formularies of the Church. The objective of the disciples of the Tractarian movement who remained in the Church of England was, in Ryle's words,

> to bring back and legalize Mass in our Communion, to cancel the Act of Settlement, which requires our Sovereigns to be Protestants, and finally, to bring about reunion between the Anglican Church and the Church of Rome.[1]

Characteristics of their practice were to turn the communion table into an altar, to encourage confession to a priest, to join the voice of 'the Church' with Scripture, and to hold up the Reformers for scoffing. Speaking of 'the Articles, Creeds, and Prayer Book', Ryle declared, 'he who flatly rejects them, denies them, contradicts them, and transgresses them, is in his wrong place inside the Church of England'.[2]

This distinction was all right in theory but too often the line between ritualists of the old high church party, whom Ryle would count as true Churchmen, and Anglo-Catholics was uncomfortably blurred and those moving away from the Protestant faith were not so easily identified. There were also subjects on which ritualists and Anglo-Catholics would share a common opinion over against Ryle. One such opinion concerned Ryle's hope that, for the wider spread of the gospel, gifted non-ordained men ought to be encouraged to take a speaking role in the public witness of the Church. But the belief that this role belonged exclusively to bishops and clergy lingered

[1] *Principles for Churchmen*, xvii.
[2] *Charges and Addresses*, 333.

in the Church of England, and it contrasted with Ryle's belief that 'nothing ought to be done in the Church without the laity'.[1]

Ryle wanted the powers of bishops to be limited by councils which would include laymen; he had proposed in 1872 that Convocation should include laity in equal numbers with clergy; and at the Diocesan Conferences, which he instituted in Liverpool, he included two lay representatives from each parish. But change in this area soon met with obstruction in Liverpool. What Ryle could do at Stradbroke in the way of welcoming unordained evangelists he could not do in Liverpool parishes where the incumbents jealously guarded their rights. A proposal from Ryle that ordained ministers, whom he would designate 'evangelists', be at liberty to preach in any parish of the diocese was unacceptable to those jealous of their parish boundaries and to those who thought of the ministry in terms of a sacerdotal priesthood.

Ryle's view was not related to any lowering of the work of the minister. He believed it was a special office, demanding particular gifts, and had no sympathy with those who wanted

> to bring into the ministry men who know little or nothing of Latin, Greek, Church History, the story of the English Reformation, the Prayer-book, the Church Catechism, or the Evidences of Christianity, and, in short, are only godly men who know the Bible and can talk about the gospel. I think the office of the ministry demands men of a higher standard than this …[2]

Another point at which tension emerged had to do with the building of a cathedral for Liverpool. As already indicated, Ryle had no high opinion of the type of Christianity which too often went with cathedrals, and in the 1870s he had called, unsuccessfully, for significant changes in the cathedral system. Cathedrals seldom had such a

---

[1] 'The Rights and Duties of Lay Churchmen', an address in Winchester Cathedral, 1886, in *Upper Room*, 334. He argued that 'The English laity have never yet had their rightful position in the management of the Church of England.'

[2] *Charges and Addresses*, 69.

preacher as his friend Henry Law at Gloucester. In anticipation of criticism from those eager for a fine cathedral beside the Mersey, Ryle addressed the subject in his first charge to the Diocese. He was not, he made clear, against the building of a cathedral in principle but, given it would cost half a million pounds, should it be thought a priority? 'I only know that my first and foremost business, as Bishop of a new Diocese, is to provide for preaching the gospel to souls now entirely neglected, whom no cathedral would touch.'[1] More clergy and more places of worship were the first need.

Committees responsible for advancing the cathedral project were set up and debates and arguments were to continue through the twenty years of his episcopate. The site for its location was only one of the number of issues that impeded progress. Ryle left planning and discussions to others but the delay was unjustly blamed on him by critics. When a site which had been a cemetery was eventually chosen, although Ryle did not favour it, one angry correspondent accused him of being 'on the side of the devil' as it would entail disturbing the bodies of the dead in Christ!'[2]

The *Liverpool Review* in November 1884 aired a complaint that the bishop gave half-hearted support to the services of St Peter's, the building which was to act as a provisional cathedral. He was reported as being seen walking on the other side of the road at the very time a weekday service was taking place. This last criticism was related to counsel Ryle had given to his clergy earlier that year. Contrary to old rubrics, he had declined to ask his clergy,

> to have daily matins, and vespers, and saints' day services where ninety-nine out of a hundred of his parishioners cannot attend such services. He can spend his day more usefully, in going from house to

[1] *Charges and Addresses*, 14.
[2] Farley, *J. C. Ryle, First Bishop of Liverpool*, 179. The first part of Liverpool Cathedral was consecrated on 29 June 1910; the second part was completed and consecrated on 19 July 1924, twenty years after the foundation stone was laid; the building was finally completed in 1978.

house among his people … by Cottage Lectures, by Bible Classes, by Young Men's Meetings, by Temperance Meetings, by Prayer Meetings, and other well-known modern means of usefulness.[1]

Where Ryle was walking to when he passed St Peter's was of no consequence to those who gave a high place to ceremonial religion.

How many of his clergy were out of sympathy with their new bishop is not on record, but there is no lack of information on the man who became a leader in obstructing Ryle. The case of the Rev. James Bell Cox, the incumbent at St Margaret's, Toxteth, became the *cause célèbre* in Ryle's whole episcopate.

It all began quietly enough and very soon after Ryle's arrival in Liverpool. After reading a report of a service at St Margaret's, Ryle wrote to Cox on 26 July 1880,

> Dear Mr Cox,
> I should feel obliged if you would call on me on Saturday next at 11. There is a matter about which I wish to have some friendly discussion with you.

The nature of their discussion can be gathered from a follow-up letter from Ryle on 31 July.

> Dear Mr Cox,
> I trust you will find your congregation ready to meet my expression of wishes about the four points I named, viz.:—lighted candles, cope, biretta, and incense. But I trust you will not forget that no wish of your congregation can exonerate you from responsibility for anything that happens in your church. I say this as your friend and bishop.[2]

This was but the beginning of an extended correspondence which went on until the end of October 1880 by which time the disagreement had reached an impasse. It was clear Cox's position was outside

---

[1] *Principles for Churchmen*, xvi.
[2] The whole correspondence, at the request of Cox, was published in *The Record*, 1 Dec. 1880, under the heading 'Ritualism in Liverpool'.

the comprehensiveness which Ryle was seeking to maintain. As a bishop, Ryle could depose only curates, not incumbents. The only way to prevent the continuance of Cox was to prosecute him in the Church courts which had come down from Medieval times. This Ryle declined to do and matters at St Margaret's stayed as they had been. Why Ryle declined to take legal action is not clear. It was not that he had changed his mind on the practice of the Church Association in initiating law suits. In 1872 he was thankful that by such procedure, 'The Association had obtained decisions in its favour on forty-five points.'[1] In 1880, when he resigned from the Association, he explained: 'I have altered no opinions I have felt or expressed about Ritualism, and have nothing to regret in having worked with your Association. But I cannot be a judge and a member of the Church Association: so I must withdraw, and work in other ways.'[2] He foresaw that if the Association brought actions against clergy in his diocese he could not belong to it and exercise the judicial role which could be required of him.

In 1885, an evangelical medical doctor, James Hakes, acting in the name of the Church Association, proceeded to institute a formal prosecution of Cox. This placed Ryle in a difficult position. He had authority to stop the prosecution if he so chose. But, believing that Cox's practice was illegal in the Church of England, and that every Englishman had the right to appeal to law, he allowed the case to go forward to the Chancery Court at York after further personal appeals to Cox had failed.

Cox declined to obey Ryle's wish with respect to Roman ritual on the same grounds as the Tractarians protested against the secularization of the Church. He told his bishop:

> I cannot recognise the spiritual authority of what his Lordship calls the Queen's Courts of Law in Ecclesiastical matters. His lordship

[1] *Church Association Monthly Intelligencer*, 1872-3, VI, 71.
[2] *Ibid.*, 1880, XVI, 135.

cannot claim canonical obedience when he is simply enforcing the decrees of secular courts.

Ryle did not know how to answer this other than to say, 'Laws and legal decisions may be bad, but so long as they are not repealed, or reversed, they must be obeyed.'[1]

The evidence brought forward by Dr Hakes was unambiguous. At St Margaret's, the administration of the 'blessed sacrament' at 'a very magnificent altar' was the daily practice, conducted with words and ritual in harmony with the Roman Missal. Preaching was of the same type. A curate was reported to have said that the jailer at Phillippi 'was saved, but not by his belief. Baptism intervened, and that made him a Christian, introduced him into the church, and saved him.'[2]

The outcome was an ineffective trial at which Cox was admonished. After repeated refusal to act on the court's warning, he was eventually sentenced for six months for contumacy and contempt. He went to comfortable accommodation in Walton prison, but only to be quickly released on grounds of a technicality, and so to the resumption of his labours at St Margaret's just as before. The whole saga led Ryle to the conclusion that no arrest of anti-Protestantism was to be expected from the Church, and that 'we are practically in a state of anarchy about ecclesiastical discipline'. In the sections of the press already critical, it was Ryle rather than Cox who stood condemned. The bishop should have exercised his veto on the prosecution. 'His name will stink in history,' *Figaro* believed (14 May 1887). Ryle also had criticism from the evangelical side for appointing the curate at St Margaret's, A. H. Paine, to officiate in the absence of Cox, and an application for his licence to be revoked was refused. Machray, not normally critical of Ryle, writes, 'The reasonableness of the Evangelical attitude was demonstrated ten or eleven years later when Mr Paine was openly "received" into the Church of Rome.'[3]

[1] Letter to Cox, 31 August 1880, in *The Record*, 1 Dec. 1880.
[2] Farley, *J. C. Ryle of Liverpool*, 212.
[3] Machray, *First Bishop*, 28. Ryle contributed to the expenses faced by Hakes for the court cases.

* * *

In later years, Herbert Ryle wrote in a comment on his father's experience, 'The High Church writers deliberately sought to destroy his position by detraction.'[1] One particular criticism was that he stood aloof from his clergy, distant, and poor in personal contacts. For support a few sentences from his autobiography have been quoted where he said that, after his arrival in Helmingham,

> I must honestly confess that I never felt drawn to be socially intimate with any of the clergy or their families. I soon got the reputation, which I never lost, of being unsociable, distant, reserved, and indisposed to encourage friendship …

But this was a reflection on his circumstances rather than his character. At Exbury he had been constantly in and out of the homes of his people. Arriving at Helmingham, guest of the Tollemaches, son of a celebrated, financially ruined family, his name had gone before him and he shrank from being an exhibit. Nor, it would seem, did he have much in common with neighbouring clergy.[2] He admitted that there was some lack of courtesy in his response to invitations, 'but after all I think it was fault on the right side'. It was based on the conviction that time is to be redeemed and 'that what was called social intercourse was an immense waste of time'. It remained a lifelong conviction that spiritual usefulness in ministers was ever related to a guarded use of time. He reminded the clergy to whom he spoke at Weston-super-Mare that the preachers who led the evangelical revival 'were not diners out. They were not men who sought the entertainments of the great and the rich.'

This is a principle which has nothing to do with being distant from people. That Ryle drew close to very many is very clear in the

[1] Fitzgerald, *Memoir of H.E. Ryle*, 134.
[2] With a touch of humour he once described neighbouring clergy in East Anglia as '"Nimrods, Ramrods, or Fishing rods", i.e. given to hunting, shooting or angling'. M. Guthrie Clark, *John Charles Ryle*, 36.

manner in which he befriended and made common cause with people of other denominations in Liverpool who were seeking to address the social and moral conditions. In this respect he remedied the limitations he faced among strong nonconformists in a manner few, if any, of his episcopal colleagues could have done. Within a short time he was engaged with the leaders of many agencies.

One of the first links was with a Mrs Birt who had organized a Sheltering Home for children and struggled for support. This work centred on arranging the emigration of children, orphan or destitute, to homes in Canada and to adoptive parents who would be 'orderly and churchgoing'. Between 130 and 160 were sent out each year, an estimated 2,000 in seventeen years. Ryle was said never to miss the agency's annual meeting in twenty years. At one point Ryle was criticized for his support for Mrs Birt on the grounds that she was not a member of the Church of England. To which charge

> He honestly confessed that he did not know to what denomination [she belonged], but he did know that she belonged to the Holy Catholic Church of Christ and was endeavouring to do a Christian work in a Christian way … he believed her great desire was to do them good in body and soul.[1]

Letters back from Canada documented the success of Mrs Birt's work. She was not alone in this field and the bishop also supported an Anglican scheme run by the Society for Promoting Christian Knowledge (SPCK), taking services on board ship before groups left Liverpool and providing Bibles and Prayer Books for the children.

In the work of helping needy women and girls, Ryle took second place to his wife, who was active in several societies, as well as his daughter Isabelle. Farley names three such agencies, with the Church of England Zenana Missionary Society heading his list. This was the Society with whom Amy Carmichael would go to India in 1895. An invitation from Ryle to Miss Ellice Hopkins led to the setting up

[1] *Daily Post*, 17 Jan. 1885, quoted by Farley, J. C. Ryle, *First Bishop of Liverpool*, 129.

of a Midnight Mission to prostitutes in Lime Street, Liverpool, and between fifty and sixty women were said to have been reclaimed in four months. Ryle's friendship with Charles Garret, president of the Wesleyan Methodist Conference in 1882, was productive of good in more than one direction. Garret's 'Waterloo' battle against corruption made noteworthy inroads on the demoralizing influence of the drink industry and drunkenness—'that cancer', in Ryle's words, 'of society in Britain at this moment'. Garret had Ryle's hearty co-operation when he started a workman's Public House Company, established to provide accommodation where cocoa and other refreshments would be served. It was soon reported that no fewer than 30,000 persons were using these places daily.

Machray records that when the Wesleyan Conference met in Liverpool Ryle welcomed the president and other members at his home 'and gave his benediction with a cordiality born of inmost conviction and sincerity'.[1]

Still more prominent than Garret in work to raise the lives of men, women, and children was Alexander Balfour, a successful shipping owner, town councillor, and one of 'the princely merchants of the great city'. Like others of that group, he was a Scot, and once a member of M'Cheyne's Bible Class in Dundee. He was a member of Fairfield Presbyterian Church in Liverpool and when Ryle was appointed bishop one of his first actions had been to send a 'thanksgiving gift' of £100 for Ryle via his minister, the Rev. R. H. Lundie. Of Balfour it was written:

> He might be said to have constituted himself by his rich benevolence an honorary member of all Christian organizations … The Liverpool Evangelization Society; the Medical Mission; the Stranger's Rest; Mrs Birt's Children's Refuge; Bands of Hope; Sunday free breakfasts; Ragged Schools; and many other institutions—counted him as their unfailing friend.[2]

[1] Machray, *First Bishop*, 40.
[2] *Christian Portrait Gallery*, 16.

With Samuel Smith MP, Balfour established the Liverpool YMCA, with its fine building, and helped in the founding of University College.

Friendship with Balfour drew Ryle into numbers of these enterprises. Both men had a special interest in the welfare of seamen. When Balfour booked the great St George's Hall for a meeting to promote the spiritual welfare of sailors, it was Ryle who was there to speak, and it was the same when Balfour opened the Seaman's Institute in 1885. The sailors upon whom Britain depended were a too-largely-forgotten part of society. After Balfour established the Liverpool Seamen's Orphanage, records kept showed that over the next sixteen years, 66,667 sailors died in English ships abroad, of whom 40,551 were drowned. Homes were suddenly left without the only bread-winner and children without a father. Lundie said of Balfour,

> To provide for the sailors' orphans, and to do it on a scale worthy of the great port of Liverpool, was his consuming desire. … No business aim, no prospect of advantage for himself, ever took possession of him as this object did. … It was almost impossible to escape the contagion of a compassion like his.[1]

Taken suddenly ill in 1886 at the age of sixty-one, Balfour had to undergo serious surgery from which he did not recover. On the morning of the operation, his family heard him pray, 'Lord, remember the great community of Liverpool.' His last act before the operation was to write to a young clergyman he was seeking to help. Ryle took the service at his friend's funeral, where 'the mourning was mingled with a thankful joy, that God had given such a man to bless and to ennoble the world'.[2] The lesson was read by Lundie who would also write the biography. He quoted the words of his late friend, 'Thoughts of the marvellous progress of God's work in Liverpool afford me more

---

[1] R. H. Lundie, *Alexander Balfour: A Memoir* (London: Nisbet, 1888), 128.

[2] *Ibid.*, 318. Also at the funeral was Dr John Roxburgh, his father-in-law, who had been minister of St John's, Dundee, at the time of M'Cheyne.

comfort and rejoicing, than the perusal of any poem, or the reading of any novel.'

In that progress Ryle had played a significant part and the co-operation continued which had been forged with Balfour's circle of friends. One common endeavour was the public preservation of the Lord's day, and two years after Balfour's death we find Ryle writing to Lundie on November 28, 1888:

> Dear Mr Lundie,
>
> If the 'Daily Post' Article is correct in its Report that our Mayor has withdrawn from the Presidency of the coming Art Congress on account of the 'Sabbath Picture Gallery' being about to be opened, I really think he ought to be supported by all faithful ministers and Christians. But what can be done? The time is short, and the Congress begins next Monday.
>
> I shall hope to preach about it at the Cathedral next Sunday afternoon.
>
> I will ask you to accept the enclosed though I know you do not need what it contains.
>
> Yours sincerely
>
> J. C. Liverpool[1]

Machray affirms that Ryle had 'the esteem of all the Nonconformist bodies'. Certainly it could be said of a number of their ministers as Robertson Nicoll says of the Rev. John Watson (Sefton Park Presbyterian): 'he had a very hearty friendship with the Bishop of Liverpool, the stout-minded English Evangelical, better known as J. C. Ryle.' When Watson shot to fame as an author in 1894, writing under the pseudonym of 'Ian Maclaren', Ryle thanked him for the gift of *Beside the Bonnie Brier Bush* in a note of 29 December:

> Dear Mr Watson,—You must let an old minister thank you very much for 'Ian Maclaren's' book; it has touched my heart, and brought

---

[1] The mayor, J. B. Morgan, stood with Ryle, who preached the following Sunday on 'The Sabbath was made for man'. He held that operas, plays and art did not provide the spiritual good for which one day in seven is intended. See Farley, *J. C. Ryle, First Bishop of Liverpool*, 156.

more tears to my eyes than anything I have read for a long time. May God bless your pen and make use of it for His own glory.[1]

The cordiality of Ryle's inter-denominational friendships does not fit the picture of a reserved and distant man. But, lest it be thought this picture speaks only of his relationship with his peers, there is more to be said. When he and his family chose not to worship at St Catherine's in Abercromby Square, they settled instead at the church which Richard Hobson had begun in a cellar twenty years earlier. The bishop's first visit to that church was on 13 March 1881, the occasion being a Sunday evening service at which he was to preach for the Irish Church Missions and administer the Lord's Supper. Hobson, the vicar, recalled:

> That was an evening never to be forgotten in the history of the parish; for truly we felt the Saviour's presence, in answer to much prayer, and in fulfilment of His own promise. The service began at 6.30 o'clock, and it was past 10 o'clock when the Bishop left. In the vestry he said, 'I make much of hands, and I conclude that five out of every six of your communicants are working people. St Nathaniel's is an answer to those who say the Church of England is not suited for working people.'[2]

For Ryle 'working people' was an honourable term for poor people who were in employment:

> The working man may live in a poor dwelling, and after toiling all day in a coal-pit, or cotton mill, or iron foundry, or dock, or chemical works, he may look rough and dirty. But, after all, he is flesh and blood, like ourselves.[3]

Just such people, along with 'only small shop keepers' and 'artisans', Ryle would later tell the Church Congress in Derby, made up St

---

[1] W. Robertson Nicoll, *Ian Maclaren: Life of the Rev. John Watson* (London: Hodder & Stoughton, 1908), 169.
[2] *Hobson of Liverpool*, 145.
[3] *Ibid.*, 334.

Nathaniel's, 'with not a rich man in it'. He said he had distributed the bread and wine at the Lord's Table to 395 people, half of whom were men, and remarked, 'I saw the hands which received them, and I know by those hands that many of them were dock-labourers and foundry-men.'[1]

Richard Hobson's congregation warmed to Ryle and he warmed to them. It could have been here that one working man of Scots descent was heard to exclaim, 'Yon mon's na Bishop; I can understand every word!' St Nathaniel's became the spiritual home for the Ryle family. In Hobson's words, he took the church 'under his episcopal wing, to the great encouragement of my loving toilers and myself'. On a later occasion when Ryle came to address men employed in the coal-yards near the parish, 'they cheered him lustily on both arrival and departure'.

This same supposedly unapproachable bishop took his daily exercise by walking the busy streets to the Landing Stage at the Mersey, and he made it known to his clergy that he was available every Tuesday morning to see any of them. His successor Francis J. Chavasse had cause to write of Ryle:

> His affection for Liverpool and his Diocese amounted to a passion. He began his work as a Bishop at an age when most men are beginning to think of rest, and he laboured on 'without hasting and without resting' so long as his brain could think, and his hand could write.[2]

[1] Hobson of Liverpool, 335.
[2] Liverpool Diocesan Conference, 1900, quoted by Russell, Man of Granite, 209.

Part of a press cartoon of 1883 on the struggle for controlling the direction of the Church of England: Ryle (17), Spurgeon (15), Charles Garret (12)

II

Standing Firm under Darkening Skies

At his desk in later years

R YLE'S attachment to the Church of England was strong and clearly argued. Whatever its faults, the Church had great benefits: a Prayer Book which required constant Old and New Testament readings in its services; Thirty-nine Articles of Religion which were clearly Protestant; a constitution which gave a national expression to the Christian Faith—these were no small things to be preserved. As noted, Ryle worked hard for a comprehensive Church which would stand limited by its formularies. For the sake of unity he urged toleration over what was not fundamental, and by his example, as we have noted, he encouraged attendance at mixed gatherings such as Convocations and Church Congresses.

We are all affected by our surroundings. This is to be seen in Ryle's life and it enters into the changes which occurred in his view of the policy evangelicals should pursue. In the 1850s he did not speak of the need for evangelical clergy to look for greater unity between all Churchmen. On the contrary, addressing fellow evangelical clergy at Weston-super-Mare in 1858, he said:

> No doubt we all love unity; but we must distinctly maintain, that true unity can only be built on God's truth. No doubt we must not withhold the right hand of fellowship from any faithful brother, because he does not think exactly like us; but we must understand who the men are to whom we extend the right hand. Many are saying now-a-days, that 'after all, there is no great difference between one clergyman and another. Some speak of a thing by one name, and some by another; but, after all, they mean the same.' It is not uncommon now to hear of high churchmen saying to evangelical clergymen, as was said in the time of Ezra and Nehemiah, by Sanballat and Tobiah—'Let us build with you.' But let us not be taken in by such

sophistry. Better build by ourselves, better let the work go on slowly, than allow Sanballat and Tobiah to come and build by our side. I believe that all communion of that sort, all interchange of pulpits with unsound men, is to be deprecated, as doing nothing but harm to the cause of God. I believe that by so doing we endorse the sentiments of persons who have no real love of Christ's truth. We enable the high church party to manufacture ecclesiastical capital out of the evangelical clergy, and to make people believe that we are all one in heart, when, in reality, we differ on first principles. From such unity and co-operation may we pray to be delivered.[1]

In the next two decades he did not withdraw such words but the emphasis changed. I have noted above how in the 1860s Ryle disagreed with a number of fellow evangelicals over a greater involvement in the Church. In particular, he wanted their attendance at the annual Church Congresses. Eugene Stock, commenting on an address Ryle gave at the Islington Conference in 1872, writes:

He was audacious enough to blame Evangelicals for misjudging High Churchmen, told them to attend Church Congress and learn better, assured them he had not himself 'caught any theological disease' by attending, advocated as much unity in the Church as was possible, and made the following notable suggestion:—

Let a few Churchmen of mark from each school be got together quietly. … Let them be put down in Cumberland, at the Borrowdale Hotel; keep away from them letters, newspapers … give them nothing but their Bibles, their Prayer-books, pens, ink and paper; and ask them to talk matters over quietly among themselves, to find out wherein they differed and wherein they agreed, and to put it down in black and white. That such a report would bring to light clear evidence of a vast amount of unity, he firmly believed, and should continue to believe until the experiment proved the contrary.[2]

There is similar hopefulness in the Preface to his third volume of his *Expository Thoughts on John* (1873):

---

[1] 'What Is Our Position?' *Home Truths*, seventh series, 257-8.
[2] *History of the Church Missionary Society*, vol. 3, 8-9.

there are many Christians whose hearts are right in the sight of God, while their heads are very wrong. I am more and more convinced, that the differences between schools of religious thought are frequently more nominal than real, more verbal than actual …[1]

The fullest statement of his thinking on greater unity came in an address given to a gathering of evangelical clergy in Southport in 1878, in which he defended attendance at Church Congresses. It was published in a thirty-two-page booklet under the title already mentioned, *Shall We Go?*[2] These gatherings were widely attended, by lay Christians as well as clergy. Held in various locations, they were organized by local committees who only appointed the opening and the closing speakers. All other speakers were called by the chairman after they had handed in their names. Ryle argued that nothing was conceded by attending, that a valuable opportunity was provided for evangelicals to present their 'distinctive principles', and that all was conducted fairly. Falling back on a lesson from school days, he believed, 'We have not had just cause to complain. We had our innings as well as others, and if we did not always bowl well and make long scores, and if we missed some catches and fielded badly, the fault was our own.'

> A Church Congress, with three or four thousand people present, is a very soul-stirring and extraordinary sight. The immense majority of the audience, we must remember, are educated people, and each is a little centre of influence. Hundreds of them are in a floating and undecided state of mind about Church questions, and are ready to receive impressions for good or ill, which may influence the whole course of their future lives. Is it wise, is it kind to give them over entirely to High Church and Broad Church speakers, and not let them hear some clear distinct Evangelical testimony? I cannot see it.

[1] *Expository Thoughts: John*, vol. 3, vi.
[2] *Shall We Go? Being Thoughts about Church Congresses, and Our Duty with Regard to Them, from the Standpoint of an Evangelical Churchman* (London: Hunt, 1878).

He conceded to brethren who disagreed over attending such gatherings, that there could be circumstances where attendance would be a compromise. If, for instance, the promoters of the Congresses gave the platform to 'extreme Ritualists, whom I am unable to distinguish from Papists, and extreme Broad Churchmen, whose views appear to me painfully like Socinianism',[1] in brief, those who do not love the Church's 'Articles and her Prayer-book', then evangelicals should not be there. There had been, he admitted, occasional instances when 'objectionable and unsound men' were heard, but he expected 'fewer mistakes' of that kind in the future.

The composition of the Congresses, he thought, represented no such heretical standpoint:

> There are myriads of Churchmen in this day who, while they occupy different standpoints, are honestly agreed in certain common fundamental principles. They love the Church of England. They have a common belief in the Trinity, the Atonement and the Divine authority of Scripture.

This was not to deny that there were real differences between them:

> I believe that the Evangelical view of the Articles and Prayer-book is the true and correct view. But surely we are going too far if we maintain that those who do not see exactly as we do are not Churchmen at all.

He told his evangelical hearers at Southport:

> There are scores of English clergymen, at this very day, who do not profess to belong to our school, and yet preach as sound a Gospel as we do ourselves. Go into their churches blindfold, *on some days*, not knowing where you were, and you would think you were hearing some follower of Bickersteth[2] or McNeile. Of course *on other days* they may preach about the Church, the ministry, and the sacraments,

---

[1] Socinus, the name of an uncle and nephew whose writings against the deity and the atoning work of Christ fuelled anti-evangelical thought in the sixteenth century. There is full refutation in John Owen, *Works*, vol. 10 (repr. Edinburgh: Banner of Truth Trust, 2000).

[2] Edward Bickersteth Jr.

which you could not receive for a moment. But to say that they never preach Christ, and salvation by grace, and repentance, and faith, and to condemn them wholesale as unsound, because on some points they are in error, is, in my mind, neither liberal nor fair. Surely we might remember that even Luther held consubstantiation, and John Wesley was an extreme Arminian. But who dare say they preached no truth and did no good? While we lament what we consider the defects in the teaching of our brethren of other schools, and while we maintain firmly that we cannot co-operate with them, and interchange pulpits, let us honestly and manfully acknowledge that they often preach a great deal of truth, and do a great deal of work, and let us thank God for it.

This statement is significant in its importance. While Ryle was not denying the Christianity of brethren of defective views, he was asserting that the differences were serious enough to warrant not teaching alongside them in the work of the Church. He saw a Congress as 'neutral ground', and 'fairly conducted' without favour to one side or the other. He was not advocating a measure of compromise or 'departure from the old paths of Evangelicalism in order to gain a hearing'. On the contrary; 'I want no new flag. I am not recommending my brethren to hoist new colours for the sake of unity. I am no advocate of peace at any price.' No man was to put evangelical views

in his pocket when he meets men of other schools. Rather let him bind them to his forehead, and own them boldly, firmly and decidedly … Let those who please twit us with only holding half the truth. We may answer boldly that we are the men who hold the *whole* truth, and that the views we object to are additions to the faith.

He closed this address at Southport with some words of caution 'to my Evangelical brethren': 'I offer them as one who is no longer young. But "days should speak", and after thirty-seven years' service in the Evangelical ranks, I hope I have learned something.' 'Let us', he urged, '*beware of narrow-mindedness in our judgment both of rivals and friends.* I do not forget that the way of life—the good old way—

is narrow; but I am afraid we are often tempted in these days to walk in it with a narrow mind.' As an example he referred to a meeting with the archbishop of Canterbury at Lambeth Palace in December 1877. One hundred and twenty clergy were invited to attend, including twenty-five evangelicals, of whom Ryle was one. Of this meeting he said:

> We went in perfect ignorance of what was going to happen. We went without the slightest concert or communication with men of other schools. We came away, after three or four hours' talking, without anything having been done, but not without a plain declaration to the Archbishop and the meeting, first made fully and manfully by my friend Joseph Bardsley, and afterwards more briefly by myself, that *unity with 'Romanizers' was flatly impossible!*

Yet, following this meeting, he went on to say

> reports were industriously circulated all over England that we were ready to sell the pass, and strike our Protestant colours, for the sake of apparent unity. I make no comment on those absurd and baseless reports. I simply mention them as a specimen of the unhappy spirit which is abroad.

I give these quotations to show the burden of his thinking in the mid-1870s. They represent no doctrinal difference but there is a change of mood. Greater unity, and better relationships with other Churchmen, came more to the fore in his view of things, as the subjects of his addresses at the Islington Conference showed. His subject at the 1868 conference was published under the title, *We Must Unite*. In 1870 he spoke on 'How may we promote greater unity of action among those Churchmen who hold the distinctive doctrines of the Reformation?' At the 1872 conference, already quoted above, his title was, 'Can a greater amount of unity be obtained among zealous and pious Churchmen of different schools of thought?'

What prompted this emphasis? Islington was the centrepiece of the evangelical clergy and in the 1860s, it is said, 'pessimism fell on the conferences'.[1] In that decade liberal theology as well as Anglo-Catholicism was making headway in the Church of England. In 1869, under Gladstone's influence, the Irish branch of the Church of England was disestablished and disendowed. For the men at Islington, including Ryle, this was a major setback for Protestant Christianity. He feared that disestablishment could take place in England, 'and where will the Evangelical body be then, if we are not trained, drilled, and prepared for the struggle?' These dangers all pointed him to the need for closing ranks as far as possible. He was speaking to the times, and also to the needs of evangelical Churchmen.

It may be that there was a measure of misjudgment in Ryle's hopefulness over the number of other Churchmen, faithful to the fundamentals, with whom evangelicals could unite more closely. Later events would show they were not the 'myriads' of which he spoke. Perhaps the favourable reception of his speeches to the thousands at the Church Congresses, where he was listened to with attention and admiration, over-influenced his thinking. Unlike the experience of some evangelicals who spoke at the Congresses, Ryle found himself welcome. The historian George R. Balleine said that at these gatherings he 'proved himself to be a born debater. Quick, incisive, good-humoured and never at a loss, he soon became one of the most popular of the Congress speakers.'[2] In the midst of sometimes dull occasions, the rector of Stradbroke kept everyone awake with his 'fluent, forcible and effective' words. Even a Ryle might mistake an admiration for his gifts and personality with a sympathy for his convictions. Maybe he was not so much on his guard now as he was when he first encountered popularity in London in the 1850s and about which he said: 'I always felt that popularity, as it was called, was a very worthless thing and a very bad thing for a man's soul'.

[1] David Bebbington writing on 'The Islington Conference', in *Evangelicalism and the Church of England in the Twentieth Century*, eds. Andrew Atherstone and John Maiden (Woodbridge, Suffolk: Boydell Press, 2014), 54.

[2] G. R. Balleine, *History of the Evangelical Party in the Church of England* (London: Longmans, 1933), 272.

I offer this comment with hesitation. Ryle had large vision and was never looking only in one direction. That he was in no way pre-occupied with the subject of unity is very clear. The very year 1878, when he spoke in Southport on 'Shall We Go?', was the one when, a few months earlier, he gave a rousing warning at the Islington Conference on, 'The Importance of the Clear Enunciation of Dogma in Dispensing the Word, with Reference to Instability among Modern Christians'. Danger was in their midst as well as in the Church at large: 'A strong dislike to all "dogma" in religion is a most conspicuous and growing sign of the times.' This was promoting a 'jelly-fish' Christianity,

> without bone, or muscle, or power. … We have hundreds of 'jelly-fish' clergymen, who seem not to have a single bone in their body of divinity. … We have thousands of 'jelly-fish' sermons preached every year, sermons without an edge, or a point, or a corner, smooth as billiard balls, awakening no sinner, and edifying no saint.[1]

He feared evangelicals were in danger from this spirit and pleaded, 'For Christ's sake let us beware of trying to heal our breaches by lowering our standard of doctrine, and watering our statements of truth in order to avoid giving offence.'[2]

This shows how Ryle could be found defending different issues at the same time. Again, while he spoke to evangelical weakness at Islington in 1878, the next year, in the columns of *The Times*, he defended the current strength of the evangelical party in the national Church.

I am not, therefore, about to argue that Ryle was dominated by another and a different emphasis in the last twenty years of his life as bishop of Liverpool, but I believe the evidence points to another change of mood. It was noted by his contemporary and sympathizer, Machray, who wrote: 'It must be said that towards the end of his

---

[1] *Principles for Churchmen*, 97.
[2] *Ibid.*, 109.

episcopate Ryle became rather pessimistic in his views as to the future of the Church of England.'[1] Instead of the greater unity for which he had hoped and worked, his experience compelled further thinking. In the Introduction to his book *Principles for Churchmen*, written in May 1884, he gave as his opinion, 'at the rate we are going now, the end of our good old Church, unless God interferes, will be either Popery or infidelity'.[2] In an address on 'Can There Be More Unity Among Churchmen', while still advising attendance on Congresses, it was with less assurance of success, and for himself he said, 'I do not particularly like Congresses. I never expect them to do very much for the Church.'[3] There is also in this address a four-times repeated encouragement for evangelicals to meet with men of different beliefs 'on neutral ground'. In other words, such meetings were not an expression of spiritual unity.

In 1886 he said bluntly, 'The horizon is black.' His practice also indicated some change of thought in the 1880s. He appears to have attended only one Congress after 1880, and, after looking at the records, Farley concluded he was not 'a particularly good attender' at the meetings of the Upper House of Convocation in York.[4] After being present at one meeting of bishops in London, he reported to his son, Herbert, that it had come to 'a weak, evasive, and impotent conclusion … I came away vexed and annoyed, and I am not at all disposed to go up again to London for one night for such waste of time.'[5] At the Lambeth Conference of 1888 he chose to leave before the end of the proceedings. That gathering of bishops went on to issue a letter ('Encyclical Quadrilateral') which spoke vaguely of the need for reunion with non-Protestant churches, and was ordered to be read in all churches. Ryle was no longer present when the letter

[1] Machray, *First Bishop*, 24
[2] *Principles for Churchmen*, xxvi.
[3] *Ibid.*, 78.
[4] Farley, *J. C. Ryle, First Bishop of Liverpool*, 232.
[5] Fitzgerald, *Memoir of H. E. Ryle*, 133.

was drawn up, and on 14 August 1888 he wrote to *The Record* dissociating himself from its contents and the impression that it had the approval of all the bishops:

> Allow me to state that this is a complete mistake. I myself, for one, had no voice or hand in drawing up the Encyclical … I only wish the public to understand that the Encyclical is not the united and harmonious voice of all the Bishops of the Anglican Communion.

He went on to deplore the absence of attempts to address the

> unhappy divisions which are at this moment convulsing the Church of England … To my eyes they are of cardinal importance and appear to require far more attention than the condition of the Scandinavian or Greek Churches, or the Old Catholic movement. Some expression of humble regret for these divisions, some properly-defined conditions of peace, some proposal to attempt the restoration of godly discipline and the creation of satisfactory Ecclesiastical Courts, some bold declaration that, with the utmost degree of toleration, our Church will never re-admit the mass and auricular confession or go behind the Reformation—a few plain statements of this kind would have immensely improved the Encyclical, greatly strengthened the Church of England, and cheered the hearts of myriads of loyal Churchmen. Alas! about all these points the Encyclical is painfully silent.

A response to Ryle from Edward W. Benson, archbishop of Canterbury, reported in *The Times* (17 August 1888) was not in the more usual conciliatory episcopal tone. He said that the Encyclical was approved by all the bishops present when it was adopted, and it was Ryle's fault if he was not there: 'We did not unfortunately have the advantage of his presence for cooperation and criticism on that day … If he preferred to be on holiday in Scotland rather than at Lambeth that was his fault.'[1]

---

[1] Reported in *The Times*, 17 August 1888, quoted by Russell, *Man of Granite*, 191. Elsewhere Ryle had written that it would be a sin to belong to the Greek Orthodox Church.

In a short response to this in *The Record* (24 August), Ryle by-passed the 'holiday' jibe with the words, 'If I had been present at Lambeth, instead of being detained at Liverpool by pressing diocesan engagements, I could not have voted for the Encyclical.'[1] The isolation that he felt is clear enough in the further words:

> I suppose I must now assume that the Encyclical was approved by all the 137 Bishops who were present when it was finally adopted, and that it represents their united judgment. Of course, if this interpretation is correct, I find myself in the unpleasant position of being one of a very small minority. But even if I stand alone I cannot change my opinion.

Lesser men than Ryle would have kept silent at the rebuffs he received. Ryle did not. In 1890 a conference of 'Churchmen in Council' met in London and addressed the subject of the 'wounds' in the Church and how to make an end of disputes. After reading a report of their conclusions, Ryle told the readers of *The Record,* 'I could not have believed, until I read it, that so many able and good men would have gravely propounded remedies for the "present distress" so unpractical, so defective, and so unlikely to do any good.' After various observations, he concluded,

> For one thing, at any rate, I heartily thank Churchmen in Council. Their proceedings show that at least other people beside advanced Protestants and Evangelicals are beginning to be concerned, troubled and alarmed about the condition of the Church of England. I am glad of it. I wish they had opened their eyes and seen our dangers long ago. The miserable policy of sitting still, doing nothing, crying peace, and snubbing anxious Protestants has utterly failed and broken down, as many foresaw it would. We are in troubled waters, and our good old ship is in imminent danger. But I cannot for a moment see that the proposals of Churchmen in Council are likely to prevent shipwreck.[2]

[1] As Ryle had written his letter of 14 August from Pitlochry in Scotland, Benson had wrongly concluded that holidays were the reason for his shortened stay at Lambeth.

[2] 'Churchmen in Council', *The Record*, 28 February 1890. One of their proposals

The so-called Lincoln case which ran from 1888 to 1892 troubled Ryle still more. It arose out of an action by the Church Association, with its Protestant membership, which charged Edward King, the Anglo-Catholic bishop of Lincoln with condoning ritualistic practices in connexion with the Lord's Supper for which there was no justification in the Church of England. Initially, and for only the second time since the Reformation, the archbishop of Canterbury took the case in his own court, sitting as the sole judge. Lincoln was cleared of the charges, but evangelicals were dismayed at the procedure followed. While previous judgments of the Court of Appeal were set aside, it was allowed that papal decrees and pre-Reformation precedents be taken as evidence for the existing 'law' of the Church of England. The Church Association then appealed to the Privy Council who upheld Benson's verdict with a trifling variation.[1] Ryle wrote in *The Record:*

> The Judgment is a direct help and encouragement to that mischievous party of Churchmen which is 'compassing sea and land' to drive the Evangelical clergy out of the Church of England, and to bring back into our Anglican worship the Mass and the confessional … Some writers have had the face to tell the public the old story that the Ritual prosecutions are all about mere outward trifles, forgetting that it has been shown a hundred times that the points in dispute are not trifles, but great principles lying at the foundation of the Christian faith. Some writers have proclaimed that the Judgment brings in a glorious reign of universal toleration. The Church is to become like Israel in the latter days of the Judges, and every clergyman is to do and teach what is right in his own eyes.
>
> It is disagreeable to feel that we are at variance with the Archbishop of Canterbury and nearly all the bench of Bishops. It is

---

would later succeed in the 1970s: it was to seek an Act of Parliament to allow measures for changes in the Church to pass Parliament without its scrutiny and consideration.

[1] Benson had ruled that lighted candles 'on the altar' did not break the law, provided they were not lighted ceremoniously. The Privy Council believed that the bishop had not lit the candles at all; it was the work of the incumbent of the parish!

disagreeable to feel that in almost every diocese we shall henceforth be regarded as a troublesome, defeated minority, tolerated but not trusted, and liable more than ever to be frowned on, cold-shouldered, snubbed and silently persecuted … I stand alone, and lay no claim to infallibility. But I will speak what I think.[1]

Ryle was convinced that the Lincoln judgment, while only *permitting* rather than *enforcing* what had previously been judged illegal, would inevitably deepen existing division:

The plain truth is, that a Church in which two opposite views of such cardinal subjects as the Lord's Supper and sacerdotalism—*the very keys of the great Romish controversy*—are formally declared to be not illegal, is not a Church in which the clergy can work very cordially and comfortably together, and its thinking laymen will gradually separate into two camps.[2]

As with the Bell Cox case in Liverpool, the fact that the State—the Privy Council—was the final authority in the Lincoln decision, a decision with which he did not personally concur, had to be some embarrassment to Ryle. He told his clergy, 'the Judgment is the decision of the highest Court of the realm … As a law-abiding Englishman and a believer in the Royal Supremacy, I submit, though I cannot approve or admire.'[3]

* * *

What had happened by this date was that two formerly separate influences had gathered strength and converged in opposition to the evangelical understanding of Scripture. Speaking to evangelicals

---

[1] 'The Lincoln Judgment', *The Record*, 12 August 1892. It bears the signature, 'A Northern Churchman', the name attached to a number of items from Ryle.

[2] *Charges and Addresses*, 250.

[3] *Ibid.*, 248. Ryle's respect for the law's authority over a national Church was also shown north of the border in Scotland. When Anglo-Catholics chided him that on his Scottish holidays in Pitlochry, he chose attendance at the Church of Scotland, not at Holy Trinity, the Episcopal Church, his answer was that it was the former which was established by the State, north of the border.

in 1858, Ryle had identified the two rising dangers in the Church. He believed that Tractarianism had 'power over a large body in the Church of England'. This has been already sufficiently noted, but of the second more needs to be said. It came from some, he said at that date,

> who are called Church-of-England men, who publicly and privately put forward strange and unscriptural views about the atonement, about the vicarious sacrifice of Christ, and about His substitution for us on the cross. There are clergymen in England, who hold strange views about inspiration, and the eternity of punishment which Scripture speaks of as being the desert of unbelief. These men go on unrebuked. No effort is made to put them out of the Church.[1]

In the next thirty years men of laxer approach to biblical truths multiplied. I noted above Ryle's response to John Colenso, bishop of Natal, who justified disbelief in parts of the Old Testament. Coupled with a lowered view of Scripture there came a diminishing regard for definite doctrinal beliefs. When Frederick Temple, bishop of Exeter, confessed his acceptance of evolution in 1884, his son, William Temple, would later note, 'it provoked no serious criticism'. In that decade it began to be said openly that scholarship had rendered it no longer possible to treat the inspiration of Scripture as a fundamental doctrine. German learning had supposedly rendered untenable the old belief in the Old Testament as the inerrant word of God. William Robertson Smith had been deposed from his professorship in Scotland for his Higher-Critical view of Scripture, only to remove to the University of Cambridge where he advocated that the new understanding of the Old Testament was in no way detrimental to Christian piety.[2]

Tractarian leaders such as Edward B. Pusey and Henry P. Liddon were no supporters of disbelief in the Bible. Liddon's hoped-for

---

[1] *Home Truths*, seventh series, 256-67.
[2] I have written on the Scottish part in the rise of Higher Criticism in 'The Tragedy of the Free Church', *A Scottish Christian Heritage* (Edinburgh: Banner of Truth Trust, 2006).

successor in leading that party was Charles Gore, but in the publication *Lux Mundi* (1889), Gore, writing on 'The Holy Spirit and Inspiration', was ready to treat part of Old Testament history as 'myth' and to explain Christ's 'mistaken' views on the authorship of its books in terms of the limitations he shared with other humans.[1] This was to be no temporary coalescence.

At this point Herbert Ryle, son of Bishop Ryle, re-enters the story. We last saw him beginning schooldays at Eton in 1868. After that he moved on to King's College, Cambridge, and in 1879 'swept the board of all distinctions open at Cambridge to students of Theology'. In the early 1880s he became a fellow of King's, taught theology at Emmanuel, was ordained in 1882, and in 1883 became one of his father's examining chaplains at Liverpool (a position which only required occasional visits). In 1888 he became the Hulsean Professor at Cambridge and in that position he allied himself with the view advocated by Robertson Smith and others that, 'The new learning could afford a firm foundation for Christian belief to which the old theory of verbal inspiration, irretrievably shattered by the advance of human knowledge, could never make good its claim again.'[2] He spoke to the same cause as Gore, on which point Owen Chadwick writes, 'And his utterance helped Gore less because of his scholarly reputation than because he was the son of one of Gore's strongest opponents, the Bishop of Liverpool.'[3] Fitzgerald adds, 'In Evangelical circles his very name won for him a hearing which might have been denied to others.'[4]

This must have been one of the heaviest disappointments of his father's life. Before his son's thinking became public knowledge, shortly before the latter became Hulsean Professor, the bishop had taken the very grievous step of ending his son's position as one of his

---

[1] Chadwick, *Victorian Church, Part II*, 101.
[2] Fitzgerald, *Memoir of H.E. Ryle*, 77.
[3] *Victorian Church, Part II*, 103.
[4] Fitzgerald, *Memoir of H.E. Ryle*, 92.

examining chaplains. Herbert Ryle's biographer tells us briefly, 'They agreed to differ in silence in points as to which they knew that nothing was to be gained by mutual discussion.'[1] In a letter to a friend from his father's home in Liverpool, Herbert commented: 'I write in a land where antagonistic German criticism has not obtained much foothold, even in the bookshelves.'

There was no possibility that the difference between father and son would not be public. In his diocesan addresses and charges to his clergy, Ryle repeatedly urged the seriousness of the changed view of Scripture which was becoming popular. Addressing the Liverpool Diocesan Conference in 1889 he said: 'Multitudes all over England … appear not to care what a minister holds or teaches about the Inspiration of Scripture.' He went on to 'entreat' his brethren in the ministry 'to understand the times, and to be bold and faithful witnesses for God's truth':

> You cannot convert men, and give them eyes to see or hearts to feel. The Holy Ghost alone can do that. But you can be witnesses. Stand fast, both in public and in private, even if you stand alone … Stand fast in the old belief that the whole Bible from Genesis to Revelation was given by inspiration of God, and that the historical facts recorded in the Old Testament are all credible and true.[2]

Later it would be recognized by others that something momentous was happening with respect to Scripture in the 1880s, yet comparatively few leaders recognized it at the time. For Ryle, belief that Scripture is 'altogether and entirely the Word of God' was

> the very keel and foundation of Christianity. If Christians have no divine book to turn to as their warrant for their doctrine and practice, they have no solid ground for present peace or hope, and no right to claim the attention of mankind.[3]

[1] *Ibid.*, 132.
[2] *Charges and Addresses*, 198-9. Consult the Index in that volume for much more on the subject. Ryle's first full statement on 'Inspiration' was published in *Old Paths* in 1877.
[3] 'Inspiration', *Old Paths*, 1.

To question this was not simply to question one traditional belief, it was to introduce doubt over *all* that Scripture teaches.

> A wave of colour blindness about theology appears to be passing over the land. The minds of many seem utterly incapable of discerning any difference between faith and faith, creed and creed, tenet and tenet, opinion and opinion, thought and thought, however diverse, heterogeneous, contrariant, and mutually destructive they may be. Everything, forsooth, is true, and nothing is false, everything is right and nothing is wrong. … You are not allowed to ask what is God's truth, but what is liberal, and generous, and kind.[1]

> These people live in a kind of mist or fog … They are eaten up with a morbid dread of CONTROVERSY and an ignorant dislike of PARTY SPIRIT, and yet they really cannot define what they mean by these phrases.[2]

While Herbert Ryle went on, with others, to popularize his views,[3] his father was increasingly isolated. Such as Charles Gore and Herbert Ryle would become bishops, and Frederick Temple made archbishop of Canterbury. Maurice Fitzgerald believed, 'They are fortunate indeed if they live to see the "heresy" of their youth accepted as the "orthodoxy" of their old age.'[4]

Herbert Ryle's policy was the opposite of his father's. His father saw the strength and unity of the Church in a return to definite evangelical doctrines. Herbert saw the Church attaining peace and unity by the allowance of a broad doctrinal liberty. So when he spoke at

[1] *Principles for Churchmen*, xix.
[2] *Ibid.*, xxii.
[3] Herbert Ryle's books included *Narratives of Genesis* and *The Canon of the Old Testament*. The greater part of his father's conference address on 'The Higher Criticism of the Old Testament Scriptures' was printed in 1893, and can be found in *Charges and Addresses*, 253-67. He refused to believe that it was only contemporary Hebrew scholars who were competent interpreters of the Old Testament, and he regarded a belittling of the authority of the Old Testament as contrary to the express testimony of Christ.
[4] Fitzgerald, *Memoir of H.E. Ryle*, 89.

the Islington Conference in 1900 it was a message very different from his father's.[1] It was not, of course, a message original to Herbert Ryle. It was rather the norm for the bishops who would hold power for more than a century to come. When Michael Ramsey, archbishop of Canterbury (1961–74), was asked about bishoprics being open to evangelicals, he gave the reply which had long been standard. Evangelicals could 'of course be made bishops; but such a man would need to be able to work with others not of his own stamp.' He recommended Cyril Bowles as bishop of Derby, a 'very broad-minded Evangelical' who would be able to 'get on with and gain the confidence of churchmen of different kinds of outlook'.[2]

Yet a century is a small time in the history of the kingdom of God. It takes the long term to judge what is of enduring value. Herbert Ryle's last book, a *Commentary on the Minor Prophets*, on which he spent many years, was never published. It found no publisher; the 'latest scholarship' was already out of date by the time of his death in 1925. His father as a teacher rested on a different authority and, as one who delighted in the law of the Lord, he inherited the promise, 'He shall be like a tree planted by the rivers of water, that bringeth forth his fruit in his season; his leaf also shall not wither' (Psa. 1:3).

[1] See below, Appendix 2.
[2] *Evangelicalism and the Church of England*, 175.

12

The Last Years

Three generations of Ryles: Herbert, Edward, and JCR

HENRIETTA RYLE, the much-loved wife of nearly thirty years, died on 6 April 1889. Her health had not recovered from a downturn in 1886. 'On the day of her funeral', Eric Russell writes,

> between five and six thousand people stood in Abercromby Square with heads bared to witness the cortège leave the Bishop's Palace, and pay their respects to a greatly loved Christian lady who had devoted much of her life to the spiritual and moral welfare of ordinary people. Among the wreaths placed near the grave was one from Liverpool railwaymen, a body of men whom Mrs Ryle had sought to help through the distribution of tracts and homely comforts.[1]

After her burial at Childwall, Ryle spoke quietly to those gathered around the graveside:

> I feel so much in my heart that indeed I must say a few words to you. … You do not know the extent of the loss you and others in the diocese have sustained in the removal of her by whose grave you now stand. She always rejoiced in your successes; she was always concerned in your every difficulty; and she bore you, and everyone who was working for the Master, from the richest to the poorest unstintingly on her heart to the King of kings. … Her faith was simple, and in that faith she lived and died.[2]

Then, with a last look at the grave as he left, he said with deep emotion, 'Till the Lord Jesus comes, we part.'[3] It is said that, whenever possible, he would visit the grave weekly during the remainder of his life.

[1] Russell, *Man of Granite*, 184.
[2] *Ibid.*, 185.
[3] *Ibid.*, from the *Liverpool Daily Post*, 13 April 1889.

He used to tell others that a good wife brings her husband nearer to heaven. Such had been his own experience. He would later say, 'Life has never been the same thing, or the world the same world, ever since my wife died.' But his daughter Isabelle, one with him in Christ, was to be at his side as a constant helper. Besides being, in her brother's words, 'a real good Christian girl and woman all her life', she was 'a quite splendid secretary and factotum to my old father after mother's death in 1889'.[1] For father and daughter Keswick, in the Lake District, remained a favourite retreat. They either rented or owned what Catherine Marsh called 'their lovely home on Skiddaw', and at this period she visited him and his daughter for perhaps the last time. Forty years had passed since their first meeting: 'Before we left he prayed with us, such a patriarchal, patriotic, and personal prayer.'[2]

Ryle was to express regret that he had not come to Liverpool as a younger man when he would have been able to do more. His strong frame of six feet two inches, and near sixteen stone, was to wear down like that of any other man.

In 1891 Ryle suffered a slight stroke, but against expectation, after recovery at a home he had at Lowestoft, on the Norfolk coast, he resumed his work. Four years later he could say, 'I am a wonder to myself in my ability to do so much without fatigue.'[3] No doubt the physique of youth helped him in age. His interest in, and encouragement of, cricket did not wane. Reflecting on England's defeat in a Test match, he wrote to his son Herbert, 'Stoddart and Co. made a sad business of the last Australian match.' This correspondence contained important advice for a grandson: 'You may tell him from me that he will never make a good batter, unless he learns to bring forward his left shoulder and play with a straight bat. The last innings I

[1] Fitzgerald, *Memoir of H. E. Ryle*, 358.
[2] O'Rorke, *Catherine Marsh*, 324.
[3] Fitzgerald, *Memoir of H. E. Ryle*, 133.

ever got was at Lincoln, when I got 88 runs, not out, and played with left shoulder forward the whole time.'[1]

At this period he continued to provide the hospitality for an annual social event for his clergy. He called it a 'quiet day', while some of his men designated it the 'presbyters' party'. As an indication of Ryle's alleged remoteness, Farley instances the way this gathering was held, not at his home, but in the mission hall of St Barnabas'. But the critic missed the words of a contemporary. W. F. Machray recorded in the *Liverpool Courier*, 'The Palace in Abercromby Square was not large enough for this meeting, and that was the only reason why it was held in a mission room.'[2]

On 10 May 1896, Liverpool clergy and laity marked his eightieth birthday by presenting him with an illuminated address. It contained the words:

> The deep sympathy of your clergy went forth to you at the time of your bereavement, and it is now with true pleasure that we unite as one body in expressing our warm appreciation of your Lordship's personal work, your kindly feeling with and for us in times of sorrow and joy alike, and your active interest in all that makes for the well-being of the community; and we rejoice that it has pleased Almighty God to continue to you the inestimable boon of health and strength at an age which comparatively few are permitted to attain.[3]

A few days after receiving this presentation, Ryle, moved by the affection shown by so many, recalled to the archdeacon of Liverpool,

> I came among you as a man of very decided opinions, and I think it likely that many of you would have preferred a bishop of a different school of thought; with rare exceptions I have found no difficulty in working with you all.[4]

---

[1] *Ibid.*, 133.
[2] Machray, *First Bishop*, 33.
[3] *Ibid.*, 34.
[4] Russell, *Man of Granite*, 193.

That statement had received confirmation from the presence and warm handshake of James Bell Cox. In later years, after Ryle's death, Cox was seen raising his hat as he passed the bishop's house in Abercromby Square. 'Was that in honour of Chavasse?' a companion asked. 'No,' was his response, 'it was to the memory of Bishop Ryle.' Richard Hobson noted:

> It was clear that towards the end of his episcopate some of those who had shown him scanty respect began to understand him. One of them, a Canon, said to me, 'Though we differ from him we have learned to love him.'[1]

One could wish that sentiment had been more general. It does not appear to have been evident at the York Convocation of bishops to which Ryle belonged. Farley documents Ryle's attendance record at York and notes its infrequency. He believed 'Ryle failed to use convocation[2] as a means to curb ritualism and "define" the Church of England.' He 'did not get on well with other bishops … When he was in opposition to the majority view he had no persuasive impact.' But this is to ignore how few of them were near his wavelength, although he tells us that William B. Carpenter, bishop of Ripon, represented Ryle as saying, 'If the Bible told me that Jonah swallowed the whale, I would have believed it', and this learned man reflected 'how readily a man might reach a position of authority and responsibility without having greatly exercised his brain'.[3]

In 1896 Ryle introduced more than one proposal at Convocation and saw both rejected by the majority. In his Liverpool Diocesan Conference, in November of that year, he told his brethren:

> A Christian Church utterly destitute of order does not deserve to be called a Church at all. … The Church which regards Deism, Socinianism, Romanism, and Protestantism with equal favour or equal

---

[1] *Hobson of Liverpool*, 294.
[2] 'Conversation' in Farley's book here must surely be a typographical error.
[3] See Farley, *J. C. Ryle, First Bishop of Liverpool*, 232-4.

indifference, is a mere Babel, a 'city of confusion', and not the city of God. … If any one tries to persuade me that I ought to smile and look on complacently, with folded arms, while beneficed or licensed clergymen teach Deism, Socinianism, or Romanism, I must tell him plainly that I cannot and will not do it. He may tell me that I am a 'troubler of Israel', and a bitter controversialist; but I repeat that, when truth is in danger, I cannot and will not sit still. At this rate the apostles ought to have left the world alone eighteen centuries ago. … The English Church must either have doctrinal 'limits' or cease to exist.[1]

In 1898, his last attendance at Convocation, he introduced a proposal calling on bishops—at whose consecration they all accepted the duty 'to banish and drive away all erroneous and strange doctrine contrary to God's word'—to be more active against the current lawlessness in the Church. He instanced the increasing use of incense, Mariolatry, prayers for the dead and so on. 'He had', says Farley, 'publicly denounced the Lambeth Conference for being silent on the last issue, and he was keen that the voice of the Church should be heard on this matter.'[2] It would not be heard at York. The archbishop of York described some of Ryle's statements as extreme, 'the dream of a moment of excitement'. An amendment was substituted for the proposal, which included the words 'due regard being had … to modern needs and the reasonable liberty which has always obtained in the Church of England'. The amendment, on which Ryle declined to vote, was carried. Ryle failed, comments Farley, because of his 'isolation from his fellow bishops and his own weak debating skills'.[3]

[1] *Charges and Addresses*, 332-3, 336-7.
[2] Farley, *J. C. Ryle, First Bishop of Liverpool*, 233. 'Denounced' is an exaggerated word. Ryle was not present at the Lambeth Conference of 1897 but in a comment on its published discussions he said at the Liverpool Diocesan Conference: 'I must deeply regret that the Lambeth Conference completely ignored and passed over the "unhappy divisions", both about doctrine and ritual, of the Church of England in the present day.' *Charges and Addresses*, 341.
[3] Farley, *J. C. Ryle, First Bishop of Liverpool*, 232-4. Others have taken a very different view of Ryle's debating ability, e.g., Balleine, quoted above, 185. Farley tells us

On such matters Ryle's voice was heard for the last time at the Diocesan Conference held in November 1898. One can only admire the patience and moderation with which he spoke. He reminded his brethren that he had not been protesting about trifles over which no question of doctrine was involved. He listed six major points[1] at which the Church was allowing a departure from the Reformation, and expressed his grief that

> in the present state of ecclesiastical discipline, when absolute liberty seems the only rubric, it is a waste of time to do more than express regrets. ... No doubt, at first sight the policy of universal toleration looks very specious. It suits the temper of the times. What more likely to provide peace and stop quarrelling than to declare the Church a kind of happy family or Noah's ark, within which every kind of opinion and creed, and every animal, shall dwell safe and undisturbed ... If the Church of England long survived such a chaotic state of things it would be a miracle indeed. When there are no laws or rules, there can be no order in any community. When there is no creed or standard of doctrine, there can be no church, but a Babel. Let men say what they please. A ship without a compass, a light-house without a lantern, a locomotive express engine without a fire, would not be more useless than a Church would be without Creeds, Articles, or Rubrics, and sailing under the flag of universal toleration.[2]

* * *

By the beginning of 1899 Ryle's health was in evident decline although, when he spoke at another 'presbyters' party' in January of that year, Hobson says, 'his words were weighty, faithful, and encouraging as ever'. On 8 January 1899, he preached at St Nathaniel's on the words of John 17:15. It would be his last time in that

---

that in his proposal Ryle was supported by the bishops of Manchester (Moorhouse), Durham (Westcott) and Sodor and Man (Bardsley). The last gave detailed figures on the growth of ritualism, as it effected vestments worn, from 336 in 1882 to 2,026 in 1898, and the use of 'hidden' manual acts, at the Lord's Supper, from 1,662 to 7,044.

[1] *Charges and Addresses*, 359-60.

[2] *Ibid.*, 360, 363-6.

pulpit. 'Truly', Hobson noted, 'whenever he came to us he brought a blessing with him.'

In April he attended the Centenary Commemoration of the Church Missionary Society in London. In presiding at one of the meetings, he recalled it was thirty-seven years since he had first preached the annual sermon. He was still attending public meetings, though against the wishes of some of his friends, in the week ending 13 May 1899. In the last of these meetings he spoke in St George's Hall, Liverpool, in support of the closing of public houses on Sundays. The next Sunday, 14 May, he preached on behalf of the Church Missionary Society at a service at St Silas', Toxteth. His text which was to be the termination of his preaching ministry, was from words in Colossians 2:23: 'A shew of wisdom in will worship.' An observer noted:

> The church was crowded in the evening, as it always was when the Bishop preached. He was evidently very unwell, but his voice came out with vigour in the pulpit … The Bishop told the people that a nurse had sent a postal order for 23s. [shillings] to represent her sympathy with the great missionary cause, and after the sermon it was found that someone had placed a gold chain in one of the collecting boxes in response to the Bishop's touching and earnest appeal.[1]

Machray noted that

> Dr Ryle attributes his long and healthy life not only to a naturally fine constitution, to regular habits, and to temperance in all things, but also to the constitutionals [walks] he took almost unfailingly every day on the Landing Stage until within the last few months. When he first found his way there it is difficult to know. The banks of the Mersey had an attraction for him even in his youth.[2]

The summer of 1899 saw the discontinuance of Ryle's Tuesday meetings with individual men at his office. The location, in the

---

[1] Machray, *First Bishop*, 37-8.
[2] *Ibid.*, 38.

Registry Office, had not suited the needs of the diocese and Ryle had set on foot a proposal which began to see fulfilment in August 1899 when the foundation stone was laid for a Church House.[1] It would be a three-story building on an excellent site. Ryle contributed £1,200 towards the cost and bequeathed his valuable library of over 5,000 books,[2] as well as paintings.

* * *

At this point Ryle's work as the bishop was virtually over. How his episcopate is evaluated depends on the standpoint of the commentator. He was both loved and hated, with, no doubt, a number of uncommitted in between. The *Liverpool Review* (21 November 1885) early expressed the opinion, 'Dr Ryle is simply about the most disastrous episcopal failure ever inflicted upon a long-suffering diocese … he is nothing better than a political fossil.'[3] Farley believes: 'His episcopate is shrouded in an image of drab ineffectiveness in a perpetual battle against overwhelming odds.'[4] This also reflects the view of his religious critics who judged him by such things as the Bell Cox law case, the lack of provision of a new cathedral, and his silence on the need for daily matins in parish churches. Not surprisingly, the late Marcus Loane, archbishop of Sydney and primate of Australia who shared Ryle's doctrinal convictions, saw it in a very different light. He wrote:

[1] Church House was to be the administrative centre of the diocese, containing offices, meeting rooms, and a library.

[2] Russell, *Man of Granite*, 194, writes: 'Some in the diocese disliked the particular brand of theology embodied in Ryle's library, and some years later it was alleged [*The Record*, 25 July 1940, and 11 July 1941] that without diocesan authority or public discussion many of the more pronounced Protestant and Evangelical tomes had been removed and replaced by more liberal works.' Whatever there was of his library was destroyed along with Church House by German bombing in 1941.

[3] Farley, *J. C. Ryle, First Bishop of Liverpool*, 236.

[4] *Ibid.*, 239. Farley goes on to say: 'The church today faces essentially the same problems as those of a hundred years ago. We could learn much from Ryle.'

It is doubtful whether any Victorian bishop gave his people such clear spiritual leadership as did Ryle, and on balance it may be safely said that when he laid down his office, the Diocese of Liverpool was one of the best organized sees in England.[1]

'Ryle was at heart an evangelist', Loane affirmed. For him, either as a curate or a bishop, the gospel came first, and he led by example, preaching in the yards of coal miners, on the decks of ships, as well as in the churches to the last year of life. This concern governed his selection of priorities. As said in a quotation already given, 'He is one of the messengers of the good news sent to the fallen races of mankind, and he simply applies himself to the work of his commission.'[2]

The same spirit lay behind his support for foreign missions, and for the many local evangelical agencies led by men or women, irrespective of their denomination.

In his diocese he saw forty-four new churches opened and fifty-nine mission halls built. The number of incumbents increased from 170 to 206, and of curates from 120 to 230.[3]

Not all who came to him for ordination were accepted. Some were turned down, it might be for 'utter ignorance' or 'sad unsoundness in doctrine'. His gospel convictions would live on in a number of his men, and their influence played a part in the protest of nearly a thousand clergy in 1927 that they would leave the Church of England rather than accept the introduction of a new Prayer Book.[4] Guthrie Clark believed:

Liverpool became a stronghold of Evangelical truth as perhaps no diocese has been either before or since. ... Ryle attracted an

[1] Loane, *John Charles Ryle*, 104.

[2] Quoted by Machray, *First Bishop*, 45.

[3] The temporal needs also had his attention. He was one of the first bishops to create a pension fund for clergy aged and infirm.

[4] Marcus L. Loane, *Makers of Our Heritage* (London: Hodder and Stoughton, 1967), 135-6. New liturgies came later, the *Alternative Service Book* in 1980, and *Common Worship* in 2000. While the Prayer Book of 1662 is now very commonly disused, the approval of Parliament for its removal was not sought or given.

extraordinarily fine lot of young men into the ministry. I could name twenty who were ordained by him; probably hundreds are still alive. I often think that the Revised Prayer Book was defeated by Ryle's men.[1]

For the same gospel reason, he raised the importance of the work of Scripture Readers and Bible women and urged their place in working together with ministers. While there were only two or three such workers when Ryle came to Liverpool in 1880, by 1887 there were forty-five Scripture Readers and thirty-one Bible women.[2]

* * *

In September 1899 Ryle was resting in Lowestoft. On one of his regular visits his son, Herbert, found him that month 'so evidently enfeebled in step, in hearing, and memory' that he advised his resignation. One is happy to note that the bond between father and son had not failed. They remained close. Ryle practised in the family the maxim he taught others, 'People will stand almost anything without taking offence, if they are convinced you love them.'

Ryle returned to Liverpool in the autumn of 1899, where, Hobson noted, for some months he was 'very low'. It was therefore the more unexpected for the vicar of St Nathaniel's that, when he responded to a knock on his vestry door, before the 11 o'clock service on Christmas Day 1899, 'to our utter amazement, there was the Bishop, quite bent, with his family, including his son the late Bishop of Winchester'.[3] Ryle,

> as was his custom, sat in the corner where good Mrs Ryle used to sit. The congregation were visibly affected at seeing their dear Bishop,

[1] M. Guthrie Clark, *J. C. Ryle*, 13, words written in 1947.
[2] *Ibid.*, 29.
[3] Herbert Ryle moved from Winchester to be dean of Westminster Abbey in 1911 where he remained until his death in August 1925. Of his two brothers very little is recorded. Reginald, a physician, died in 1922, and Arthur, an artist, in 1915. Herbert spoke of them as 'two such loving brothers as few men ever had', but sadly they made no profession of faith in Christ. Fitzgerald, *Memoir of H. E. Ryle*, 358.

always so straight and commanding, now bowed down; yet delighted to have seen him once again in the church he loved so well.[1]

After the service he reached out his hand to Hobson, with the words, 'This is the last time; God bless you; we shall meet in heaven.'[2]

Surprisingly even at the beginning of a new century, there was another volume of Ryle's sermons to be published. The initiative came from his friend, Thomas J. Madden, archdeacon of Warrington, who asked permission to look at the bishop's unpublished manuscripts with a view to presenting them as a 'memorial' of his sixty years' ministry. This was granted and, as Ryle wrote to Madden, the suggestion was appreciated:

> It is a great relief to me that you have carried off my old sermons. You have my full permission to do what you will with these. Not a few were written long ago before I was 35! And now I am an old sinner of 83. Not a few were written in my first living in Helmingham and the earliest of all in my first curacy at Exbury in the New Forest and are *very raw*. Not one was written after I became a Bishop. Some of them are very unfinished and only fit to be burned … Show them no mercy. My first was preached in 1842 and now it is 1900. They are all my own and I never copied any one's.[3]

Hobson and Ryle were to meet one more time, on 22 January 1900. Of that meeting his friend recorded:

> Calling at the hour he had fixed for seeing me, I found him in his study: he was very bright and as was his wont, he inquired after my health and about the parish. On remarking how touched we all were by seeing him with us at St Nathaniel's on Christmas morning, he smilingly replied, 'Yes, I said to my children, "Let us go to St Nathaniel's this morning, for I am sure we shall be welcome there."'[4]

[1] *Hobson of Liverpool*, 287.
[2] *Ibid.*
[3] Quoted by J. I. Packer, *Faithfulness and Holiness*, 65, from the original in the possession of the Rev. Arthur B. Turton. The sermons referred to are the ones published as *The Christian Race* (1900).
[4] *Hobson of Liverpool*, 288.

Then he gave Hobson the Bible he had used in his study for fifty years and said, 'Now let us have a parting prayer.' 'I knelt by his chair', wrote his friend, 'and oh, what a prayer he offered for me! I shall never forget it.'[1]

Ryle also had another Bible to place where he knew it would be treasured and, three days after Hobson's visit, he wrote to another good friend on 25 January 1900:

> My Dear Honeybourne,
> I send you, as a parting gift, a *marked* copy of 'The Best of Books', and ask you to accept it from me (with all its marks of daily reading) as my grateful remembrance of helps given by you, and received by me during my life in Liverpool.
> I am a very old man, and we are not likely to meet much more in a changing dying world. But you must let me wish you a full measure of health, happiness, grace & usefulness in this life and I trust we shall yet meet again in that better world where there will be no partings or separations.
> Believe me always,
> Yours most sincerely
>
> J. C. Liverpool

A week later, on 1 February 1900, with his resignation fixed for the end of that month, Ryle wrote a letter of farewell to his 'Reverend and dear Brethren':

> After filling unexpectedly the office of your Bishop for nearly twenty years, I am about to resign a post which years and failing health at the age of eighty-three told me I was no longer able to fill with advantage to the diocese or to the Church of England. ... I am conscious that I have left undone many things which I hoped to have done when I first came to Liverpool. ... But I am thankful that our God is a merciful God. I can truly say that my approaching separation from Liverpool will be a heavy wrench to me. ... I had ventured to hope that I might be allowed to end my days near the Mersey, and to die in harness. But God's thoughts are not as our thoughts, and he has

---

[1] *Hobson of Liverpool*, 289.

gradually taught me by failing health that the huge population of this diocese requires a younger and stronger Bishop.[1]

The letter went on to contain final, characteristic exhortations. Let his brethren never neglect their preaching. People

> will not be content with dull, tame sermons. They want life, and light, and fire, and love in the pulpit as well as in the parish. Let them have plenty of it. … Be at peace among yourselves … Never forget that the principles of the Protestant Reformation made this country what she is, and let nothing ever tempt you to forsake them.
>
> In a little time we shall all meet again; many, I hope, on the King's right hand and few on the left. Till that time comes I commend you to God and the word of his grace.[2]

On 5 March he wrote one of his last letters from Abercromby Square. It was to thank clergy and laity of the diocese for a gift and their greetings, and concluded:

> I ask you one and all to believe that my heart is deeply grateful, and while life lasts I shall remember Liverpool. Life is uncertain, and I am a very old man, but as long as I live I shall remind my children that their old father was the first Bishop of the new diocese on the Mersey.[3]

He had planned to leave Liverpool for Lowestoft the next day, but illness prevented his departure with Isabelle until 22 March. Their home at 58 Kirkley Cliff Road, Lowestoft, aptly named 'Helmingham House' after former memories, overlooked the North Sea where he had enjoyed his father's yacht in his childhood. He had once said, one supposes in humour, that had it not been for his height he would have been a seaman. Here, back in East Anglia, he had constant care from his faithful daughter, and also Nea, Herbert's wife, with their son Edward. Passing his eighty-fourth birthday on 10 May, he died

[1] *Charges and Addresses*, 367-8.
[2] *Ibid.*, 368.
[3] Machray, *First Bishop*, 48.

on Sunday, 10 June. His sons had been summoned the day before but none could be there in time. Herbert, who was only an hour late, wrote to a friend:

> The sudden blow—however long expected—comes suddenly and is a blow to which nothing can be compared. You have been through the experience, and know what it all means. And I to whom it was an intense stimulus to think of pleasing my father as a boy and a young man, feel how greatly he has always filled up the picture of life.
>
> In the country life of Suffolk he was everything to us—taught us games, natural history, astronomy, and insisted on our never being idle, and carefully fostered our love of books. To us boys he was extraordinarily indulgent. And he was tolerant to a degree little known or recognized. … And since the time I went to school at the age of nine and a half I never received from him a harsh word. … It was a merciful end, for the powers were used up, and there was no pain.[1]

The Wednesday following, his body was taken by the 7:57 am train from Lowestoft to Liverpool, to be buried the next day in the churchyard of All Saints, Childwall. The day was wet yet it did not prevent thousands coming from central Liverpool by special trains. 'The graveyard was crowded', Herbert wrote, 'with poor people who had come in carts and vans and 'buses to pay the last honours to the old man—who had certainly won their love.'[2]

Many could not be contained within the church and could only have heard from a distance the singing of 'Rock of Ages' (his favourite hymn), and 'Come, Let Us Join Our Friends Above'. In time to come they would speak of being there when their bishop, his 'preaching Bible' in his hands, was committed to the ground in anticipation of the resurrection day.

Richard Hobson wrote:

> There was, as usual, the general chorus of lamentation, joined in, forsooth, even by certain portions of the religious press which had

[1] Fitzgerald, *Memoir of H. E. Ryle*, 134-5.
[2] *Ibid.*, 135.

so maligned that great and good man, whose praise was 'in all the churches'. The head and front of his offending was his able champ- ionship of thorough Protestant evangelical principles. Bold as a lion for the truth, he was yet tender, even to those who could not see anything good in him, or in his work as a Bishop.[1]

Of all the tributes paid to the memory of John Charles Ryle, none said so much in few words as that of Francis Chavasse. Ryle was, said his successor, 'that man of granite with the heart of a child'.

Madden's selection of Ryle's sermons was published later in 1900 with the title *The Christian Race*. The book was a true memorial, beginning with sermons on regeneration and ending with 'Ready to Be Offered', Paul's parting words of assurance in 2 Timothy 4:6-8. Ryle's sermon on those verses gives us a testimony which may stand both as a summary and a conclusion to his life. 'Assurance', he wrote, gives a child of God

> joy and peace in believing. It makes him patient in tribulation, con- tented in trial, calm in affliction, unmoved in sorrow, not afraid of evil tidings. It sweetens his bitter cups, it lessens the burden of his crosses, it smooths the rough places on which he travels, it lightens the valley of the shadow of death. It makes him feel as if he had something solid beneath his feet and something firm under his hand, a sure Friend by the way and a sure home in the end. He feels that the great business of life is a settled business—debt, disaster, work, and all other business is by comparison small.[2]

Many years earlier, in 1858, Ryle asked for prayer for himself and for all gospel ministers. For him the petitions of that prayer were all answered by 10 June 1900. Let us take up the same prayer:

> Pray that we may be kept humble and sensible of our own weakness, and ever mindful that in the Lord alone can we be strong.—Pray that we may have wisdom to take the right step, to do the right thing in the right way, and to do nothing to cause the Gospel to be blamed.

[1] *Hobson*, 293.
[2] *The Christian Race*, 298.

Pray, above all, that we may go straight on, even unto the end—that we may never lose our first love, and go back from first principles,—that it may never be said of us, that we are not the men we once were, but that we may go on consistently and faithfully, die in harness, and 'finish our course with joy, and the ministry which we have received of the Lord Jesus, to testify the Gospel of the grace of God'.[1]

Graves of John Charles and Henrietta Ryle,
All Saints' Church, Childwall, Liverpool

[1] 'What Is Our Position?', *Home Truths*, seventh series, 268.

What Does Ryle Say for Today?

J. C. Ryle, First Bishop of Liverpool

I F THE question is put with respect to Ryle's churchmanship in the Church of England, the answer has to be largely a negative one. His policy cannot fit a national Church scene now so different from the one he knew. His boundary for evangelicals in the Church was the principle, 'So long as the Articles and Prayer-Book are not altered we occupy an impregnable position.'[1]

That boundary no longer has any effective existence. In 1975 a new Declaration of Assent to be taken by clergy replaced the former subscription. In its Preface, the Thirty-nine Articles are named as among the 'historic formularies' of the Church of England which bear witness to the faith 'set forth in the catholic creeds', and the Declaration proceeded:

> 'I, A B, do so affirm, and accordingly declare my belief in the faith which is revealed in the Holy Scriptures and set forth in the catholic creeds and to which the historic formularies of the Church of England bear witness; and in public prayer and administration of the sacraments, I will use only the forms of service which are authorized or allowed by Canon.'

Let the language be read carefully. Just how much or how little in the Thirty-nine Articles bears witness to 'the catholic creeds' is unstated. It is left to the individual to decide. The current Canon A2 says that the Articles 'may be assented to with a good conscience', leaving the option to others not to affirm its statements if they wish. That liberty was already being taken by many before 1975.

---

[1] *Principles for Churchmen*, xxvii and often repeated. In 1968 the Lambeth Conference recommended that the various Anglican provinces no longer print the Articles with their Prayer Books or require ordinands to subscribe. See Andrew Atherstone, 'The Incoherence of the Anglican Communion', *Churchman* 118 (Autumn 2004), 239.

Geoffrey Fisher, archbishop of Canterbury, far from believing the statement of Article XXXI that 'sacrifices of masses' were 'blasphemous fables and dangerous deceits', declared in 1957, 'We should like to see the Church of England, Scotland, the United States and other countries, bound together in one body. If the Pope would like to come in as chairman, we should all welcome him.'[1] On 2 February 1960, a service of Requiem Mass was held for the late Earl of Halifax in Westminster Abbey. What happened in 1975 was only a formalizing of a position which already existed. It was confirmed in 1985 when the General Synod approved the Final Report of the *Anglican/Roman Catholic International Commission* (ARCIC), upon which *The Times* reported, 'The Church of England, through its representative body, declared its willingness to take into its system the office of universal primate, the Bishop of Rome.'[2]

But the release from the Protestantism of the Thirty-nine Articles took place following the removal of another safeguard which was integral to Ryle's churchmanship. In his lifetime, according to the Act of Uniformity, all authority in the Church was subject to 'the Queen's Majesty, with the Advice of her Commissioners, appointed and authorized … for Causes Ecclesiastical'. As we have noted, to change this situation, giving the Church liberty to regulate her creed, was one of the primary objectives of the Tractarian movement. This could only be achieved by an Act of Parliament which would change the law of the land. For this liberty the spiritual independence of the Church was pleaded, while Ryle, and evangelicals, argued that Church means laity as well as clergy and that their interests, and the nation's Protestant constitution, were better safeguarded by Parliament. Behind the evangelical case was the pragmatic recognition that, given the minority influence which evangelicals had among clergy

---

[1] *Church Times*, 31 May 1957.

[2] Quoted by David Samuel in 'J. C. Ryle's Significance for Today', *Banner of Truth*, Nov. 2000, 23.

and bishops, for authority to be transferred to them would be like leaving 'an innocent body of passengers to the charge of a mutinous and unfaithful crew'.[1] So Ryle stood for the *status quo* and argued, 'The true Churchman [i.e. the evangelical] occupies an impregnable position so long as the law is unaltered.'

Were the law to be changed, and the Church given freedom to determine its faith, then a situation would arise for which Ryle's thinking made no provision. This is what finally happened in 1974 when Parliament, with royal assent, gave to the General Synod of the Church of England the authority to change the assent/subscription required of clergy.[2] The next year saw the change put into effect as stated above. The General Synod was thus made the final arbiter of the doctrine of the Church of England and on that no legal challenge to its ruling would thereafter be possible.

It would be a mistake to deduce from this that Ryle was short-sighted. He was not. He foresaw better than most what was likely to happen. He understood that the law that was upheld by the State would, under God, depend ultimately on public opinion, and that the day was passing when Crown and Parliament could be said to be the voice of the laity in the Church of England. He knew that there were only three million communicant members of the national Church at a time when the population of the land stood at thirty million, and drew the lesson:

> The pleasant old theory that Church and State are co-extensive and identical has long since vanished into thin air, and is a thing of the past. The House of Commons ... is no longer an assembly of none but 'Churchmen'. Moreover, it is notorious that there is no subject the House of Commons cares so little to discuss as religion.[3]

---

[1] The words come at the conclusion of his letter to *The Record* on the Lincoln Judgment, 12 August 1892.
[2] See 'Church of England (Worship and Doctrine) Measure 1974 (No. 3)'.
[3] *Upper Room*, 328.

The last quotation comes from the year 1888. Yet Parliament had not yet finished with its role. In February 1898 it debated 'lawlessness in the Church of England', during which Samuel Smith gave lengthy quotation from 'the venerable Bishop Ryle', one 'of the few Protestant Bishops we still have on the Bench'.[1] Smith also reminded the House that in the Coronation Oath, 'The Archbishop shall say to the Sovereign—"Will you to the utmost of your power maintain the laws of God, the true profession of the Gospel, and the Protestant Reformed religion established by law?"'

But the last supportive action by Parliament in favour of the traditional and Protestant position came with the defeat of the Anglo-Catholic attempt to revise the Prayer Book in 1928. By that date, however, the Coronation Oath had already been revised (1910), to make it Christian rather than Protestant. It was a trajectory which would prevail. In 1964, when Parliament voted to allow clergy to wear vestments previously seen as symbols of Roman Catholic doctrine, it was passed by 205 to 23, 'with barely a flicker of Protestant feeling'—'The death knell for nearly a century of evangelical parliamentary strategy.'[2]

Ryle's anticipation of what would happen if the law was changed was correct. As long as clergy professed agreement to formularies authorized by the law of the land there was some common bond. Without that bond the only unity which could replace it would be a comprehensive one in which a minimum of doctrinal agreement would be required. This is exactly what happened. The quest of the bishops through the twentieth century would be for a synthesis of beliefs which would ensure the peace of the Church. The programme was already in formation in 1900 as will be seen below in the address of Herbert Ryle at the Islington Clerical Conference.

---

[1] *Lawlessness in the Church of England: Speech by Samuel Smith MP* (London: Thynne, 1899), 6. Sixty thousand copies were printed.

[2] I quote from John Maiden, in *Evangelicalism and the Church of England*, 148-9.

So Ryle's churchmanship passed into history. He stuck to it, despite the flaw he had seen, because he knew no better alternative *in their hands*. But there was an alternative in the hands of God. Ryle had not ceased to pray. In the darkening Church scene of which he spoke in 1897, he had asked:

> Can nothing be done to … restore health to our Zion? I answer, Nothing, in my opinion, but an outpouring of the Holy Spirit. More schools and universities will not set us right. They touch heads but not hearts. Spiritual is the disease, and spiritual must be the remedy. In plain words we need among us more of the 'real presence' of the Holy Ghost. For this let us all pray and besiege the throne of grace continually.[1]

Ryle had no developed theory of revival. He knew history and Scripture too well to believe that it depended on human effort. At the same time he took very seriously the truth that disobedience to Scripture is disobedience to God. Churches stand or fall by faith or unbelief. Far more than questions of churchmanship, it burdened him that the movement which questioned the trustworthiness of Scripture, begun in the universities and spreading in the land, would bring spiritual desolation. Through forty years he had taught that Scripture gives us, not 'the words which man's wisdom teacheth, but which the Holy Spirit teacheth' (1 Cor. 2:13). 'He that holds a Bible in his hand should remember that he holds not the word of man, but of God. He holds a volume which *not only contains, but is God's word.*' 'To me and many others it is God's mouth-piece to a dark and fallen world.' 'I abhor the idea of a fallible Bible almost as much as the idea of a fallible Saviour.'[2]

The denial of this belief ushered in one of the greatest changes in British church history. Yet it was a change which church leaders and writers sought to play down as they treated the inerrancy of Scripture

---

[1] *Charges and Addresses*, 352.
[2] I quote from the extensive sections on the subject in three of his *Charges and Addresses* (1890, 1892, 1893), 210, 262, 263.

as a tiresome deviation from orthodoxy recently invented by 'funda-
mentalists'. History has recorded a sounder verdict. In his history
of this era, Professor A. J. P. Taylor of Oxford wrote of the religious
change and decline in Christianity as a change 'as great as any in English history since the conversion of the Anglo-Saxons to Christianity'.
And as a component of that change he identified 'the higher criticism
which discredited the verbal inspiration of the Bible—a hard knock
especially against Protestantism'.[1]

The older language on Scripture might sometimes be still
employed in the churches, as when the Moderator of the Church of
Scotland hands a Bible to the monarch in the coronation service with
the words, 'these are the lively oracles of God',[2] but the language was
now hollow.

To this erosion of faith evangelicals were not immune. More than
any other factor, a retreat from commitment to all Scripture would
bring disunity and disruption into evangelical institutions. In the
mid-twentieth century the Inter-Varsity Fellowship and its publications were almost alone in still holding to the infallibility of Scripture
and much opprobrium was its reward. For the title Fundamentalism
and the Word of God (IVF, 1958) the author, J. I. Packer, earned for
his writings the description 'very narrow and rigid'.[3] It was clear that
critics of the Church's synthesis would not be welcome to share in its
unity and such was the ecumenical pressure that a neo-evangelicalism,
prepared to make no issue over inerrancy, was sanctioned in 1967. To
this policy even Packer for a time acquiesced, to his later regret.[4]

The spiritual need in Britain will not be met at the level of organ-
ization. What must come before that is clear, strong gospel truth.

---

[1] *English History 1914–1945* (Oxford: Clarendon Press, 1965), 168.
[2] Quoted in the Preface to the ESV. 'Oracles of God' = divine communications
spoken and written (Rom. 3:2).
[3] Michael Ramsey, quoted in *Evangelicalism and the Church of England*, 173.
[4] J. I. Packer, *Truth & Power: The Place of Scripture in the Christian Life* (Guildford:
Eagle, 1996), 91.

What Ryle put first must be first today: 'We want a great increase of plain, thorough, unmistakeable Evangelical teaching.'[1] This has always been God's order for restoring the church in the past—first the recovery of the authority of Scripture, along with the raising up of men, anointed with the power of the Holy Spirit, under whose preaching there comes new life, and new rallying points—churches which are 'the pillar and ground of the truth'.

* * *

I have conceded that Ryle is not the right starting point when it comes to the formulation of a policy for evangelicals within the Church of England today. In this regard he was a man who served his own generation. But while he loved the national Church, he had a higher priority than denominational loyalty:

> I am not ignorant of those magic expressions, 'the parochial system, order, division, schism, unity, controversy,' and the like. … False doctrine and heresy are even worse than schism. If people separate themselves from teaching which is positively false and unscriptural, they ought to be praised rather than reproved. In such cases separation is a virtue and not a sin. … Unity which is obtained by the sacrifice of truth is worth nothing. It is not the unity which pleases God.[2]

Certainly Ryle did not doubt that church questions are significant and have their place, but the focus of his ministry lay elsewhere. He remembered that the gospel ministry is a work for eternity (Dan. 12:3). He held in view the day when no one will say he is an Episcopalian, a Presbyterian, an Independent or a Baptist, or other current names, and he asked: 'After all, what shall we hear about most of

---

[1] 'Chief Wants of the Church of England' in *Bishop, Pastor, and Preacher*, 29.
[2] 'The Fallibility of Ministers', *Knots Untied* (1885), 375-6, as quoted by David Samuel in 'Ryle's Significance for Today', *Banner of Truth*, Dec. 2000, 9, the last of three valuable articles.

these differences in heaven? Nothing, most probably: nothing at all. *Does a man really and sincerely glory in the cross of Christ? That is the grand question.*[1] To Ryle was given a large measure of the wisdom of those who 'turn many to righteousness', and there are multitudes who will ever be thankful that *preaching Christ* was the main substance of his ministry.

Notwithstanding this, Ryle's writings were to fall into neglect, even among evangelicals, on account of the report that his teaching was dated. Such a feeling has persisted in some circles. One of his recent biographers has observed, 'Today some of the issues he regarded as important, such as Sabbath Observance, Worldliness, and Election and Predestination, are regarded as dated and irrelevant.'[2] But those who so think about his books are commonly those who have never read them seriously, and it is observable that those who relish his writings are those who share his commitment to Scripture.

In conclusion, I want to emphasize three truths prominent in his writings yet frequently missing in pulpits today.

First, *the human race was created in the image of God for the glory of God*. Worship, adoration and praise therefore belong to the essential meaning of life; the first commandment addresses the purpose of our being: 'Thou shalt worship the Lord thy God, and him only shalt thou serve' (Matt. 4:10). The obligation rests upon all, for all owe their existence to him: 'kings of the earth, and all people; princes, and all judges of the earth: both young men, and maidens; old men, and children. Let them praise the name of the Lord: for his name alone is excellent; his glory is above the earth and heaven' (Psa. 148:11-13). It is therefore the starting point, not only of the *Shorter Catechism* but of all true theology, to say, 'Man's chief end is to glorify God, and to enjoy him for ever.' And the depravity of fallen man is nowhere more profoundly stated than in the words, 'when they knew God, they

---

[1] *Old Paths*, 242-3.
[2] Russell, *Man of Granite*, 210-11.

glorified him not as God, neither were thankful; … who changed the truth of God into a lie, and worshipped and served the creature more than the Creator, who is blessed for ever' (Rom. 1:21, 25).

The instinct to worship remains in every human heart yet it leads not to God. One condemnation belongs to all races, whether in Samaria or at Athens: 'Ye worship ye know not what' (John 4:22; Acts 17:23). The place which the subject has in Ryle's writings corresponds with the central place it has in Scripture. In this connection he spoke often of conditions in England before and after the Reformation, not from some cultural Protestant tradition, but because it demonstrated so graphically the difference which Scripture draws between false and true worship. Before the Reformation the prevailing worship 'filled the land with superstition, ignorance, formalism, and immorality. It comforted no one, sanctified no one, elevated no one, helped no one toward heaven.'[1] It was religion which put the visual before the spiritual, outward ritual before inward grace. There was no lack of shrines, colourful vestments, crucifixes, pictures, incense, and even bread and wine said to be the very body and blood of Christ; but to it all the rebuke of Christ belonged, 'In vain they do worship me, teaching for doctrines the commandments of men' (Matt. 15:9).

Those who think Ryle's Protestantism belongs with circumstances of long ago miss that it has to do with how we are to think of God, and the proneness to adopt a form of worship which results from ignorance. False religion is an abiding danger.[2] Christ confronted it,

---

[1] 'Worship' in *Knots Untied* (1885), 291-4. This is one of Ryle's most important chapters for today. He believed, 'Next to the Word of God there is nothing which does so much good to mankind as public worship … There is a special presence of Christ in religious assemblies.' He quoted the words of Stephen Charnock, 'The natural inclination to worship is as universal as the notion of a God; else idolatry had never gained a footing in the world.' *Worship: Its Priority, Principles and Practice* is also available as a 32-page booklet (Edinburgh: Banner of Truth Trust, 2005).

[2] He noted the 'falling away from old-fashioned Protestantism' of those who like 'lively, sensational worship, and dislike anything which seems plain and dull'. *Charges and Addresses*, 361-62. As T. E. Peck once observed, 'The true glory of

and so did the apostles, among both Jews and Gentiles. Men take readily to 'a sensuous, histrionic religion'.[1] 'It is the religion that the natural heart likes, but it is not the religion of God.'[2]

> There is a natural proneness and tendency in us all to give God a sensual, carnal worship, and not that which is commanded in His Word. We are ever ready, by reason of our sloth and unbelief, to devise visible helps and stepping-stones in our approaches to Him … Any worship whatsoever is more pleasing to the natural heart, than worshipping God in the way which our Lord Jesus Christ describes, 'in spirit and in truth' (John 4:23).[3]

Today there are numbers of evangelicals who suppose the subject of the worship of God is quite secondary to the gospel message. They could have sympathy with the question which the Anglo-Catholic, Lord Halifax, put at the time of the Bell Cox controversy: 'Why is not everything which art, music and outward splendour can contribute to be enlisted in the service of the sanctuary?'[4]

The answer is that Scripture must draw the line between the false and the true, and for drawing that line many gave their lives in the sixteenth century. They recognized this was no secondary issue; rather as Calvin affirmed, 'It [the worship of God] is to be preferred to the safety of men and angels.'[5] Both the glory of God and the salvation of men is involved. The exposure of the false is necessary if people are to understand their need of Christ, and that Christians are those

---

Christian worship consists in the presence and power of the Holy Ghost … it must have the Spirit to work it or be nothing.' *Memorial Volume of the Semi-Centennial of the Theological Seminary at Columbia, South Carolina* (Columbia, SC, 1884), 30.

[1] *Light from Old Times*, 253.

[2] 'Evangelical Religion', in *Knots Untied* (1885), 15 fn.

[3] *Knots Untied* (1885), 405.

[4] Farley, *J. C. Ryle, First Bishop of Liverpool*, 215. Pictures supposedly of Christ are sometimes popular but they were rightly condemned by the Book of Homilies. Ryle believed 'Pictures and statues never brought one soul to God.' *Old Paths* (Edinburgh: Banner of Truth Trust, 2013), 254.

[5] John Calvin, 'Concerning Antidote to the Council of Trent', *Tracts and Letters* (repr. Edinburgh: Banner of Truth Trust, 2009), vol. 3, 260.

'which worship God in the spirit … and have no confidence in the flesh' (Phil. 3:3).

Ryle would have us understand that how God is worshipped is a fundamental issue. It radically affects how people live. 'The best public worship is that which produces the best private Christianity.' If that is not recognized, and public worship is suited to human taste and emotion, the consequence will be an absence of reverence, adoration and godliness. 'Here', he said with feeling, 'we have often felt that we stand comparatively alone, and that even in God's house the real spiritual worshippers are comparatively few.' His comfort was, 'We shall have worshipping companions enough in heaven.'[1]

Second, *God has given his law for all people.* When Ryle began his book *Holiness* with the text 'Sin is transgression of the law' (1 John 3:4) he was following a biblical order. The proof that man is not now in the condition in which he was created is that his mind 'is not subject to the law of God' (Rom. 8:7). Because the law expresses the character of God, to dislike it is to be at enmity with our Creator. Man was made to love God 'with all his heart and soul and strength'. He is worthy of supreme devotion. That is the first commandment. But sin puts self in the place of God, and we live in darkness about ourselves until the moral law is brought home to our conscience: 'by the law is the knowledge of sin' (Rom. 3:20). 'Those whom the Spirit draws to Jesus', writes Ryle, 'are those whom the Spirit has convinced of sin.' Therefore,

> Let us bring the law to the front and press it on men's attention. Let us expound and beat out the Ten Commandments, and show the length, and breadth and depth, and height of their requirements. This is the way of our Lord in the Sermon on the Mount. We cannot do better than follow his plan.[2]

With the recovery of the Bible at the Reformation, the ten commandments were commonly to be found prominently displayed

[1] *Knots Untied* (1885), 296, 297.
[2] *Holiness*, 13-14.

within the churches, in contrast with later years:

> I think it an evil sign of our day that many clergymen neglect to have
> the commandments put up in their new, or restored, churches, and
> coolly tell you, 'They are not wanted now!' I believe they were never
> wanted so much![1]

Whatever is said to the contrary, an absence of the law hinders an
understanding of the gospel. What can deliverance from the penalty
of the law signify to those who do not know what the law requires? A
gospel from which law is absent is not the apostolic message: 'Christ
hath redeemed us from the curse of the law, being made a curse for us'
(Gal. 3:13). For those who believe in Jesus as their substitute, Christ
is 'the end of the law'. He is their perfect righteousness before God,
but that does not mean the end of the law as the standard after which
their new nature is being patterned. The law is perfectly expressed
in the character of Christ, and for the righteousness of the law to be
fulfilled in us (Rom. 8:4) and to have the law written on our hearts
(Heb. 8:10), has the same high significance as being 'conformed to the
image of his Son' (Rom. 8:29). For the Christian, 'not under the law'
does not mean a life without law; rather, the gospel which redeems
'establishes the law' (Rom. 3:31). This truth, elementary in the thinking of Reformers and Puritans, and vital to evangelical belief, was in
decline before the end of the nineteenth century.

With this passing of the place of God's law, there came the failure
to recognize that the law is God-given for all mankind. But Scripture
teaches that *all* the world is 'under the law' (Rom. 3:19). None can
escape its authority. Gentiles, as well as Jews, 'shew the work of the
law written in their hearts, their conscience also bearing witness, and
their thoughts mean while accusing or else excusing one another'
(Rom. 2:15). The accountability of the creature to acknowledge and
worship the Creator remains, and both for the individual and for

[1] *Ibid.*, 405.

communities collectively. Nations are 'servants of God', 'ordained of God', and answerable to him (Rom. 13:1-4).

This means that the message of the Bible is not simply for individuals. It announces law for the structure of society. Failure to recognize this Ryle saw as disaster for Britain. It allowed professing Christians to be unconcerned whether the ten commandments were taught in schools, whether the Christian Sunday was publicly observed, and whether the Protestantism of the nation's Act of Settlement was retained.[1] Instead the idea gained acceptance that such things had no bearing on the welfare of a country, whereas, 'The Church, which only cares for saving souls, and the State, which only cares for the education of minds, are both making a vast mistake.'[2]

Ryle valued a national Church, in the first place, *not* because it might uphold his views of episcopacy and church government, but because it gave expression to England's recognition of God and his law. That recognition was much more important than questions of churchmanship. A 'secular State' is a lie. Government is a divine institution. The strength of Ryle's commitment to England having a 'national religion' established by law was not the result of his anxiety to preserve his denomination; it went much deeper. He could say:

> I had far rather see the Episcopal Establishment upset, and the Baptists or the Independents made the Established Church of England, than see the State ceasing to recognise God. I had far rather see our next Sovereign crowned in Westminster Abbey by a Spurgeon, or the

---

[1] The Act of Settlement of 1701 required that successors to the throne be Protestant.

[2] *Upper Room*, 29. This does not mean that he regarded Church and State as coextensive (*Ibid.*, 328). A. A. Hodge warned in 1890: 'The atheistic doctrine is gaining currency, even among professed Christians and even among some bewildered Christian ministers, that an education provided by the common government for the children of diverse religious parties should be entirely emptied of all religious character. ... The claim of impartiality between positions as directly contradictory as that of Jews, Mohammedans, and Christians, and especially as that of theists and atheists, is evidently absurd.' *Evangelical Theology*, 242-3.

President of the Wesleyan Conference, with an extempore prayer, and
the Archbishop of Canterbury standing as a private individual in the
crowd, than see our Government turning its back on Christianity
altogether.[1]

Some of Ryle's most forceful writing relates to this point. Against
those who wanted a severance of the connection between Church
and State—so that the State should have nothing to do with religion—he argued the consequence would be:

The Government of England would allow all its subjects to serve God
or Baal,—to go to heaven or to another place,—just as they please.
The State would take no cognizance of spiritual matters, and would
look on with Epicurean indifference and unconcern. The State would
continue to care for the *bodies* of its subjects, but it would entirely
ignore their *souls*.

Gallio, who thought Christianity was a matter of 'words and
names', and 'cared for none of these things' [Acts 18:17], would
become the model of an English statesman. The Sovereign of Great
Britain might be a Papist, the Prime Minister a Mohammedan, the
Lord Chancellor a Jew, Parliament would begin without prayer.
Oaths would be dispensed with in Courts of Justice. The next King
would be crowned without a religious service in Westminster Abbey.
Prisons and workhouses, men of war and regiments, would all be left
without chaplains. In short, for fear of offending infidels and people
who object to intercessory prayer, I suppose that regimental bands
would be forbidden to play 'God Save the Queen'. ...

Scripture teaches plainly that God rules everything in this
world,—that He deals with nations as they deal with Him,—that
national prosperity and national decline are ordered by Him, ... and
that without His blessing no nation can prosper ... Whether men
like to see it or not, I believe it is the first duty of a State to honour
and recognise God ... The sinews of a nation's strength are truth-
fulness, honesty, sobriety, purity, temperance, economy, diligence,
brotherly kindness, charity among its inhabitants. Let those deny
this who dare.—And will any man say that there is any surer way of
producing these characteristics in a people than by encouraging, and

[1] *Principles for Churchmen*, 340-1.

fostering, and spreading, and teaching pure Scriptural Christianity? The man who says there is must be an infidel.

The Government which ignores religion, and coolly declares that it does not care whether its subjects are Christians or not, is guilty of an act of suicidal folly. Irreligion, even in a temporal point of view, is the worst enemy of a nation … In what manner God would punish England, if English Governments cast off all connection with religion, I cannot tell. Whether he would punish us by some sudden blow, such as defeat in war, and the occupation of our territory by a foreign power,—whether He would waste us away gradually and slowly by placing a worm at the roots of our commercial prosperity,—whether He would break us to pieces by letting fools rule over us and allowing Parliaments to obey them, and permitting us, like the Midianites, to destroy one another,—whether He would ruin us by sending a dearth of wise statesmen in the upper ranks, and giving the reins of power to communists, socialists, and mob-leaders,—all these are points which I have no prophetical eye to see, and I do not pretend to determine. God's sorest judgments, the ancients said, 'are like millstones, they grind very slowly, but they grind very fine'. The thing that I fear most for my country is gradual, insensible dry-rot and decay. But of one thing I am very sure,—the State that begins by sowing the seed of national neglect of God, will sooner or later reap a harvest of national disaster and national ruin.[1]

We may not agree with all that Ryle says on the relationship between Church and State but let the basis of his thinking be understood. It was not any kind of national Church that he stood for. 'I have come to one decided conclusion. I say, give me a really Protestant and Evangelical Established Church, or no Established Church at all.'[2]

[1] 'Disestablishment' in *Principles for Churchmen*, 315-42. Ryle gives some space to the question whether or not Christianity may prosper without any national recognition by the State, and instances the case of the United States, but in relation to that subject he quotes the words of George Washington: 'Let us with caution indulge the supposition that morality can be maintained without religion. Whatever may be conceded to the influence of refined education on minds of peculiar structure, reason and experience both forbid us to expect that national morality can prevail to the exclusion of religious principle' (339). See also, *Charges and Addresses*, 119-20.
[2] *Principles for Churchmen*, 389. See also the chapter, 'The Church's Distinctive Principles'.

* * *

The modern Christian may react with incredulity to such statements as I have quoted above. The words sound as unfamiliar as if they belonged to another world. And there are those who would say that Ryle has left his calling as an evangelist when he talks of law for nations and not gospel faith for individuals. He would answer that to frame the issue in those terms is a false antithesis. Certainly, it is grace, not law, which changes the individual, but has the public recognition of Christianity, the upholding of one day in seven for worship, and the upholding of biblical morality, no bearing on the spread of the gospel? The gospel may succeed in lawless paganism, but does that mean that Christians need not pray for conditions which support 'godliness and honesty' (1 Tim. 2:2)? Can the Christian be unconcerned whether Christ is publicly honoured or not? Does it make no difference whether society at large acknowledges or despises the law of God? Was Ryle dreaming when he taught that from creation God appointed one day in seven to be kept holy, and that the public observance of that day has brought untold blessing to mankind? The truth is that the law of God has wider function than the promotion of conviction which leads to salvation. Where it is heard and known it acts as a restraint on sin. It speaks to the conscience of the unregenerate. Although obedience to the law may be only external, nonetheless it makes for a far better country than the one where its sanctions are thrown aside. To live where God is known and where his word is heard is an inestimable blessing.

Ryle needs to be heard again on this subject. It was knowledge both of Scripture and of history which lay behind the words with which he concluded his 'Farewell to the Diocese': 'Never forget that the principles of the Protestant Reformation made this country what she is, and let nothing ever tempt you to forsake them.'

In the third and ultimate place, we need the truth that *the praise of God's grace is the great purpose of redemption*. This was what Ryle first learned on that Sunday afternoon in Oxford, in the summer of 1837, from the words 'by grace are ye saved through faith: and that not of yourselves: it is the gift of God: not of works, lest any man should boast.' From that point, the truth that it was God who had saved him governed his thinking and became the foundation of all his life and faith. Then he was brought to see that this was no exceptional experience given to him. He, like Paul, was 'to testify the gospel of the grace of God', because this was the message of the Lord Jesus for all (Acts 20:24).

While there is no uniformity in outward circumstances, what happens when anyone becomes a Christian is the same:

> the Holy Ghost always works on the heart of a man in *an irresistible manner*. ... He effects miraculous changes. He turns the character upside down. He causes old things to pass away, and all things to become new. In a word, the Holy Ghost is Almighty. With him nothing is impossible.[1]

There is no way to account for this apart from the sovereignty of grace:

> He comes to one and does not come to another. He often converts one in a family, while others are left alone. There were two thieves crucified with our Lord Jesus Christ on Calvary. They saw the same Saviour dying, and heard the same words come from his lips. Yet only one repented and went to Paradise, while the other died in his sins. ... There were many slave captains in John Newton's time; yet none but he became a preacher of the gospel.[2]

The sinner on first coming to Christ does not know it, but what has happened was not the beginning of God's grace. Slowly, it may be, his eyes are opened to learn that his conversion was part of something far greater:

> Those men and women whom God has been pleased to choose from all eternity, he calls in time, by his Spirit working in due season. He

---

[1] 'The Holy Ghost', *Old Paths*, 260-1.
[2] *Ibid.*, 259-60.

convinces them of sin. He leads them to Christ. He works in them repentance and faith. He converts, renews, and sanctifies them. He keeps them by his grace from falling away entirely, and finally brings them safe to glory. In short God's eternal election is the first link in that chain of a sinner's salvation of which heavenly glory is the end. None ever repent, believe, and are born again, except the elect. The primary and original cause of a saint's being what he is, is God's eternal election.[1]

That this truth could be misused Ryle saw clearly, and he often wrote against its abuse. That it led some to think that the gospel's invitation is not for all he understood and warned against. That it caused others to think 'that God's love is limited and confined to his own elect, and that all the rest of mankind are passed by, neglected and let alone', he instanced as contrary to Scripture. God loves all the world 'with a love of compassion'.[2] But, this said, he saw strong biblical reasons why Christians need to receive the truth of God's sovereign election.

There is a 'whole system of Christianity' revealed in Scripture, and it is needful for Christians to understand it. He believed that it is here that many are weak. Their theology is 'vague and misty':

> They have no clear idea of the nature, place, and proportion of the various doctrines which compose the gospel. Its several truths have no definite position in their minds. … Of the great systematic statements in the Epistles to the Romans, Galatians, and Hebrews, they are profoundly ignorant. … I entreat you to observe how important it is for Christians to be *sound in the faith*, and to be armed with a clear scriptural knowledge of the whole system of the gospel.[3]

A failure to give a truth in its right place confuses other truths. Thus a failure to understand that regeneration and conversion 'is a mighty

---

[1] *Ibid.*, 432.
[2] *Ibid.*, 356-7. These words need to be marked and also his comments on Manton as a Calvinist in his 'Estimate of Manton' in Manton, *Works*, vol. 2.
[3] *Old Paths*, 467, 471.

work on the heart, which none but he who made the world can effect', leads some to regard the perseverance of the saints as doubtful. They do not understand that the rebirth is part of an eternal redemption with can never be overthrown. Made alive by the grace of God, the believer will never go back but live for ever.[1]

Grace is a great practical truth for believers. In the words of Article XVII, 'Of Predestination and Election', 'our Election in Christ, is full of sweet, pleasant, and unspeakable comfort to godly persons … as well because it doth greatly establish and confirm their faith of eternal Salvation to be enjoyed through Christ, as because it doth fervently kindle their love towards God'. In Ryle's words:

> There is unspeakable consolation in the thought that the salvation of our souls has been provided for from all eternity, and is not a mere affair of yesterday. Our names have long been in the Lamb's book of life. Our pardon and peace of conscience through Christ's blood, our strength for duty, our comfort in trial, our power to fight Christ's battles, were all arranged for us from endless ages, and long before we were born. … Christians should never forget that the everlasting covenant is 'ordered in all things and sure'.[2]

Further, this truth is a special help to Christians when the times are hard and the cause of Christ may seem to go down. In his Preface to *Old Paths*, written in 1877, Ryle noted 'the extraordinary neglect into which election and perseverance of the saints have fallen'. In the years which followed, as Spurgeon also experienced, neglect turned to downright opposition to what was called 'Calvinism'. 'Men deal with doctrines they do not like, much as Nero did when he persecuted the early Christians. They dress them up in a hideous garment, and then hold them up to scorn and run them down.'[3]

Ryle lived to see an impending collapse of churches into apostasy. While it grieved him deeply, he was not dismayed or alarmed. Visible

---

[1] *Ibid.*, 470.
[2] *Upper Room*, 260.
[3] *Old Paths*, 455.

churches may pass away, but the church remains of which Christ says, 'I will build … and the gates of hell shall not prevail against it' (Matt. 16:18).

Grace is the steadying truth for hard times. God is in no need of permission from man to build his kingdom. 'All who are given to Christ will come to him. No obstacle, no difficulty, no power of the world, the flesh, and the devil, can prevent them.'[1] What he had begun he will complete. What Satan seeks to do will all be put down for ever when Christ chooses to finish his work. Then praise will be for ever. In that calm assurance Ryle ended his words to all his brethren and friends in Liverpool:

> In a little time we shall all meet again; many, I hope, on the King's right hand and few on the left. Till that time comes I commend you to God and the word of his grace, which is able to build you up, and give you an inheritance among them that are sanctified.[2]

'The last words of Mr Honest', wrote John Bunyan, 'were *Grace Reigns*: So he left the World.' Ryle called Bunyan 'that mighty master of theology'. They were both participants in the grace that takes Christians home.

---

[1] *Expository Thoughts: John*, vol. 1, 263.
[2] *Charges and Addresses*, 368.

APPENDIX 1

Extracts from Ryle

A page from *Home Truths*

The Cross of Christ

Let others, if they will, preach the law and morality; let others hold forth the terrors of hell, and the joys of heaven; let others drench their congregations with teachings about the sacraments and the church; give me the cross of Christ! This is the only lever which has ever turned the world upside down hitherto, and made men forsake their sins. And if this will not, nothing will. A man may begin preaching with a perfect knowledge of Latin, Greek and Hebrew; but he will do little or no good among his hearers unless he knows something of the cross. Never was there a minister who did much for the conversion of souls who did not dwell much on Christ crucified. This is the preaching which the Holy Ghost delights to bless. He loves to honour those who honour the cross.

Whenever a church keeps back Christ crucified, or puts anything whatever in that foremost place which Christ crucified should always have, from that moment a church ceases to be useful. Without Christ crucified in her pulpits, a church is little better than a cumberer of the ground, a dead carcase, a well without water, a barren fig tree, a sleeping watchman, a silent trumpet, a dumb witness, an ambassador without terms of peace, a messenger without tidings, a lighthouse without fire, a stumbling-block to weak believers, a comfort to infidels, a hot-bed of formalism, a joy to the devil, and offence to God.

'The Cross of Christ', *Old Paths*, 240-2.

The New Birth

The change which our Lord here declares needful to salvation is evidently no slight or superficial one. It is not merely reformation, or amendment, or moral change, or outward alteration of life. It is a thorough change of heart, will, and character. It is a resurrection. It is a new creation. It is a passing from death to life. It is the implanting in our dead hearts of a new principle from above. It is the calling into existence of a new creature, with a new nature, new habits of life, new tastes, new desires, new appetites, new judgments, new opinions, new hopes, and new fears. All this, and nothing less than this is implied, when our Lord declares we all need a 'new birth'. … Heaven may be reached without money, or rank, or learning. But it is clear as daylight, if words have any meaning, that nobody can enter heaven without a 'new birth'.

Expository Thoughts: John, vol. 1, 86-87 (John 3:1-8).

We maintain that to tell a man he is born of God or regenerated while he is living in carelessness or sin, is a dangerous delusion and calculated to do infinite harm to his soul. We affirm confidently that fruit is the only certain evidence of a man's spiritual condition; that if we would know whose he is and whom he serves, we must look first at his life. Where there is the grace of the Spirit, there will be always more or less the fruit of the Spirit. Grace that cannot be seen is no grace at all, and nothing better than Antinomianism. In short, we believe that where there is nothing seen, there is nothing possessed.

Quoted in M. Guthrie Clark, *J. C. Ryle*, 24.

Election to Eternal Life

Election to eternal life is a truth of Scripture which we must recognize humbly, and believe implicitly. Why the Lord Jesus calls some and does not call others, quickens whom he will, and leaves others alone in their sins, these are deep things which we cannot explain. Let it suffice us to know that it is a fact. God must begin the work of grace in a man's heart, or else a man will never be saved. Christ must first choose us and call us by his Spirit, or else we shall never choose Christ. Beyond doubt, if not saved, we shall have none to blame but ourselves. But if saved, we shall certainly trace up the beginning of our salvation to the choosing grace of Christ. Our song to all eternity will be that of Jonah, 'Salvation is of the Lord' (Jon. 2:9).

Expository Thoughts: John, vol. 3, 84-85 (John 15:12-16).

Who those are who are given to Christ by the Father, we can only certainly know by outward evidences. But that all believers are so given by the Father, predestined, elect, chosen, called by an everlasting covenant, and their names and exact number known from all eternity, is truth which we much reverently believe, and never hesitate to receive. So long as we are on earth we have to do with invitations, promises, commands, evidences, and faith; and God's election never destroys our responsibility. But all true believers, who really repent, and believe, and have the Spirit, may fairly take comfort in the thought, that they were known and cared for and given to Christ by an eternal covenant, long before they knew Christ or cared for him.

Expository Thoughts: John, vol. 3, 134 (John 17:1-8).

Why an Assured Hope Is Rare

I know that many have never attained assurance, at whose feet I would gladly sit both in earth and heaven. *Perhaps* the Lord sees something in some men's natural temperament which makes assurance not good for them. Perhaps to be kept in spiritual health they need to be kept very low. God only knows. Still after every allowance, I fear there are many believers without an assured hope, whose case may too often be explained by causes such as these:

1. One common cause, I suspect, is a defective view of the doctrine of justification. I am inclined to think that justification and sanctification are in many minds insensibly confused together. They receive the gospel truth that something must be done *in us*, as well as something done *for us*, if we are true believers; and so far they are right. But then, without being aware of it perhaps, they seem to imbibe the idea, that this justification is in some degree affected by something within ourselves. They do not clearly see that Christ's work and not their own work, either in whole or in part, either directly or indirectly, alone is the ground of our acceptance with God; that justification is a thing entirely without us, and nothing is needful on our part

but simple faith, and that the weakest believer is as fully justified as the strongest. They appear to forget sometimes that we are saved and justified as sinners, and only as sinners, and that we can never attain to anything higher if we live to the age of Methuselah. Redeemed sinners, justified sinners, and renewed sinners doubtless we must be, but sinners, sinners always to the very last. They seem, too, to expect that a believer may some time in his life be in a measure free from corruption, and attain to a kind of inward perfection. And not finding this angelical state of things in their own hearts, they at once conclude there must be something wrong, go mourning all their days, and are oppressed with fears that they have no part or lot in Christ. ...

2. Another common cause, I am afraid, is slothfulness about growth in grace. I suspect many believers hold dangerous and unscriptural views on this point. Many appear to me to think that, once converted, they have little more to attend to—that a state of salvation is a kind of easy-chair, in which they may just sit still, lie back, and be happy. They seem to think that grace is given them that they may enjoy it, and they forget that it is to be used and employed, like a talent. Such persons lose sight of the many direct injunctions to increase, to grow, to abound more and more, to add to our faith and the like; and in this do-little condition of mind I never marvel that they miss assurance. ...

'Give diligence,' says Peter, 'to make your calling and election sure.' ... There is much truth in the maxim of the Puritans, 'Faith of adherence comes by hearing, but faith of assurance comes not without doing.'

3. Another common cause is an inconsistent walk in life. With grief and sorrow I feel constrained to say, I fear nothing in this day more frequently prevents men attaining an assured hope than this. Inconsistency of life is utterly destructive of great peace of mind. ... A vacillating walk, a backwardness to take a bold and decided line, a readiness to conform to the world, a hesitating witness for Christ, all these make up a sure recipe for bringing a blight upon the garden of your soul. It is a vain thing to suppose you will feel assured and persuaded of your pardon and peace, unless you count all God's commandments concerning all things to be right, and hate every sin whether great or small. ...

I bless God our salvation in no sense depends on our own works. 'By grace are we saved'; not by works of righteousness that we have done, through faith, without the deeds of the law. But I never would have any believer for a moment forget that our *sense* of salvation depends much on the manner of our living. … 'To him that ordereth his conversation aright will I show the salvation of God.' Paul was a man who exercised himself to have a conscience void of offence toward God and man; …

Hear the conclusion of the whole matter. The nearest walker with God will generally be kept in the greatest peace. The believer who follows the Lord most fully will ordinarily enjoy the most assured peace.

'Ready to Be Offered', *The Christian Race*, 305-11.

Marks of True Zeal

If zeal be true, it will be a zeal *about things according to God's mind, and sanctioned by plain examples in God's Word.* … Such zeal will make a man hate unscriptural teaching, just as he hates sin. It will make him regard religious error as a pestilence which must be checked, whatever may be the cost. It will make him scrupulously careful about every jot and tittle of the counsel of God, lest by some omission the whole gospel should be spoiled. Is not this what you see in Paul at Antioch, when he withstood Peter to the face, and said he was to be blamed (Gal. 2:11)?

Furthermore, if zeal be true it will be a zeal *tempered with charity and love.* It will not be a bitter zeal. It will not be a fierce enmity against persons. It will not be a zeal ready to take the sword, and to smite with carnal weapons. The weapons of true zeal are not carnal, but spiritual. True zeal will hate sin, and yet love the sinner. True zeal will hate heresy, and yet love the heretic. …

It will expose false teachers, as Jesus did the Scribes and Pharisees, and yet weep tenderly, as Jesus did over Jerusalem when he came near to it for the last time. … True zeal will speak truth boldly, like Athanasius, against the world, and not care who is offended; but true zeal will endeavour, in all its speaking, to 'speak the truth in love'.

Furthermore, if zeal be true, *it will be joined to a deep humility.* A truly zealous man will be the last to discover the greatness of his own attainments. All that he is and does will come so immensely short of his own desires, that he will be filled with a sense of his own unprofitableness, and amazed to think that God should work by him at all. Like Moses, when he came down from the Mount, he will not know that his face shines. Dr Buchanan[1] is one whose praise is in all the churches. He was one of the first to take up the cause of the perishing heathen. He literally spent himself, body and mind, in labouring to arouse sleeping Christians to see the importance of missions. Yet he says in one of his letters, 'I do not know that I ever had what Christians call zeal.' Whitefield was one of the most zealous preachers of the gospel the world has ever seen. … Yet he says after preaching for thirty years, 'Lord help me to begin to begin.' M'Cheyne was one of the greatest blessings that God ever gave to the Church of Scotland. Few men ever did so much good as he did, though he died at the age of twenty-nine. Yet he says in one of his letters, 'None but God knows what an abyss of corruption is in my heart. It is perfectly wonderful that ever God could bless such a ministry.'

'Zeal', *Practical Religion*, 183-4.

Defects and Remedies in Contemporary Evangelism

For want of 'counting the cost', hundreds of professed converts, under religious revivals, go back to the world after a time, and bring disgrace on religion. They begin with a sadly mistaken notion of what is true Christianity. They fancy it consists in nothing more than a so-called 'coming to Christ', and having strong inward feelings of joy and peace. …

[Footnote] For true revivals of religion no one can be more deeply thankful than I am. … But it is a melancholy fact that, in a world like this, you cannot have good without evil. I have no hesitation in

---

[1] Claudius Buchanan (1716–1814), a Scot encouraged by John Newton to serve in the Church of England, named in the *Dictionary of Scottish Church History & Theology* as 'the outstanding missionary publicist of his day, at a time when interest in missionary activity was viewed by many as suspect'.

saying, that one consequence of the revival movement has been the rise of a theological system which I feel obliged to call defective and mischievous in the extreme. The leading feature of the theological system I refer to, is this: an extravagant and disproportionate magnifying of three points in religion,—viz., instantaneous conversion,—the invitation of unconverted sinners to come to Christ,—and the possession of inward joy and peace as a test of conversion. I repeat that these three grand truths (for truths they are) are so incessantly and exclusively brought forward, in some quarters, that great harm is done. ...

The defects I have in view appear to me to be these: (1) The work of the Holy Ghost in converting sinners is far too much narrowed and confined to one single way. Not all true converts are converted instantaneously, like Saul and the Philippian jailor. (2) Sinners are not sufficiently instructed about the holiness of God's law, the depth of their sinfulness, and the real guilt of sin. To be incessantly telling a sinner to 'come to Christ' is of little use, unless you tell him why he needs to come, and to show him fully his sins. (3) Faith is not properly explained. In some cases people are taught that mere feeling is faith. In others they are taught that if they believe that Christ died for sinners they have faith! At this rate the very devils are believers! (4) The possession of inward joy and assurance is made essential to believing. Yet assurance is certainly not of the essence of faith. There may be faith when there is no assurance. To insist on all believers at once 'rejoicing', as soon as they believe, is most unsafe. Some, I am quite sure, will rejoice without believing, while others will believe who cannot at once rejoice. (5) Last, but not least, the sovereignty of God in saving sinners, and the absolute necessity of preventing grace, are far too much overlooked.[1] Many talk as if conversion could be manufactured at man's pleasure, and as if there was no such text as this, 'It is not of him that willeth, nor of him that runneth, but of God that showeth mercy' (Rom. 9:16). ...

The antidotes to the state of things I deplore are plain and few. (1) Let 'all the counsel of God' be taught in scriptural proportion; and let not two or three precious doctrines of the gospel be allowed

---

[1] 'Preventing' is here used in the older sense of 'to go before'; God's grace 'anticipating human action or need'. *Shorter Oxford English Dictionary.*

to overshadow all other truths. (2) Let repentance be taught fully as well as faith, and not thrust completely into the background. Our Lord Jesus Christ and St Paul always taught both. (3) Let the variety of the Holy Ghost's works be honestly stated and admitted; while instantaneous conversion is pressed on men, let it not be taught as a necessity. (4) Let those who profess to have found immediate sensible peace be plainly warned to try themselves well, and to remember that feeling is not faith, and that 'patient continuance in well-doing' is the great proof that faith is true (John 8:31). (5) Let the great duty of 'counting the cost' be constantly urged on all who are disposed to make a religious profession, and let them be honestly and fairly told that there is warfare as well as peace, a cross as well as a crown, in Christ's service. …

I have not much faith in the soundness of conversions when they are said to take place in masses and wholesale. It does not seem to me to be in harmony with God's general dealings in this dispensation. … The healthiest and most enduring success in mission fields is not when natives have come over to Christianity in a mass. The most satisfactory and firmest work at home does not always appear to me to be the work done in revivals.

'The Cost', *Holiness*, 101-3.[1]

Faith, the Secret of Usefulness

We think too much, and talk too much about graces, and gifts, and attainments, and do not sufficiently remember that faith is the root and mother of them all. In walking with God, a man will go just as

---

[1] These words, among the most important and discriminating Ryle ever wrote, come from a footnote, yet they accord with his entire ministry. By 'revivals', it has to be understood, he is referring to the mass evangelism of evangelistic campaigns, to which the word 'revival' was identified by C. G. Finney in the 1830s and became a popular usage. The method of an evangelist calling for an immediate, physical sign of acceptance—treated as 'coming to Christ'—became almost universally popular, not because it was argued from Scripture but because it appeared to promise greater success in terms of results. It was scarcely to be challenged in the 20th century until the ministry of Martyn Lloyd-Jones, who would write a chapter on 'Calling for Decisions' in his *Preaching and Preachers* (London: Hodder & Stoughton, 1971).

far as he believes, and no further. His life will always be proportioned to his faith. His peace, his patience, his courage, his zeal, his works,— all will be according to his faith.

You read the lives of eminent Christians perhaps. Such men as Romaine, or Newton, or Martyn, Scott, or Simeon or M'Cheyne; and you are disposed to say, 'What wonderful gifts and graces these men had!' I answer, You should rather give honour to the mother-grace which God puts forward in the eleventh chapter of the Epistle to the Hebrews,—you should give honour to their faith. Depend on it, faith is the mainspring in the character of each and all.

'Faith's Choice', *Home Truths*, first series, 228.

Readiness for Christ's Appearing

I believe this is the standard Paul sets before us when he says the Thessalonians were 'waiting for the Son of God from heaven', and the Corinthians 'waiting for the coming of our Lord Jesus Christ' (1 Thess. 1:10; 1 Cor. 1:7). And surely this is the standard Peter sets before us, when he speaks of 'looking for and hasting unto the coming of the day of God' (2 Pet. 3:12). I believe it is a mark, that every true believer should be continually aiming at,—to live so as to be ready to meet Christ. ...

It is useless to tell me that, in asking this, I put before you too high a standard. It is vain to tell me that a man may be a very good man, and yet not be ready for the kingdom of Christ. I deny it altogether. I say that every justified and converted man is ready, and that if you are not ready you are not a justified man. I say that the standard I put before you is nothing more than the New Testament standard, and the Apostles would have doubted your religion, if you were not looking and longing for the coming of the Lord. I say above all that the grand end of the Gospel is to prepare men to meet God. What has your Christianity done for you if it has not made you meet for the kingdom of Christ? Nothing! Nothing; nothing at all! ...

Live as if you thought Christ might come at any time. Do everything as if you did it for the last time. Say everything as if you said it for the last time. Read every chapter in the Bible as if you did not know whether you would be allowed to read it again. Pray every prayer as if you felt it might be your last opportunity. ... This is the way to turn Christ's second appearing to good account. ...

Yet a little while and the last sermon shall be preached,—the last congregation shall break up. Yet a little while and carelessness and infidelity shall cease and pass away. The believers among us shall meet with Christ, and the unbelievers shall be in hell. The night is far spent, and the day is at hand.

Coming Events and Present Duties, 34, 66-7, 92-3, 88.

Doctrine/Dogma

I say that the advocates of dogma can turn boldly to the whole history of the progress and propagation of Christianity, from the time of the apostles down to the present day, and fearlessly appeal to its testimony. ... It was 'dogma' in the apostolic age which emptied the heathen temples, and shook Greece and Rome. It was 'dogma' which awoke Christendom from its slumbers at the time of the Reformation, and spoiled the Pope of one-third of his subjects. It was 'dogma' which ... revived the Church of England in the days of Whitefield, Wesley, Venn, and Romaine, and blew up our dying Christianity into a burning flame. It is 'dogma' at this moment which gives power to every successful mission, whether at home or abroad. It is doctrine—doctrine, clear ringing doctrine—which, like the rams horns at Jericho, cast down the opposition of the devil and sin. ...

Well says Martin Luther: 'Accursed is that charity which is preserved by the shipwreck of faith or truth, to which all things must give place; both charity, or an apostle, or an angel from heaven.' Well says Dr Gauden: 'If either peace or truth must be dispensed with, it is peace and not truth. Better to have truth without public peace than peace without saving truth.'

'The Importance of Dogma',
Principles for Churchmen, 103, 107, 109.

APPENDIX 2

Herbert E. Ryle

T O FOLLOW the thinking of Herbert Ryle is to be led not only into the extent of the difference between father and son but right into the great change then taking place among leaders of the churches. It was not a difference between one generation and another—it would affect many generations to come—but a difference between what Protestantism had been and what it was becoming; between Scripture as the authoritative word of God, and Scripture re-interpreted by new principles. Herbert Ryle was representative of a current of belief that would carry almost all before it for more than a century to come.

On 9 January 1900, the year in which his father died, Herbert was the speaker at the Islington Conference of evangelical clergy. The invitation was given to him to give one of four addresses on the subject, 'The Church of England: Catholic, Apostolic, Reformed, and Protestant'.[1] For numbers, a synthesis of all four features was the way ahead, and with that in view who better to handle 'The Protestantism of the Church of England' peacefully than the son of England's foremost Protestant? So the forty-four-year-old Cambridge teacher, shortly to be appointed bishop of Exeter, was given the controversial subject. With the hope of supplying a better understanding, Herbert Ryle introduced his subject with the 'three great distinctive principles' of Protestantism. He believed they were:

1. Scripture as the one absolute standard of Christian doctrine and conduct.

---

[1] The subjects and speakers at the Islington Conference, from 1856 to 1982, are all helpfully listed by Andrew Atherstone in *Evangelicalism and the Church of England*, 268-96. H. E. Ryle published his address in *On the Church of England: Sermons and Addresses* (London: Macmillan, 1904), 32-57.

2. Complete liberty of conscience and the right of private judgment.

3. A national Church independent of all foreign control.

While the first principle is meant to secure the faith of the evangelical, the second wins the sympathy of others by allowing liberty of thought. So letting both be accepted was presented as the way to peace and unity in the Church. The thesis was attractively and carefully stated, but it left the main question unanswered, namely, What is the standard of doctrine taught in Scripture? In what creed is it best expressed? On this the speaker was silent but it emerged that there was no *Protestant* creed which he wanted enforced on the teachers of the Church. In his whole book of sermons and addresses *On the Church of England* he says nothing in support of the Thirty-nine Articles. Speaking of the revision of the Articles which had taken place in 1865, he revealed the motive behind it. Until that date the subscription required of clergy at their ordination included the words that 'all and every one of the Articles … are agreeable to the Word of God'. At the revision these words were replaced by a more general statement calculated to support the 'spirit of broad comprehensiveness' (104-5).[1] Not a word does Herbert Ryle say of the distinctive Protestant belief recovered at the time of the Reformation. He seemed to see no necessity for any creedal statements other than the brief résumé of the historical facts confessed in the so-called Apostles' Creed (232), and the Nicene Creed with its statement on the deity of Christ (106). These creeds say nothing on how Christ becomes the Saviour of the individual.[2]

In reality, Herbert Ryle's second principle overrode his first. As Protestant belief on such points as justification by faith was contrary

[1] Clergy were now only required to say, 'I believe the doctrine of the Church of England as therein set forth to be agreeable to the Word of God', which is not the same as asserting that the doctrine of the Articles *is* the doctrine of the word of God.

[2] In one sermon, there is a protest against 'the cry for a creedless Christianity' (246), yet those two brief creeds are judged to be enough as far as any enforcement for clergy is concerned.

to the 'private judgment' of many, the second principle must have priority over the first. Otherwise unity would never be possible, there being so many diverse opinions within the Church that 'the devout Catholic Churchman' (most largely represented by Anglo-Catholics) and 'the sturdy Protestant … will never coalesce, they will never understand one another'. Another approach was necessary. It was to recognize that while their words and opinions cannot be harmonized, 'we need them both', for 'they are both members of the same Church, both servants of the same Lord' (249). Parties in the Church are not to be suppressed; on the contrary, in their existence is 'the very security for freedom and comprehensiveness' (88). 'We want the strength of all parties and the tyranny of none' (16). Nor is it only 'Catholic' and 'Protestant' who are to be part of an inclusive Church. There must be room for all the spiritual movements which have been 'the prevalent dominant influences of different periods—Reformers, Laudians, Platonists, Non-jurors, Evangelicals, Oxford Movements, Liberals' (115). All should be seen as 'the emergence of the Spirit force' (171).

But what is to happen to the 'absolute' standard of Scripture if conflicting schools of thought are all to have their place? The preacher did not explain; instead he introduced his belief that Scripture is not the *only* standard. There is a continuing revelation of the mind of God. He saw the progression of knowledge in the nineteenth century as part of the evolution of man, led by the Spirit 'that sanctifies our progress into fuller truth and larger hope' (79). So there must be advance in the Church's belief also; the 'word of God' was not yet complete:

> Our witness is to be the declaration of 'the word of God', which is Christ in us and in our world; a new life not a dead tradition … the Christ of our country and of our century … it shall ever be that there will be truths both new and old revealed by the Spirit to successive generations (76-7).

Christ reveals Himself to each age and generation through the medium of its best thought. Compare the terms in which any standard work by a responsible teacher would now handle such varied topics as Eternal Punishment, Verbal Inspiration, the Creation of the Universe, or the Atonement, with the language used in the middle of the [nineteenth] century, and you will realise in some measure how the change which has passed over the mind of the religious world coincides with the expansion of thought during the past generation. It has meant a victory of the Spirit over the formalism of tradition (210).

So it is not unfaithfulness to the word of God to accept 'the interpretation of doctrine in terms of modern thought' (17). Indeed that must be the way, for not to do so is to be left with 'some very narrow isthmus of traditional orthodoxy' (49), with theology which 'knows no expansion' and 'no room for intellectual freedom' (209).

Two things stand out in the case presented throughout his book:

1. The *interpretation of history* as between father and son is markedly different. The son praises men in church history whom his father censured or ignored, such as Laud and the Restoration divines, George Bull and John Cosin. But there is the opposite of praise for Puritans. The Commonwealth period is described as guided by 'the fanaticism of partisanship', 'when Presbyterian was in conflict with Independent, and Independent with Presbyterian; and both in league to compass the destruction of the Church' (231).[1] 'The carelessness and frivolity' of the Restoration period was said to be 'in fatal reaction from Puritan strictness and gloom' (63).

But the most striking difference between father and son in their understanding of history concerns the third principle which, Herbert told the Islington Conference, is distinctive of Protestantism, namely, the independence of the national Church from foreign control. That

---

[1] This is assuming a different interpretation of 'Church' than the one set down in Article XIX of the XXXIX Articles: 'The visible Church of Christ is a congregation of faithful men, in the which the pure Word of God is preached.'

is surely a misleading explanation of the Reformation. The momentum of the Reformation in England was not primarily political or ecclesiastical but spiritual and biblical. Herbert's so-called third principle is no answer at all to the question his father addressed, 'Why Were the Reformers Burned?'[1] They were burned for upholding the truth of the New Testament gospel, not for the sake of national independence. For Herbert Ryle to have accepted his father's understanding would have been to see biblical doctrine at the centre of the sixteenth-century division. Instead he approved the answer of Bishop George Bull to the question, 'Where was your Church before Luther?': 'Our Church was then where it is now, even here in England. She hath not changed one thing of what she held before, any way pertaining either to the being or well-being of a Church'; yes, Bull goes on to add, she dropped some ceremonies and traditions, 'greatly prejudicial to both', but he says nothing about the Reformation being a recovery of *the gospel*. In the same way H. E. Ryle saw no fundamental difference between what was believed in England before the Reformation, when possessors of any Scripture in English were burned, and after, when the message of the New Testament brought a new day. He saw nothing wrong in identifying the pre-Reformation bishop John Fisher, who supported the Pope, with Thomas Cranmer, who called him 'Christ's enemy and Antichrist' (204). Similarly, Robert Farrar, the Marian martyr, is linked with Laud (61). It is a reading of history in which the meaning of the gospel is passed over. Rather opponents are simply to be seen as men of their times who shared the common mistake of putting dogma before love and unity.

In the Ryles, father and son, we have two well-educated men, who read the same history, coming to very different conclusions. How that is to be explained leads to the next difference.

2. The *handling of Scripture* by the two men is basically different. Scripture did not control the thinking of Herbert Ryle as it did that

---

[1] See the chapter in *Light from Old Times.*

of his father. Yet he told his 'reverend brethren' at Islington that, 'by the modern study of Holy Scripture, the Bible has become to some of us, and I believe to thousands of my own and a yet younger generation, a more living, a more powerful, and a more sacred volume … I humbly ask that you will do justice to the motives of English scholars' (50-51). His sermons do not support this claim. Had they done so there is no way he could have treated contemporary human wisdom as the vehicle for the revelation of the Holy Spirit with such statements as, 'The Christianity which does not commend itself to the reason is not of God; for the reason is of God' (130). This is flatly contradictory to Scripture (i.e. 1 Cor. 2:12-13). Instead of welcoming biblical testimony, the mind of unregenerate man is alienated from God and at enmity with him. Herbert Ryle can write, 'Men have begun to realise the presence of a Divine Power in the world around them as well as in the Church … The conscience of mankind responds to the witness of the Divine Spirit, that our God is in the universe, in history, and in the heart' (241). Is that the teaching of John 3:3-13 or of Roman 1:19-22; 3:11?

The volume from which I have been quoting is largely made up of sermons which begin with the announcement of a biblical text. A number are texts on which his father would have relished preaching, but in the case of Herbert the striking feature is not how he lets the text speak, but the way he 'spiritualizes' the words in order to a view of things patently remote from the meaning of the original author. Thus Peter's deliverance from prison by an angel, recorded in Acts 12:7, is made the basis for a lesson on the Church's deliverance from the 'chains of party spirit and indifference' (85-6). In application of that supposed lesson, he presses the question, 'Shall we follow the guidance of the angel? Shall we accept the open gates of better knowledge, and with the gift of larger freedom go forth …? When we pass through the barriers of ignorance and prejudice there is a wide door open to those who will move forward' (89-90).

There are a number of similar examples of the misuse of Scripture. I quote only one more where the text is 2 Kings 2:9-10, and the sermon title, 'Elijah's Mantle'. From the prophet's prayer, 'Let a double portion of thy spirit be upon me', one might have expected an emphasis on the continuity of the church's work and witness, or the nature of the prophetic office, but that is not at all what the preacher had in mind. From this text he told the men whom he was ordaining for the Christian ministry that when God withdraws 'a generation that has served its day' it is not the mantle of former teachers that they need; rather,

> There is more to be done, in a new way, and with altered thoughts and habits and tastes, with larger knowledge and wider tolerance. The age alters, but not the Christ … The law of evolution gets a stronger hold upon the thought and belief of mankind … In the light of science both the books of Scripture and the book of Nature are illuminated with new power of revelation … Gone is the old witness; there is but a faint glow where the vanishing wheels of flame disappeared from sight. What have not seventy-five years brought! New science, new philosophy, new criticism … Only let men see in the change the chariot of God, only recognize the new call, that England in the new age may not be wanting (153-4).

That Herbert Ryle was sincere in so reading the Bible and church history I do not doubt. He believed that he had been privileged beyond his father in the advance of knowledge which his age had come to possess. In these sermons he mentions his father only once, in a passing reference. Their convictions moved in opposite directions. While J. C. Ryle held that the way forward for the Church demanded doctrinal teaching, definite and clear, H. E. Ryle saw such a proposal as the thinking of a bygone age. While the father anticipated the direction the Church of England was moving with dismay, the son could say, 'When I hear or read of men speaking with despondency and even despair of our National Church … I confess I do not understand them' (48).

Herbert Ryle proposed a successful future for the Church of England to lie in the coexistence of differing parties, with an 'equilibrium' held between them. He saw no prospect for the school of belief for which his father spoke. He thought of those suspicious of change as being like nervous people moving in the dark who 'cannot see what is in front of them. We, my friends, who live in this twentieth century, are moving; but is it in the dark? ... let us see where we are and timidity and nervousness will quickly evaporate' (175).

The light assured for the twentieth century did not arise. Instead, in the words of Professor A. J. P. Taylor, already quoted, Britain was to see in the decline of Christianity a change 'as great as any in English history since the conversion of the Anglo-Saxons to Christianity'.[1] Herbert Ryle's generation, which believed that the demonic had vanished from history, needed to be taught afresh that it was not the fall of man which is a myth but man's evolutionary progress. The evidence of history was soon to be before them. The centenary of the birth of J. C. Ryle fell at a time when immense casualties were being suffered on the battlefields of Europe. His son wrote in his diary for 10 May 1916, 'Centenary of my dear Father's birthday! how constantly one's thoughts go back to him!'[2]

True Christians can make terrible mistakes, and when those mistakes are carried into the teaching of the churches, the harvest in history is tragedy. All Christians rest on the one foundation of the person and work of Christ. To pass from death to life the believer need have no larger body of knowledge than was possessed by the penitent thief at Calvary. But for those holding the teaching office in the church it is 'all the counsel of God' which is required (Acts 20:27). J. C. Ryle was not challenging Herbert's faith in Christ on the sad day he ended his position as one of his examining chaplains. He was acting on the truth that once commitment to all Scripture is

---

[1] *English History 1914–1945* (2013).
[2] Fitzgerald, *Memoir of H. E. Ryle*, 350.

given up by would-be teachers of the church, there is no saying what darkness will follow.

There are aspects of the difference between father and son which it is not for any to judge but, for this writer, one lesson has to be that of the New Testament warning:

> For other foundation can no man lay than that is laid, which is Jesus Christ. Now if any man build upon this foundation gold, silver, precious stones, wood, hay, stubble; every man's work shall be made manifest: for the day shall declare it, because it shall be revealed by fire; and the fire shall try every man's work of what sort it is. If any man's work abide which he hath built thereupon, he shall receive a reward. If any man's work shall be burned, he shall suffer loss: but he himself shall be saved; yet so as by fire (1 Cor. 3:11-15).

INDEX

Act of Settlement, 229

Act of Uniformity (1662), 75, 153, 218

Anglesey (nr. Gosport), 50, 64, 82

Anglo-Catholic/ism, 31, 33, 35, 88, 89, 117,128,146, 147-8, 149, 151, 159, 163, 185, 190-1, 220, 226

Anglo-Catholic Library, 88

Apostolic Succession, 102, 146, 148

Arkwright, R. 9
(and family), 3, 18, 21

Arkwright, Mrs Henry, 45

Arminians/ism, 74, 138, 183

Arnold, Thomas, 11

Athens, 115-6

Atherstone, A., xi, 4n, 185n, 251n

Atonement, 76n, 138, 192

Augustine, 151

Autobiography (Ryle's), xi, 112, 169

Balfour, A., 171-3

Balleine, G., 185, 203n,

Baptist, 57, 159, 223, 229

Baxter, R., xiv, 75, 86, 100, 105

Bardsley, J., 66, 90, 184

Beaumaris, N. Wales, 44

Benson, E. W. (Abp), 188, 190

Berridge, John, 55n

Bible:
    Commentaries on, 122
    Criticism of, 116, 192-5, 221-2
    Inspiration of, 122n, 192-4, 221
    Liberal view of, 252-4, 256
    Provided, 170

Bickersteth, E., 72, 76-7n, 88, 98, 140
    E., Jr, 182n

Birmingham, 78,
    St Martin's, 114, 125

Birt, Mrs, 170-1

Book of Martyrs (Foxe), 143

Borrowdale, Cumbria, 180

Bowles, C. 196

Bradford, John, 83
    Writings of, 151n

Bradleys (of Leamington), 62

Bridges, Charles, 76

Bridlington, Yorks, 5

British and Foreign Bible Soc., 32

British Medical Association, 61n

Brooks, T., 98

Buchanan, C., 244

Bull, G. (Bp), 254-5

Bullinger, H., 151

Bunyan, John, xiv, 76-7, 236

Burnet, John, 21

Caesar (dog), 45-6, 49

Calvin, John, 77, 151n, 226
  Calvinistic/ism 74, 235

Cambridge University, 190

Canada, 170

Canon Christopher (J. S. Reynolds), 66n, 145n

Cardiphonia, 72

Carmichael, Amy, 170

Carpenter, Wm. (Bp), 202

Catechism of the Catholic Church, 35

Cecil, Richard, 32, 75

Chadwick , Owen, 120n, 193

Charles I (King), 104

Charles II (King), 73

Charnock, S., 77, 105, 225n

Chavasse, F. (Bp), 177, 202, 213

Cheltenham, 120

Chester, 129

Christian Professor, 72

Christian Student, 72, 76, 98, 140n

Christopher, A. M. W., 20-21, 23, 66, 116, 144-5

Church Association Monthly Intelligencer, 167n,

'Churchmen in Council', 189

Church History (Milner), 72-3

Church, Dean R. W., 159

Church of Scotland, 191n, 222

Church Times, 127, 159, 218

Church of England:
  ARCIC 218
  Baptismal Regeneration, 65, 147-53n
  Benefits of, 179
  Calvinism, 73-4
  Church Association, 117-18, 167, 190
  Church Pastoral Aid Society, 21n, 32, 117
  Church Missionary Society, 32, 75n, 80, 115-7, 180, 205
  Clergy criticised, 37, 86, 135, 141, 169n, 186
  Comprehensiveness, 162-3, 196, 204, 220, 253, 258
  Congress, 161, 174, 180-3, 185, 187
  Convocation (York), 202-3
  Declaration of Assent (new), 217
  Eclectic Soc., 32, 87
  Fears of future, 187, 188-9,

Infant baptism, 147, 151, 152, 152n
Irish Church Missions, 117
Lambeth Conference, 187-9, 203n, 217n
Prayer Book, 27, 146, 149-51, 163, 170, 207, 217n, 220 (revised)
Reunion with Rome, 35, 163, 218
Ritualism, 30, 64-5, 118-9, 167, 202, 204n
And the State, 28, 167-8, 218-19
SPCK, 170
Thirty-nine Articles, 27, 29, 31, 68, 71-2, 150, 148, 162-3, 217, 254
Zenana Missionary Soc., 170
Close, Francis, 120
Colenso, John (Bp), 116, 118, 192
Confession of Faith (Scots), 29
Constable, John, 79
Cooper, A. A. (Lord Shaftes-bury), 89
Coronation Oath/Service, 220, 222
Cosin, John (Bp), 254
Coote, Algernon, 22, 83
Cox, J. B., 116-8, 191, 202, 226
Cranmer, T. (Abp), 73, 150-1, 255

Cromwell, Oliver, 105

Daintry, John S., 3, 44, 48
Derby, 174
St John's, 125
Disraeli, B. (Prime Minister), 125, 127-8, 159
Dissenters (Nonconformists), 74, 76, 102-3, 146, 170, 173
Dundee, 83

Edward VI (King), 147, 152
Elizabeth I (Queen), 28, 101, 153
English Reformers, 87, 98, 103
Eton College, 8, 22, 113, 193
Cricket, 10
Debating Soc., 10, 33
Hawtrey, E. (housemaster), 8, 11, 27
Keate, J. (headmaster), 8, 9
Newcastle Scholarship, 10, 27
Evangelical
Abandoned, 33-5
Criticised, 36, 67, 159, 189-90
Defined, 161-2
Revival (18th century), 32, 73, 139, 141n, 169
Evangelicalism and the Church of England, 185n, 196n, 220n, 222n, 251n
Evangelical Magazine, 84
Evangelical Theology, 144n, 229n
Evolution, 192, 257-8

Exbury, 54, 57, 60-5, 169, 209
Exeter, 'A Clergyman …', 100

Faithfulness and Holiness, xiin, 75n, 126n, 209n
Fairclough, 99
Family Treasury, The, 123
Farrar R., 255
Fathers of the English Church, 87
Fawley, Hants, 55-7
Fisher, J. (Bp), 255
Fisher G. (Abp), 218
Fitzgerald, M., 96n, 113n, 121n, 129, 169n, 193n, 195
Flavel, John, 77, 98, 152n,
Foxe, John, 143
Fredville Manor, 82
Froude, R. H., 28, 29, 32
Fundamentalism and the Word of God, 222
Furse, C. W. 11n

Garnham (coachman), 120
Garret, C., 158, 171, 176
George IV (King), 6
Gibson, Wm., 55, 57
    Mrs, 58
Gladstone, W. E., 8, 33, 55, 128, 159, 185
Gloucester, 165
Goode, Wm., 89, 152
Goodwin, Thomas, *Works of*, 115
Gore, C. 193, 195

Great Yarmouth, 84
Greek Orthodox Church, 188
Gurnall, Wm., 99, 102

Hadleigh, 99
Hakes, J., 167-8
Hall, Joseph (Bp), 87
Halifax (Earl of), 218, 226
Harcourt (Admiral), 45, 79-80
Helmingham, 66, 70, 79, 82, 84, 93-99, 110, 121, 169, 209
    Hall (Castle), 79, 97
    St Mary's Church, 70, 79
Henbury Hall, 26, 38, 44, 49
Herbert, George, xiv
High Church, 159, 163, 169, 179-81
History of the Church of Christ, 73n, 146n
Hobson, R., xin, 129, 174-5, 204-5, 208-10, 212
Hobson of Liverpool, xi, 129n, 174n, 202n, 209n, 210n, 213n
Hodge, A. A. 144n, 229n
Honeybourne, Mr, 210
Hope, Henry (Admiral), 45, 79-80
Hopkins, E. (Bp), 87
Hopkins, Ellice, 170
Hoxne, 120
Hull, 120
Hunt, Wm., 83

Hurt (Family), 18
  Susanna (see Ryle), 3, 50
Hyper-Calvinist, 138

Inter-Varsity Fellowship, 222
Ipswich, 84, 85, 96
  Ipswich Journal, 98
Ireland, 128n,
Irish Church Missions, 174
Isle of Wight, 57, 87,

Jackson, J (schoolmaster), 6-7
James, J. A., 72-3
Jephson, H. (Dr), 62
Jewel, John (Bp), 87n
Jonah, 202, 241
Julian (Emperor), 144

Keats (Lady), 40
Keble, John, 28, 29, 34
Keswick, 200
  Convention, 137
Knox, John, 29n, 152
Knox, Ronald, 30

Latimer, Hugh, 86, 144
Laud (Abp), 88, 103, 153, 254-5
Law, Henry, 114, 122n, 165
Lawrence, M., 99
Leamington, 62, 78
Leycester:
  'Miss Leycesters', 17
  Charlotte, 45, 51, 77
  Emma, 45

Liddell, H., 16, 116
Liddon, Henry, 194
Life of William Marsh, 78n
Lincoln, 201
  Bp. of, 159
  Lincoln case, 190-1, 219n
Liverpool, 132, 134, 142
  Abercromby Square, 161, 174, 199
  Bishopric of, 127-31
  Bootle, 6
  Cathedral, 164-5, 173,
  Childwall, 199, 212
  Church House, xiv, 206
  Crosby, 6, 46
  Diocesan Conference, 162-3, 164, 175n, 194, 202-4
  Drink Industry, 171
  Evangelical Agencies, 170
  Evangelical growth, 207-8
  Fairfield Presbyterian Church, 171
  Landing Stage, 156, 175, 206
  Liverpool Courier, 43n, 161n, 201
  Daily Post, 173, 199n
  Liverpool Review, 165, 206
  Midnight Mission, 171
  St Barnabas', 201
  St Catherine's, 163, 174
  St George's Hall, 157, 172, 205
  St Margaret's, 166-8

St Nathaniel's, 174-5, 204,
209
St Peter's, 160-1, 165-6
St Silas', 205
Seamen, 158, 172
Sheltering Home, 170
Walton prison, 168
Lightfoot, J. B., 148n,
Lloyd-Jones, D. M., xiii-xiv,
246n
Loane, M. L. (Abp), xii, 109
London:
Drury Lane Theatre, 40
Islington Clerical Confer-
ence, 115, 180, 184-6, 196,
220, 251, 254
Lambeth Palace, 184
Lincoln's Inn, 43
St Bride's, 115
St John's, Bedford Row, 44,
125
St Mary Woolnoth, 72
St George's, Southwark, 125
Oxford and Cambridge
Club, 43
Ryle in, 43-4, 94-5
Smithfield, 144
Lowestoft, 200, 208, 211, 212
Lundie, R. H., 171-3
Luther, Martin, 83, 183, 248, 255,
Lux Mundi, 193
Lyndhurst, Hants, 50

Lyme Hall, Cheshire, 46

Macclesfield:
Christ Church, 2, 4
Clergy, 18
Macclesfield and Cheshire
Bank, 3, 46-7
Macclesfield troop, 46,
'Daintry and Ryle Bank', 44,
47
Methodists in, 18-9
Park House, 2-4, 17, 38-9
Silk mill, 19
St George's, 21-2, 39
M'Cheyne, R. M., xiv, 83-4n,
171-2n, 244, 247
McNeile, Hugh, 77, 114-15, 120,
182
Madden, T. J., 209, 213
Malvern, 17, 45
Manchester, 47-8
Manning, H. E. (Cardinal), 34,
64
Manton, Thomas, 60n, 75, 77,
98, 102-3, 105, 234n
Margaret Chapel, London, 31
Marsh, Wm., 77-8, 83, 110-11,
122, 136
Catherine, 45, 51,78, 200
Marshall, S., 99
Massey, Mrs, 45
Mass, the, 150-1, 163, 188, 190,
218, 246

Martyr, Peter, 151
Mary Tudor (Queen), 143
Memoir of Rev. Josiah Pratt, 30n,
  34n, 37n
Memoir of Herbert Edward Ryle
  (Fitzgerald), 96, 113n, 121n,
  169n, 187n, 193n, 200n, 208n,
  212n, 258n
Methodists, 18, 20, 37, 57, 67,
  143, 158-9, 171
Mexican Reformed Church, 90
Miller, John C., 115-5
Milner, Joseph, 72-3
  Isaac, 145
Milnor, James, 63-4n, 77n,
Mohammedan, 229n, 230
Moody, D. L., 134, 158
Moore, G., 122
Moses, or the Zulu? 116
More, Hannah, 87-8

Newman, J. H. (Cardinal), 28,
  29, 31-35, 88
Newton, John, 72, 233, 246n
Newsome, David, 34, 37
Nicoll, W. Robertson, 173, 174n
Nisbet, James, 103
Noel, J. B., 44, 148
Nonconformists (see Dissenters)
Norwich, 119-20

Oakeley, F., 27, 31
Over, Cheshire, 6-7

Overton, J. H., 75
Owen, John, xiv, 75, 77, 98, 105,
  182n
Oxford:
  Balliol, 24, 34
  Brasenose, 24
  Christ Church, 15,17, 22, 24,
    33, 116, 145
  Convocation, 31
  Craven Scholarship, 16
  Oriel, 28, 33-4, 37
  St Edmund's Hall, 37
  Wadham, 37
  St Aldate's, 20, 116, 145
  St Mary's, 22, 28, 116
  St Peter's, 22
  University XI, 16

Packer, J. I. (see under Ryle,
  biographers)
Paine, A. H., 168
Parker, Colonel, 4-5, 17
Parker Society, 88-9, 98
Parliament, 33, 43, 48, 57, 60,
  78, 142n, 190n, 207n, 218-20
  House of Lords, 118
Parting of Friends, The, 34, 37
Paul (Apostle), 20, 85n, 90,
  115-16, 118, 133, 148n, 213, 233,
  243, 246-7
Pearsall Smith, R. and H., 137
Peck, T. E., 225n

Peckforton Castle, 97
Peel, R. (Prime Minister), 33, 55
Pelham, John (Bp), 109, 119-20
Pictures of Christ, 226n
Pilgrim's Progress, 76
Pitlochry, 199n, 191n,
Pius IX, 31
Plumptre, John, MP, 80, 82, 83
    Matilda (see Ryle)
Poole, M., 122n
Pope, and Popery, 10, 30, 37,
    104, 118, 143n, 187, 218
Practical View of Christianity,
    72, 87
Pratt, Josiah, 29-30, 33, 34n, 87
Presbyterian, 102, 146, 223
Privy Council, 120, 190n, 191
Protestant Reformation Society,
    80
Protestantism, 105, 119, 147, 202,
    218, 222, 225n, 251-4
    Opposed, 29, 168
Pusey, E. B., 28, 31, 33, 101, 192
Puritan, 73-7, 88, 98-106, 115,
    153, 228, 242, 254
    Authors and leaders listed,
    75, 77, 105

Ramsey, M. (Abp), 196
Ravenscroft, Mr, 47
Record, The, 20, 21n, 66n, 117n,
    123, 145, 166n, 168n, 188-90,
    206n, 219n

Reformation, 29, 34, 73, 76-8,
    117, 143, 147, 148, 152-3, 164,
    184, 188, 190, 204, 211, 225,
    227, 232, 239, 255
Religious Tract Society, 58, 85
Reply to Bishop Tomline, 72
Richmond, Legh, 87-8
Ridley, N. (Bp), 88, 144
Rome/Romanism, 33, 64, 146-7,
    167-8, 202-3
    Reunion with, 35, 163
Roman Catholic, 27, 30-31
    Sacramental teaching, 34-5,
    191
Royal Supremacy, 191, 218
Rutherford, S., 137
Ryder, G. H., 34

RYLE, JOHN CHARLES
Family:
    John (grandfather), 19-20, 47
    John (father), 3-5, 4, 5, 6, 17,
        19n, 20, 38-9, 43, 44, 47-9,
        64
    Susanna (mother), 3-5, 64, 95
    Frederic (brother), 3, 64-5n
    Mary Anne (sister), 3, 49-50,
        58
    Susan (sister), 3, 21-2, 39
    Emma (sister) 3, 5, 58
    Caroline (sister) 3, 95
    Matilda (1st wife), 80-2, 93
        Georgina (daughter), 82

Jessy (2nd wife), 93, 96-7
Jessy Isabelle (daughter),
93, 170, 200, 211
Reginald (son), 93, 208n
Herbert Edward (son; Bp),
93, 96, 112, 169, 187,
193-6, 198, 200, 208,
212, 251-59
Edward (grandson), 198,
211
Arthur (son), 94, 208n
Henrietta (3rd wife), 111, 115,
172, 201, 216
Ryle, views on:
Articles (39), and Prayer
Book, 72, 147-50, 163, 179,
182, 217
Assurance, 213, 235-6, 241-3
Baptismal regeneration, 23,
65, 148-50, 153
Bible, 23, 116, 122, 194-5n,
210, 221
Cheshire, 38, 57
Children, 112-3
Church history, 144, 164
Church and State, 218-9, 230
Commentaries, 109-11-n, 122
Congress, 119, 180-3, 185, 187
Convocation, 164, 202-3
Comprehensiveness, 162-3,
180-4, 202-4
Contemporary evangelism,
244-6

Cricket, 10, 201-1
Disestablishment, 185, 231n
Doctrine, definite, 186, 248
English Reformation, 164, see
Reformation
Evangelists, 164
Faith, 246-7
Hell, 138-9
Infant baptism, 148-50, 153
Laity, 164
Lambeth Conference, 187-9,
203n,
Law:
English, 118-9, 168, 189
Ten Commandments,
136-7, 227-9, 232
Lord's Day and Sabbath, 47,
173, 229, 231-2
Love of God, 138, 234
Marriage, 44, 65, 80, 139
Methodists, 143
National Church, 239-32
New birth, 23, 239-40
Pastoral visitation, 59, 63-4,
141-2
Puritans, 75-77, 98-9, 103-6
Preaching, 60-1, 94, 140, 211,
239
Reformation (Protestant), 211
Revival, 139, 221
Ritualism, 167
Tract ministry, 58, 85, 121

Unity, 184, 223
Vestments, 160-1
Worship, 224-7
Second Advent, 136, 247-8
Sovereignty of grace, 233-36
Zeal, 243-4

Ryle, biographers of:

Clark, M. Guthrie, xii, 169n,
207-8, 240

Farley, I. D., xiii, 11n, 135n,
142n, 157n, 158n, 165n,
168n, 170, 173n, 187, 201-3,
206, 226n

Loane, M. L., xii, 90, 206-7

Munden, A., xiii, 50n, 93n,
110n

Machray, W. F., 43n, 90, 123,
128n, 168, 171, 173, 186,
201, 205, 207n, 211n

Packer, J. I., xiin, 75n, 126n,
209n, 222,

Toon, P. and Smout, M., xii,
15n, 23n, 95n, 115n, 128n,
129n, 158n

Russell, E., xii, 46n, 81, 112n,
125n, 127n, 161n, 175n,
188n, 199, 201n, 206n,
224n

Ryle, works by:

Books:

*Bishop, the Pastor and the
Preacher, The*, 74, 86,
124, 153n, 223n

Charges and Addresses,
141n, 142n, 143n, 144n,
160n, 162n, 163n, 164n,
165n, 191n, 194n, 195n,
203n, 204n, 211n, 221n,
225n, 231n, 236n6n, 213,
223n, 228n, 233n, 238n

*Christian Leaders of the
Eighteenth Century,* 75n,
97n, 123-4, 141n

Christian Race, 61, 67,
140n, 209n, 213, 243

*Coming Events and Present
Duties*, 88n, 124, 136n,
138n, 248

*Expository Thoughts on the
Gospels*, 94, 121, 122, 123;
(Matt.) 50n, 86; (Mark)
86, 135n; (Luke) 86,
139n; (John) 109, 120n,
121, 122, 180, 181n, 236n,
240, 241

*Facts and Men: Being Pages
from Church History,
1553–1683*, 124

Holiness, xiii-xv, 99n, 100n,
124, 137, 227, 246

Home Truths, 83n, 84n,
85, 86n, 89n, 98n, 115n,
134n, 137n, 141n, 143n,
144n, 144n, 160n, 180n,
192n, 214n, 238, 247

Knots Untied, xii, 119n, 123, 124n, 148n, 149n, 162n, 2233n, 225n, 226n, 227n

Light from Old Times, 76n, 99n, 102n, 106n, 124, 143n, 145n, 226n, 255n

Old Paths, 121n, 124, 194n, 224n, 226n, 233n, 234n, 2235n, 239

Practical Religion, 124, 139n, 154

Principles for Churchmen, 124n, 148n, 152n, 162n-66n, 186n-7, 195n, 217n, 230n-1n, 248

Spiritual Songs, 85

Upper Room, 7n, 60n, 61n, 116n, 117n, 148n, 157n, 164n, 219n, 229n, 235n,

Other Writings:
'Estimate of Manton', 60n, 103, 234
'Memoir of Samuel Ward', 99n
Shall We Go? 120, 181, 186
Tracts, 85, 89-90, 124
What Do We Owe to the Reformation? 117
Ryle, Nea (Mrs H. E.), 213

St Mary's, Alverstoke, 64
Salisbury, Deanery of, 125-6, 127-8

Samuel, David (Bp), 218n, 223n
Sanday, W., 145
Sandon (Lord/Viscount), 127
Sandys, E. (Bp), 87
Sargent, John, 34
and family, 34
Scales, D., 24n, 118n
Scott, Thomas, 32, 72-4, 76
John, 74
Sibbes, R., 98
Simeon, Charles, 32, 75
Smith, S., (MP), 172, 220
Smith, W. R., 192-3
Socialism, 182, 202-3
Southampton, 58, 62
Southport, 181-3, 186
Spurgeon, C. H., xii, 123, 153, 176, 229, 235
Stanley, A. P. (Dean), 32
Stephen, James, 36
Stock, Eugene, 75, 116, 180
Stokes, G., 88
Stradbroke, 108-12, 120-3, 125-7, 129, 130, 134, 158, 164, 185
Sunday School, 112
Suffolk:
Suffolk Chronicle, 95n, 97
Puritans in, 99
Sunday at Home, 125n
Sunners, Ned, 134-5
Sword and the Trowel, The, 154n

Taylor, A. J. P., 222, 258

Tarporley, 97

Taylor, R., 99

Temple, F. (Abp), 192, 195
  Wm. (Abp), 192

The Times, 89, 126, 159, 186, 188

Thomas, W. H. Griffith, 21n

Thornhill, Wm. (Colonel), 50, 55, 58

Thornycroft, John, 45

Thought of the Evangelical Leaders, 32, 153n

Tollemache, John, 45, 78, 80, 93, 96-7, 169
  Georgina B., Mrs, 45, 78-81

Tomline, G. (Bp), 73-4, 76

Torquay, 93

Tory/Tories, 127-8

Tractarian movement, Tractarians, 28, 29, 30, 33, 88-9, 142, 167, 192,218

Tracts for the Times, 28

Tyndale, Wm., 89n

Usher, J. (Abp), 152

Varley, Henry, 134

Venn, Henry, 97

Victoria (Queen), 127

Walker, John, 96
  Jessy, Miss (see Ryle)

Walsh, W., 29n

Washington, George, 231n

Ward, Samuel, 99, 102

Ward, W. G., 31

Warfield, B. B., 151n

Watson, John (Ian Maclaren), 173-4n

Wellington (Duke), 11, 38

Wells, David, 144n

Wesley, John, 18-9, 36, 123, 143, 183

Wesleyan Conference, 171, 230

Westminster Abbey, 208n, 218, 230

Weston-super-Mare, 84n, 86n, 114, 143, 169, 179

Whitefield, G., 18, 36, 75n, 86, 100, 123, 134, 143, 244, 248

Whitgift, John, Works of, 151n

Wickes, Wm., 116

Wickham, Althea, 62

Wilberforce, William, 32, 37,72, 87
  (sons) Henry, 33, 64; Robert, 28, 33, 37; Samuel (Bp.), 33,37, 64-5; Robert 28, 33
  (daughter) Lizzy, 37

Winchester, 54, 62-3, 65-6, 71, 164n
  Bishop of, 56, 62, 208
  Cathedral, 164n
  St Thomas's Church, 54, 62

Windsor, 8, 12, 114

Wood, J. R. (cousin), 12n, 40, 47n, 72,

Wood (relatives), 47-8
Wycliffe, John, 124

York, 187, 202-3
  Abp of, 203

Books by J. C. Ryle
Published by the Trust

Expository Thoughts on the Gospels
(7 vols, clothbound)

Matthew

Mark

Luke
vol 1: Luke chaps 1-10
vol. 2: Luke chaps 11-24

John
vol. 1: John chaps 1-6
vol. 2: John chaps 7-12
vol. 3: John chaps 13-21

Other Clothbound Titles

Charges and Addresses

Holiness: Its Nature, Hindrances, Difficulties and Roots

Light from Old Times

*Old Paths: Being Plain Statements on Some of the
Weightier Matters of Christianity*

*Practical Religion: Being Plain Papers on the Duties, Experience,
Dangers, and Privileges of Professing Christians*

Paperbacks

Christian Leaders of the Eighteenth Century

Five English Reformers

Is All Scripture Inspired?

Thoughts for Young Men

The Upper Room: Being a Few Truths for the Times

Warnings to the Churches

Booklets

The Agency that Transformed a Nation

A Call to Prayer

Simplicity in Preaching

Worship: Its Priority, Principles, and Practice

Other Titles by Iain H. Murray

Amy Carmichael: Beauty for Ashes
Archibald G. Brown: Spurgeon's Successor
The Cross: The Pulpit of God's Love
D. M. Lloyd-Jones, vol. 1: The First Forty Years, 1899–1939
D. M. Lloyd-Jones, vol. 2: The Fight of Faith, 1939–1981
Evangelical Holiness and Other Addresses
Evangelicalism Divided: A Record of Crucial Change in the Years 1950 to 2000
The Forgotten Spurgeon
Heroes
The Invitation System
The Life of Arthur W. Pink
The Life of Martyn Lloyd-Jones
John MacArthur: Servant of the Word and Flock
Jonathan Edwards: A New Biography
Life of John Murray
Lloyd-Jones: Messenger of Grace
The Old Evangelicalism: Old Truths for a New Awakening
Pentecost—Today? The Biblical Basis for Understanding Revival
The Psalter—The Only Hymnal?
The Puritan Hope: Revival and the Interpretation of Prophecy
Rest in God or A Calamity in Contemporary Christianity
Revival and Revivalism: The Making and Marring of American Evangelicalism 1750–1858
A Scottish Christian Heritage
Spurgeon vs. Hyper-Calvinism: The Battle for Gospel Preaching
The Undercover Revolution: How Fiction Changed Britain
The Unresolved Controversy: Union with Non-Evangelicals
Wesley and Men who Followed

ABOUT THE PUBLISHER

THE Banner of Truth Trust originated in 1957 in London. The founders believed that much of the best literature of historic Christianity had been allowed to fall into oblivion and that, under God, its recovery could well lead not only to a strengthening of the church, but to true revival.

Inter-denominational in vision, this publishing work is now international, and our lists include a number of contemporary authors along with classics from the past. The translation of these books into many languages is encouraged.

A monthly magazine, *The Banner of Truth,* is also published. More information about this and all our publications can be found on our website or supplied by either of the offices below.

THE BANNER OF TRUTH TRUST

3 Murrayfield Road   PO Box 621, Carlisle,
Edinburgh, EH12 6EL   Pennsylvania 17013,
UK   USA

www.banneroftruth.org